"*Home-Cooked Vegan Comfort Food* is the ultimate cookbook for dispelling forever the myth that vegan cuisine is nothing more than 'bird food.' The industrial-strength recipes here will satisfy the biggest, most demanding appetites, and do it with plenty of popping flavors and rich textures. Highly recommended!"

—DR. WILL TUTTLE, pianist, composer, former Zen monk, co-founder of the Prayer Circle for Animals, and award-winning author of the acclaimed bestseller *The World Peace Diet*

"Move over brown rice and tofu, there's a new cookbook in town! *Home-Cooked Vegan Comfort Food* will make a believer out of anyone who is skeptical about vegan food—and that includes your stubborn uncle Rick, who still pronounces vegan 'vay-gun.' I guarantee it'll shut him up right quick."

—LAURA BECK, www.Vegansaurus.com

"Most of us have been there. A meat eater gleefully waves a burger in our faces, confident that we as vegans are missing out. Not so. The tables have turned and it's time for us to wave some 'hearty vegan' fare in their faces. The difference? They're going to like it."

—TAMASIN NOYES, author of *American Vegan Kitchen*

"This is the cookbook to consult when you absolutely must impress the guests at your table—be they dedicated herbivores or doubtful omnivores. Nobody can discriminate against delicious!"

—MICHELLE SCHWEGMANN, co-owner of The Herbivore Clothing Company, www.herbivoreclothing.com

"Celine and Joni prove, beyond the shadow of a doubt, that vegan eats are not only delicious, they are hearty! Be warned, this cookbook is not for the weak of appetite!"

—CAROLYN SCOTT-HAMILTON, www.healthyvoyager.com

"I challenge you to look through *Home-Cooked Vegan Comfort Food* without marking at least ten recipes to make this week. In typical Celine and Joni fashion, the photos reel you in, the recipe titles glue you to the pages, the ingredients are within pantry's reach, and there is no doubt that once you finally set the book down. your belly will be fully satisfied."

—ALISA FLEMING, ... of ......Free.org and author of .... .nd *Cookbook*

HOME-COOKED VEGAN COMFORT FOOD

MORE THAN 200 BELLY-FILLING, LIP-SMACKING RECIPES

CELINE STEEN AND JONI MARIE NEWMAN

AUTHORS OF 500 VEGAN RECIPES AND
THE COMPLETE GUIDE TO VEGAN FOOD SUBSTITUTIONS

FAIR WINDS
PRESS
BEVERLY, MASSACHUSETTS

© 2013 Fair Winds Press
Text © 2011 Celine Steen and Joni Marie Newman
Photography and Design © 2011 Fair Winds Press
This edition published in 2013

First published in the USA in 2013 by
Fair Winds Press, a member of
Quayside Publishing Group
100 Cummings Center
Suite 406-L
Beverly, MA 01915-6101
www.fairwindspress.com

This book was originally published with the title *Hearty Vegan Meals for Monster Appetites*
(Fair Winds Press, 2011).

17 16 15 14 13   1 2 3 4 5

ISBN: 978-1-59233-588-6
Digital edition published in 2013
eISBN: 978-1-61058-888-1

Library of Congress Cataloging-in-Publication Data available

Book layout by MeganJonesDesign.com
Photography by Celine Steen

Printed and bound in China

This book is dedicated to our mothers, for being the most rocking role models we'll ever know and for putting so much heart into the "heart"-y foods we grew up on.

CONTENTS

INTRODUCTION

Make Room For Fantastically Full

We believe that the most convincing argument for going vegan is the food. If you can serve up a delicious, hearty, filling meal to a die-hard meat eater only to hear, "Man, that was so good! I'm so full, I couldn't eat another bite," then you know just what we mean.

People go vegan for a multitude of reasons, and this book wasn't written to wax philosophical. Rather, it was written so that you can create magnificent vegan meals that will have your dinner guests wondering why they ever "needed" meat in the first place.

Eating vegan doesn't mean sacrificing flavor. Quite the opposite: Eliminating the flavors that come along with animal products means using the natural flavors in fruits, vegetables, grains, spices, herbs, and more to create enticing and familiar flavors.

We must admit that when we each decided to go vegan, our first thoughts were, "Boring food, here we come—at least the animals will be safe and we'll be healthier," followed immediately by, "How will we ever survive without cakes and other sweet treats?"

But the good news is that we've never had as much fun eating as we do now—and our family members agree! In fact, we're happy to report that our significant others and even some family members have either switched from consuming an omnivorous diet to eating solely vegan foods when at home, or have at least made great steps toward including more vegan foods in their diet, which, to us, is as great an endorsement as any!

We think you can convince your family to do the same, which is why we've written this book. Inside you'll find a vast collection of our "secret" recipes, the ones we keep in our back pockets when we know a nonvegan is coming over (or living among us) and needs to be wow-ed with straight-up great food. All said and done, this is a book full of hearty, flavorful recipes written by a couple of gals who find feeding friends and loved ones to be one of the best (and tastiest) pleasures in the world.

To anyone who's ever thought, "a meal without meat is a terrible thing to eat," we've got news for you: You're about to sink your teeth into some of the best food you've ever eaten. Food that *happens to be vegan* but is always *definitively delicious.*

CHAPTER 1

Your Complete Prep Guide to Wicked Good Meals

We know it's important to plan things, and plan them well in order to be as efficient as possible come dinnertime, especially when you have one hungry mob waiting for you to bring a steaming hot plate of deliciousness to the table.

This chapter is meant to help you accomplish the task of preparing a meal without tearing your hair out, or waving the proverbial white flag by picking up the phone to order some greasy food from the joint down the street. Show that kitchen who's boss! And while you're at it, hire any willing participant to come give you a hand in whipping up something tasty: The food will not only get to the table much faster, but you'll also get to spend quality time with family members or friends you barely get to enjoy hanging out with and talking to during the busy day. Bonus!

Things We Simply Can't Live without in Our Kitchens

Following is a list of items we use the most, and that we acquired without breaking the bank. If you are serious about cooking, or just want to be someday, having at least a few of these items on hand is sure to make your life easier.

Baked goods pans: We use standard aluminized steel pans, but never glass pans, for baking, because results aren't always satisfying with the latter.

Cast-iron skillet: A good-quality cast-iron skillet just may replace half of your other pots and pans. Oven safe, naturally nonstick, long lasting, and usually inexpensive (some of the best come from garage sales and thrift stores), these pans have become indispensable in our kitchens. Try to find one with a tight-fitting lid.

Deep fryer: While we do not advocate eating deep-fried foods every single day of the week, it's still fun to enjoy the occasional golden brown and crunchy treat. A Fry Daddy Jr. only costs about $25 and makes frying an easy task. It heats the oil to temperature within minutes and has a handy storage lid so that you can reuse the oil several times before having to throw it out.

Food processor: We've owned processors that cost us next to nothing, as well as others that almost required us parting with a limb. Truth is, we don't see a big difference between the two. The main thing you want to keep in mind when choosing a processor is size. Consider how many people live in your household and how big your batches of food will be before you buy. As an example, we both use a 10-cup (2.4-l) food processor for a household of two.

Immersion blender: This magical tool makes for speedy blending right in the bowl, no transfer of food required. We really like our Cuisinart model. It costs under $30 and is going on its sixth year of intensive use.

Food scale: Because we use both weights and measures in our cookbooks, we've grown very fond of weighing our ingredients. It makes for easier cleanup (since you can weigh everything right into the mixing bowl, rather than dealing with measuring cups), and is often far more accurate than measuring. It's possible to find scales for as low as $25 that offer excellent results. We use the Escali brand.

Good-quality chef's knife: You don't have to spend hundreds of dollars, but a good chef's knife with a heavy handle and a blade that can be sharpened at home will save you hours of aggravation, not to mention the cost of bandages from cutting yourself with a frustratingly dull, supercheap version.

Jumbo muffin tins: If you're hungry and you know it, whip out your jumbo muffin tin. Each tin yields six bakery-style muffins made of up to 1 cup (235 ml) of batter. Impressive and quite useful when appetites are extreme (or you're considering baking for profit). As a comparison, standard muffin tins use up to ⅓ cup (80 ml) of batter, so your baking time will likely need to increase by a bit if you're converting a standard muffin or cupcake recipe.

Microplane grater: Use it for citrus zest, whole nutmeg, garlic, and anything that requires a close shave.

Silicone baking mats, such as Silpat: We both swear by them, for one main reason: less waste. Unlike parchment paper, baking mats can be used repeatedly and usually perform for at least 2,000 uses.

Thermometers: Oven thermometers and instant-read thermometers are an affordable and great way to make sure your oven is well calibrated and that the liquid for your yeast bread is at the adequate temperature.

General Baking and Cooking Tips

Here are a few basic tips we find essential in making our cooking and baking experiences all the more seamless and enjoyable.

Be mindful of ingredient temperature. It's best to use ingredients that are at room temperature when baking, but even more so when dealing with yeast bread. The main exception, however, is when making pie crusts and biscuits, where the ingredients should all be very cold. Follow the recommended ingredient temperatures in each recipe–rebelling will only cause regret!

Measure flour correctly. We use a scoop to transfer flours into the measuring cup, so as not to overpack. It makes a difference in how recipes turn out, so it's a good thing to keep in mind.

Sift whenever possible. Sifting after measuring (or before, if the recipe calls for it) helps create light and airy baked goods with an even crumb. Simply use a fine mesh sieve to make sure flour, cocoa powder, baking soda, and other such dry ingredients don't get over-clumped on you.

Practice *mise en place*. This is French for "Don't be messy, fool!" (Okay, really it means "everything in place," but same idea.) To follow this rule, simply gather your ingredients on the counter (and measure out if you're really feeling organized) in advance, so you won't have to go looking for the cinnamon when your wet and dry ingredients are already mixed and need to get into the oven pronto. This way, you'll also allow for things to come to room temperature. (Just don't do that with things that actually need to be super cold, like nondairy butter for biscuits, or frozen blueberries for muffins!)

Read through recipes. It's always wise to make sure you've got all the ingredients you need and know what you're in for.

Getting to Know Your Ingredients

If you find yourself scratching the top of your head wondering what on earth maca powder and nutritional yeast are, the following list of ingredients should help you become better acquainted with items that will soon turn out to be indispensable to your vegan pantry.

A lot of the ingredients you will come across in this book can be found in any well-stocked supermarket, while less common ingredients may require a trip to your local health food store or a quick visit to the good ole Internet.

Beans: We usually go for canned beans, rinsing and draining them thoroughly to get rid of as much sodium as possible. If you happen to cook your own, we tip our hats to you. You probably already know that one 15-ounce (425 g) can of beans equals approximately 1⅔ cups (294 g) cooked beans, or ⅔ cup (120 g) dry beans.

Edible seaweed: Hijiki, dulse, and nori are three edible seaweeds that add a fishy flavor to foods without using fish.

Egg replacer: Although very rarely called for in our recipes, this powder is a handy ingredient to have around the kitchen. Ener-G and Bob's Red Mill brand egg replacers both make an easy task of replacing eggs in recipes.

Flours: If you want to get the most nutrition out of your baked goods, consider using whole wheat pastry flour instead of all-purpose flour. Whole wheat pastry flour is ground from soft wheat and is lighter than regular whole wheat flour, so it works particularly well in pastries, cookies, cakes, and the like. (It does not, however, work quite as well in yeast breads due to its low gluten content.)

If you can't find or don't have whole wheat pastry flour, you can combine equal amounts of unbleached all-purpose and whole wheat flours to get the same results (or just use all all-purpose). Most supermarkets have also started to carry *white* whole wheat flour, which we find makes for lighter and fluffier breads while still retaining all the nutrition regular whole wheat flour does. We're big fans of it and recommend using it in yeast breads for less dense results or in combination with all-purpose flour in baked goods, if available.

Liquid smoke: A condiment that's stocked near the marinades in most markets, this is made by condensing smoke into liquid form. A little goes a long way in giving a smoky flavor to many foods.

Maca powder: This dried root is somewhat of a superfood, because it is packed with vitamins (B), minerals (including calcium), and amino acids, and is said to increase stamina, reduce fatigue, and even enhance libido. It is rather expensive, but a little goes a long way. It has a nutty, almost buttery flavor. It can be sprinkled on oatmeal or other hot cereals for an added nutritional boost. We sneak it into some of our recipes to add richness and depth.

Nondairy milks: We favor unsweetened milk so that it lends itself to pretty much any use, but we aren't too picky on which kind: soy, almond, rice, whatever we have. Consider trying several to discover what your palate enjoys best.

Nut butters: Peanuts, almonds, cashews, creamy or crunchy: They're all fantastic, especially when made of nothing but nuts and a little salt. Most all-natural peanut butters have a tendency to separate in the jar, requiring a good stir; sometimes this can cause a problem in our recipes. Luckily, there are several all-natural creamy peanut butters (including Earth Balance and MaraNatha) that are clearly labeled as no-stir, and believe it or not, they really are! When necessary, we specify when no-stir peanut butter is needed in our recipes.

Nutritional yeast: This is a nonactive kind of yeast you'll either love, hate, or learn to appreciate. Its nutty and cheesy flavor is a bit of an acquired taste, so give yourself time to get used to it. Look for the vegetarian-support formula (this will be noted on the label), which is enriched in vitamin B12.

Oils: Use neutral-flavored vegetable oils (such as canola, vegetable, peanut, etc.) in baking, unless otherwise mentioned. When it comes to cooking, we favor peanut oil for dishes that involve a long frying time because it has a high smoke point. For salads, we like extra-virgin olive oil.

We recognize that some people feel that canola and coconut oil are the evil duo of the greasy world. The charges against them include GMO issues for the former, and saturated fats for the latter. If this is a concern, you can always opt to replace them with peanut or vegetable oil.

Orange marmalade: You will find this in several of our recipes, because we love its bold flavor. Look for the kind that has no sugar or artificial sweetener added: It isn't bitter at all. Try Smucker's Simply Fruit or St. Dalfour brands.

Salt and pepper: We want to respect your habits when it comes to salt and pepper, so the measurements you will find in our recipes are meant as a guideline. You will usually see "to taste" added after these two ingredients so that you can follow your needs and preferences.

The salt you are most likely to find in our kitchens is sea salt, because it retains some minerals, albeit a minuscule amount. We have been known to add a small amount of black salt in recipes that aim to replicate eggs, because it lends a delicate sulfurous flavor to foods.

Sambal oelek: Spicy sauce made of chiles, vinegar, and salt, this condiment is available at most supermarkets in the international food section.

Soy sauce: If you prefer tamari or Bragg's Liquid Aminos, they are all interchangeable. We like to use the reduced-sodium kind so as to have control over the saltiness of our food. The liquid aminos only contain a small amount of natural sodium and happen to be gluten free.

Spices and herbs: Sometimes we call for fresh herbs and spices, and sometimes we call for dried in our recipes. Unless otherwise noted, you can use either, but of course, fresh is best whenever available. As a general rule, 1 part dried herb is the equivalent of 3 parts fresh.

Sriracha: This hot sauce is made from chile peppers, garlic, vinegar, and salt ground together to form a smooth paste. Check the ingredient list carefully, because some brands contain fish sauce.

Sweeteners: We most commonly use organic evaporated cane juice (guaranteed to be vegan, as opposed to most brands of granulated cane sugar), organic beet sugar, organic brown sugar, Sucanat, and raw sugar. As for the liquid sweeteners, why not try agave nectar, pure maple syrup, and brown rice syrup? We love them, too.

Tofu and tempeh: Silken tofu is most frequently used for desserts and sauces, and extra firm or even super firm (yes, there is such a thing!) is best for frying and baking. Be sure to press the tofu if you're going to fry it, because it makes for a chewier and meatier texture. To press, drain the block and then sandwich it between either two folded kitchen towels or several folded layers of paper towels. Place a heavy object (a book or frying pan) on top to press out excess moisture, and let sit for 1 hour.

TVP (textured vegetable protein): These granules are used to replicate and replace ground meats in many of our recipes. TVP is inexpensive and found in most health food stores. Made from defatted soy flour, this gluten-free staple will become a must-have in your kitchen. We mostly stick to the small granules, but the larger chunks can also come in handy for stir-fries, soups, and curries.

Vital wheat gluten flour: A perfect source of protein, this flour is sometimes used in breads to improve texture and is also used to prepare seitan, also known as *wheat meat*. Gluten is the natural protein portion removed from whole wheat. It can be found in most grocery stores or ordered online. Keep in mind that vital wheat gluten flour is completely different from high-gluten flour: these two are not interchangeable and will not perform similarly in recipes.

Yeast: We use active dry yeast in our recipes, unless otherwise noted, because it is readily available in markets. It is sold in either strips of three envelopes or in small jars. One envelope is equal to 2¼ teaspoons (¼ ounce, or 7 g).

Food Allergies and Recipe Icons

We have done our best to label our recipes, but allergens still have a way of sneaking into ingredients. Please closely monitor all food labels, and contact food manufacturers when in doubt.

Throughout this book you will find recipes labeled in the following way:

GLUTEN FREE

Gluten Free: Recipes that do not contain gluten. Double-check ingredient labels.

QUICK AND EASY

Quick and Easy: Recipes that take less than 30 minutes to whip up, provided you have intermediate cooking and/or baking skills.

LOW FAT

Low Fat: Recipes that contain 3 grams (the equivalent of 27 fat calories) of fat, or less, per serving.

SOY FREE

Soy Free: Recipes that do not contain soy. Double-check ingredient labels.

EAT YOUR VEGGIES!

You know your mama was right all along—munching on your greens *is* important and a great way to balance out the slightly more exuberant dishes you'll just have to try out from this book. Find hints as to what veggies or salads we like to pair certain recipes with by using this sidebar as your guide.

CHAPTER 2

Down-Home Breakfasts

Fluffy pancakes, hearty bowls, delectable doughnuts, and scrumptious scrambles—sweet and savory breakfasts to fuel you up for a hectic day.

Picture this: You wake up on the wrong side of the bed and find yourself wondering how those eight restful hours could have flown by so quickly. You pull yourself out of bed with only one thing on your mind: caffeine.

Hold that thought. Is that turbo-charged, ultra-grande, soy macchiato of yours really going to nourish you? Or are we going to find you face down on your keyboard two hours from now?

Let us help by offering this tidbit of advice: Hearty breakfasts make you full. Being full makes you focused. Being focused makes the day go by more quickly. And gets you back in that warm bed of yours in no time.

Don't say we never gave you anything.

PIÑA COLADA FRENCH TOAST WITH CANDIED MACADAMIA NUTS

If you top this already crazy good brunch item with vegan whipped cream, you will get marriage proposals. (We apologize in advance if you aren't actually looking to get hitched.) The rum syrup also makes more than enough for a few breakfasts (or as a topping for ice cream).

FOR THE RUM SYRUP:

1 cup (192 g) Sucanat

¼ cup (60 ml) dark rum or nondairy milk

½ teaspoon rum extract if using nondairy milk

⅓ cup (80 ml) water

½ teaspoon ground cinnamon

FOR THE CANDIED MACADAMIA NUTS:

¼ cup (48 g) Sucanat

2 tablespoons (30 ml) water

1 cup (132 g) macadamia nuts

Pinch of fine sea salt

FOR THE FRENCH TOAST:

½ cup (63 g) all-purpose flour

2 tablespoons (24 g) Sucanat

½ teaspoon ground cinnamon

Pinch of fine sea salt

1 cup (235 ml) coconut milk

1 recipe Juliette Brioche (page 184) or French bread, stale for best results, cut into eight 1-inch (2.5-cm) thick slices

Nondairy butter, for frying

FOR SERVING:

8 slices fresh pineapple

Nondairy whipped cream, for serving (optional)

DIRECTIONS:

To make the syrup: Combine all the ingredients in a saucepan. Bring to a boil, lower the heat, and cook until the Sucanat dissolves. Set aside. Let cool completely. (Extra may be stored in an airtight container in the refrigerator.)

To make the candied macadamia nuts: Place the Sucanat, water, nuts, and salt in a saucepan. Heat over medium-high, bring to a low boil, and cook for about 4 minutes. Stir constantly, lowering the heat to medium, until the nuts get some color to them. Remove from the heat. Set aside.

To make the French toast: In a shallow dish, combine the flour, Sucanat, cinnamon, and salt. Whisk in the milk until mostly smooth. Let stand for a few minutes.

Heat a pan over medium-high heat. Dip the bread, 1 slice at a time, into the batter. You just want a thin layer of batter on the bread.

Melt a pat of butter in the pan. Cook the toast until golden and crispy, about 2 minutes on each side. Repeat with the remaining slices.

Serve the French toast topped with the pineapple slices, a drizzle of rum syrup, and a sprinkle of candied nuts. If you have whipped cream . . . you know what to do.

YIELD: 4 servings, 1 cup (235 ml) rum syrup

FRENCH TOAST DIPSTICKS

These dippers are a fun way to serve breakfast, especially for kids.
If you have a deep fryer, these will cook up in mere seconds.
If not, a frying pan filled with about ½ inch (1.3 cm) of oil will do the trick just fine.

INGREDIENTS:

Vegetable oil, for frying

1 cup (125 g) all-purpose flour

2 tablespoons (25 g) evaporated cane juice or granulated sugar

¼ teaspoon ground cinnamon

⅛ teaspoon salt

¼ teaspoon baking powder

¼ teaspoon baking soda

1 cup (235 ml) vanilla-flavored nondairy milk

½ teaspoon pure vanilla extract

1 loaf hearty artisan French bread, stale is best

Powdered sugar, for serving

Warm maple syrup, for serving

DIRECTIONS:

Preheat the oil to 350°F (180°C).

In a shallow dish, combine the flour, sugar, cinnamon, salt, baking powder, and baking soda. Add the milk and vanilla and stir to combine until there are virtually no lumps.

Cut the bread into strips about 4 to 6 inches (10 to 15 cm) long and 1 inch (2.5 cm) thick and wide. Dip each strip of bread into the batter and place in the hot oil using tongs. If using a deep fryer, it should take only 5 to 10 seconds to get nice and golden and crispy. If using a frying pan, place on one side for 5 to 10 seconds, then flip and repeat until both sides are golden and crispy.

Transfer to a plate lined with paper towels to absorb the excess oil. Sprinkle with the powdered sugar and serve with the warm maple syrup for dipping.

YIELD: 12 to 16 dipsticks

RECIPE NOTE

Funny thing is . . . French Toast isn't really French at all. The earliest references date back to the late 4th or early 5th century AD, in a collection of Roman recipes known as the *Apicius*!

THE CAPTAIN'S FRENCH TOAST

QUICK AND EASY

We call for Cap'n Crunch cereal in this recipe, but you can swap in an alternative if you prefer. Although Cap'n Crunch does appear to be vegan, it does contain an insane amount of weird things in the ingredients, so try using an all-natural variety, such as Gorilla Munch, if you like.

INGREDIENTS:

2 cups (72 g) sweet corn cereal, such as Cap'n Crunch, crushed into a powder

½ cup (62 g) all-purpose flour

¼ teaspoon baking soda

¼ teaspoon baking powder

1 cup (235 ml) vanilla-flavored nondairy milk

3 tablespoons (42 g) nondairy butter, for frying

6 slices stale French bread, about ½ inch (1.25 cm) thick

Maple syrup, for serving

DIRECTIONS:

Combine the crushed cereal, flour, baking soda, and baking powder in a shallow dish. Stir in the milk to make a thick batter.

Preheat a frying pan over high heat. Melt 1 tablespoon (14 g) of the butter for every 2 slices of French toast.

Dip each piece of bread into the batter. The batter is thick, so you may need to smear it on the bread with your fingers. Panfry for about 2 minutes per side, or until golden and crispy. Serve hot with pure maple syrup.

YIELD: 6 slices

RECIPE NOTE

In addition to butter and warm maple syrup, sliced strawberries (as shown) or fresh blueberries and a dollop of nondairy whipped cream taste spectacular served atop this sweet breakfast treat.

COCOA KAHLÚA PANCAKES

QUICK AND EASY

Ooh, yummy! Chocolate pancakes with a grown-up flair!

INGREDIENTS:

2 cups (250 g) all-purpose flour

½ teaspoon salt

1 teaspoon baking powder

1 teaspoon baking soda

¼ cup (50 g) evaporated cane juice or granulated sugar

¼ cup (20 g) unsweetened cocoa powder

1 tablespoon (7 g) instant espresso powder

⅔ cup (160 ml) vanilla-flavored or plain soymilk

2 tablespoons (30 ml) freshly squeezed lemon juice

⅓ cup (80 ml) coffee liqueur, such as Kahlúa

¼ cup (60 g) vegetable oil

1 teaspoon pure vanilla extract

Nondairy butter, maple syrup, or Chocolate Syrup (page 227), for serving

DIRECTIONS:

In a medium-size mixing bowl, sift together the flour, salt, baking powder, baking soda, sugar, cocoa powder, and espresso powder. In a separate small bowl, combine the soymilk and lemon juice. It will curdle and become like buttermilk. Add the liqueur, oil, and vanilla and stir to combine. Stir the wet ingredients into the dry and mix until there are virtually no lumps. (For the teetotalers and kiddies out there, replace the Kahlúa with strong brewed coffee. Add ¼ cup (50 g) evaporated cane juice or granulated sugar to make up for the lost sweetness.)

Preheat a nonstick skillet over high heat. Drop about ½ cup (150 g) of batter per pancake onto the pan. This batter is a bit thicker than most pancake batters, so it will need a little coaxing to spread on the pan. When the batter begins to bubble, flip and cook on the other side until golden brown. Serve immediately with whatever you fancy.

YIELD: Six 6-inch (15-cm) pancakes

SALTY SWEET OATS ▶

QUICK AND EASY   SOY FREE

Peanut butter + jelly, ice cream + cake, salty + sweet . . . these combinations just belong together, and we wouldn't have it any other way. Put these oats to good use by incorporating them into pancakes or waffles (page 26), cookies (page 248), or simply eat them by the fistful.

INGREDIENTS:

2 cups (160 g) old-fashioned oats

4 ounces (113 g) crushed pretzels

¼ cup (36 g) light brown sugar, not packed

2 tablespoons (30 ml) pure maple syrup

2 teaspoons (4.6 g) ground cinnamon

2 tablespoons (30 ml) peanut oil

2 tablespoons (30 ml) water

DIRECTIONS:

Preheat the oven to 325°F (170°C, or gas mark 3).

Place all the ingredients in a large bowl and stir to combine. Spread evenly on a large rimmed baking sheet.

Bake for 8 minutes, stirring well. Bake for another 8 minutes, or until golden brown. Let cool on the baking sheet. Store in an airtight container for up to 2 weeks.

YIELD: 4 cups (400 g)

OVERNIGHT OAT PANCAKES OR WAFFLES

Although we are big fans of typical pancakes and waffles, we wanted to make things even easier on you by creating a delicious batter you can prepare the night before and enjoy first thing in the morning. Weekend breakfasts don't get much easier than this!

INGREDIENTS:

1 cup (235 ml) light coconut milk, at room temperature, plus more for final batter

¼ cup (50 g) evaporated cane juice or granulated sugar

1 teaspoon active dry yeast

1 teaspoon pure vanilla extract

1 cup (120 g) whole wheat pastry or all-purpose flour

1 cup (100 g) Salty Sweet Oats (page 24), plus extra for sprinkling

1 teaspoon baking powder

½ teaspoon fine sea salt

Nonstick cooking spray, if making waffles

Vegetable oil, if making pancakes

Compote (page 229) or Marinated Strawberries (page 234), for serving

Nondairy whipped cream, for serving

DIRECTIONS:

Combine the 1 cup (235 ml) milk, sugar, and yeast. Let stand for 5 minutes until bubbles and foam form. Using a fork, stir in the vanilla, flour, 1 cup (100 g) oats, baking powder, and salt until combined. Cover with plastic wrap and place in the refrigerator overnight.

The next morning, remove from the refrigerator, stir the thick batter with a fork, cover again, and leave on the counter for 1 hour to bring back to room temperature.

To make waffles: Adjust the batter thinness if needed by adding extra milk so that the batter is just pourable. Following the manufacturer's instructions, coat the waffle iron with cooking spray in between each waffle, when the machine has been sufficiently preheated. Add about ¾ cup (170 g) batter per waffle in a Belgian-style waffle iron, ½ cup (113 g) per standard waffle iron. For extra crispness, toast the waffles before enjoying.

To make pancakes: Adjust the batter thinness if needed by adding extra milk so that the batter is just pourable. Heat a nonstick pan over medium-low heat and coat with 1 teaspoon oil. Add about ⅓ cup (76 g) batter, and cook pancakes for 6 minutes on each side, or until golden brown and fully cooked. Add extra oil as needed while cooking.

Serve with compote or Marinated Strawberries and nondairy whipped cream. Sprinkle extra oats on top.

YIELD: 6 to 8 medium pancakes, or 3 Belgian or 6 standard waffles

BLUEBERRY BUTTERMILK PANCAKES

QUICK AND EASY

When Joni and Celine embarked on a road trip to Portland, Oregon, Joni was on a quest to find some fluffy, delicious diner-style vegan blueberry pancakes. After being disappointed time and time again, she decided to take things into her own hands; this recipe will cook up fluffier and tastier than any pancake you've ever tried!

INGREDIENTS:

2 cups (250 g) all-purpose flour

½ teaspoon salt

½ teaspoon baking powder

½ teaspoon baking soda

2 tablespoons (25 g) evaporated cane juice or granulated sugar

1½ cups (355 ml) soymilk

3 tablespoons (45 ml) freshly squeezed lemon juice

1 teaspoon pure vanilla extract

1 tablespoon (8 g) Ener-G egg replacer powder

¼ cup (60 ml) warm water

3 tablespoons (42 g) nondairy butter, melted, optional

1 cup (145 g) fresh or thawed frozen blueberries

Nondairy butter and maple syrup, for serving

DIRECTIONS:

In a medium-size mixing bowl, combine the flour, salt, baking powder, baking soda, and sugar. In a small bowl, combine the soymilk, lemon juice, and vanilla. It will curdle and become like buttermilk. In another small bowl, whisk together the egg replacer and warm water until foamy. Add to the buttermilk mixture. Add the wet ingredients to the dry and mix until the batter just comes together. Mix in the melted butter.

Heat a large nonstick skillet over medium-high heat. (If not using a nonstick skillet, melt a little bit of nondairy butter in the pan to prevent sticking.) Ladle about ½ cup (140 g) of batter into the pan for each pancake. Sprinkle a handful of blueberries on each pancake. When the batter begins to bubble, flip and cook on the other side until golden brown.

Serve immediately with butter and maple syrup.

YIELD: Six 6-inch (15-cm) pancakes

RECIPE NOTE

If your serious about making your pancakes perfect, follow these in-depth directions: Preheat your pan, then melt the butter. Add the batter to the center of the pan, leaving ample room to flip. Watch the batter. When it begins to bubble and the edges start to look dry, use a spatula to lift the edge and check the color. If it is nice and golden brown then it is time to flip! Slide the spatula under the pancake, and in one quick, smooth motion, lift and flip the pancake. Make sure it lands back in the center of the pan. Lift the edge to check color after about a minute. Once golden, flip one last time, give it a press, and if no batter oozes, then the pancake is done!

BANANA SPLIT WAFFLES

We love to turn regular breakfast items into acceptable morning versions of our favorite decadent desserts, and it was high time banana split made our list.

INGREDIENTS:

½ cup (96 g) Sucanat

2 ripe bananas

2 cups (470 ml) nondairy milk

¼ cup (60 ml) vegetable oil

2 teaspoons (10 ml) pure vanilla extract

1 teaspoon ground cinnamon

1½ cups (120 g) old-fashioned oats

1½ cups (180 g) all-purpose flour, divided

1 tablespoon (12 g) baking powder

¼ teaspoon fine sea salt

2 tablespoons (16 g) cornstarch

½ cup (80 g) dried cherries

DIRECTIONS:

Combine the Sucanat, bananas, milk, oil, vanilla, cinnamon, oats, ½ cup (60 g) of the flour, baking powder, and salt in a large bowl. Use an immersion blender and blend until smooth. Stir in the cornstarch and cherries, along with the remaining 1 cup (120 g) flour. Let stand for 15 minutes.

Following the manufacturer's instructions, coat the waffle iron with cooking spray in between each waffle, when the machine has been sufficiently preheated. Pour about ¾ cup (180 ml) batter for Belgian waffles, about ½ cup (120 ml) for standard, adjusting to fit your waffle iron. For ultimate crispness, toast the waffles before enjoying them.

YIELD: 6 Belgian waffles or 10 to 12 standard waffles

RECIPE NOTE

Want to make something mighty tasty *even better*? Enjoy these with a big scoop of your favorite ice cream (Cake Batter Ice Cream, page 222, is pictured here), nondairy whipped cream, and Chocolate Syrup (page 227).

BREAKFAST POTATOES O'BRIEN

These are the kind of breakfast potatoes that you can order at any ole greasy spoon. Lucky for us, we can make them at home! It's up to you whether or not to leave the skins on the taters.

INGREDIENTS:

6 medium-size russet potatoes, diced (8½ cups, or 1275 g)

3 tablespoons (42 g) nondairy butter

1 medium-size yellow or white onion, diced

1 green bell pepper, cored, seeded, and finely diced

1 red bell pepper, cored, seeded, and finely diced

1 clove garlic, minced

1 jar (4 ounces, or 112 g) diced pimientos, drained

Vegetable oil, for frying

Salt and pepper, to taste

DIRECTIONS:

Soak the potatoes in cold water to prevent discoloration while the other ingredients are being prepped, and then drain and pat dry thoroughly.

Melt the butter in a frying pan over medium heat. Add the onion, peppers, garlic, and pimientos. Sauté until tender and fragrant, 5 to 7 minutes. Remove from the heat and set aside.

In a large cast-iron skillet or frying pan, pour the oil to a depth of ¼ inch (6 mm). Heat over medium-high heat. Add the potatoes and cook until golden brown and fork-tender. Carefully drain the excess oil.

Add the pepper and onion mix, season with salt and pepper, and toss, continuing to cook until completely heated through, 3 to 5 minutes.

YIELD: 6 to 8 servings

GRAMMA JO'S TATER TOT SURPRISE

Joni's Gramma Jo makes these potatoes every time the family gets together for a holiday breakfast or brunch. It makes a lot, so if you're looking for a handy way to use up the leftovers, try making a breakfast wrap. Add a pile of potatoes into the center of a soft flour tortilla, top with a little hot sauce and a few avocado slices, roll it all up and you have yourself a handy on-the-go breakfast!

INGREDIENTS:

1 large bag (32 ounces, or 900 g) tater tots, thawed

½ cup (50 g) finely chopped scallion

8 ounces (227 g) nondairy sour cream, store-bought or homemade (page 211)

2 cups (470 ml) Creamy Mushroom Soup (page 71) or store-bought vegan mushroom soup

1 cup (112 g) shredded nondairy cheese, such as Daiya

½ cup (112 g) nondairy butter, melted

4 cups (112 g) cornflake cereal, crushed

DIRECTIONS:

Preheat the oven to 350°F (180°C, or gas mark 4).

Cut each tater tot in half (this is optional, but makes it better for sure!) and add to a large bowl. Add the scallion, sour cream, soup, cheese, and melted butter and mix well, using your hands. Spread evenly in a 9 × 13 × 2-inch (22.5 × 32.5 × 5-cm) baking dish.

Top with the cornflakes and bake, uncovered, for 30 minutes. The cornflakes won't really brown, so just know that it needs to be hot all the way through. Allow to cool for about 10 minutes before cutting into squares and serving.

YIELD: 12 servings

BREAKFAST BURRITO

Scrambled tofu, potatoes, and avocado wrapped together in a tortilla?
The day ahead magically appears a tad less stressful all of a sudden.

INGREDIENTS:

2 tablespoons (30 ml) peanut oil

2 tablespoons (20 g) chopped shallot

1 cup (150 g) diced red potatoes

1 pound (454 g) extra-firm tofu,
drained, pressed, and crumbled

1 tablespoon (17 g) brown sauce, such as HP, or
1 teaspoon vegan Worcestershire sauce

15 ounces (425 g) fire-roasted or
regular diced tomatoes, with liquid

3 tablespoons (48 g) natural peanut butter

2 cloves garlic, minced

1 tablespoon (15 ml) soy sauce

1 teaspoon ground ginger

4 burrito-size flour tortillas

1 medium-size avocado, halved, pitted,
peeled, and cut into 8 slices

DIRECTIONS:

In a large skillet, combine the oil, shallot, and potatoes. Cook over medium-high heat for 10 minutes, or until the potatoes start to brown, stirring often. Add the tofu and fry until golden brown, about 10 minutes longer, stirring often.

In the meantime, in a medium-size bowl, combine the brown sauce, tomatoes, peanut butter, garlic, soy sauce, and ginger. Stir the mixture into the potatoes and tofu, and cook for 4 minutes longer, until the sauce reduces down a bit.

Divide the preparation among 4 tortillas, and top with 2 avocado slices each. Wrap up the tortillas tightly, and serve.

YIELD: 4 burritos

EAT YOUR VEGGIES!

Turn this into a complete and nutritious meal by serving alongside a freshly made and in-season fruit salad (technically not veggies, we know, but "Eat Your Produce" sounded too silly). Our favorite combo is strawberry halves and fresh pineapple chunks.

BREAKFAST CHICKEN-FRIED STEAK

The coating on this chicken-fried steak is both sweet and savory, crispy and crunchy, making it perfect breakfast fare. Serve it smothered in White Sausage Gravy (page 33).

FOR THE CUTLETS:

2 cups (288 g) vital wheat gluten flour

1 cup (120 g) whole wheat pastry flour

1 tablespoon (7 g) garlic powder

2 tablespoons (14 g) onion powder

½ teaspoon freshly ground black pepper

¼ cup (30 g) nutritional yeast

1 cup (235 ml) vegetable broth

¼ cup (60 ml) soy sauce

¼ cup (60 ml) steak sauce

2 tablespoons (30 ml) oil

1 tablespoon (15 ml) liquid smoke

FOR THE BOILING BROTH:

6 cups (1.41 l) vegetable broth

½ cup (120 ml) soy sauce

3 cloves garlic, cut in half

1 bay leaf

FOR THE CRISPY COATING:

1 cup (235 ml) plain soymilk

2 tablespoons (30 ml) freshly squeezed lemon juice

1 cup (36 g) sweet corn cereal, such as Cap'n Crunch, crushed into a powder

1 cup (125 g) all-purpose flour

¼ teaspoon paprika

½ teaspoon dried parsley

½ teaspoon garlic powder

¼ teaspoon salt

¼ teaspoon freshly ground pepper

½ teaspoon onion powder

½ teaspoon dried mustard

Oil, for frying

DIRECTIONS:

To make the cutlets: Combine the wheat gluten, whole wheat pastry flour, garlic powder, onion powder, black pepper, and nutritional yeast in a large mixing bowl.

Combine the vegetable broth, soy sauce, steak sauce, oil, and liquid smoke in a separate bowl. Add the wet ingredients to the dry and knead for about 10 minutes. You can do this right in the bowl. Let rest for about 20 minutes to allow the gluten to develop.

Divide the dough into 7 equal pieces. Form each piece into an oblong patty about ½ inch (1.3 cm) thick.

To make the broth: Add all of the broth ingredients to a large pot. Bring to a boil. Reduce to a simmer.

Carefully place each patty into the simmering broth, cover, and simmer for 30 minutes. Return occasionally to gently stir and prevent the steaks from sticking to the bottom and each other.

Remove the steaks from the broth and set aside. Reserve 1 steak (unfried) to be used in the gravy.

To make the crispy coating: In a shallow dish mix together the soymilk and lemon juice; it will curdle and become like buttermilk. In a separate shallow dish, mix together the crushed cereal, flour, and spices.

Pour the oil to a depth of about ½ inch (1.3 cm) into a deep fryer or a frying pan and heat to 350°F (180°C).

Take 1 steak and dip into the buttermilk mixture to coat, then dredge in the cereal mixture for a nice thick coating. Carefully place in the oil and fry until golden brown and crispy.

Remove from the oil and place on a paper towel-lined plate to absorb the excess oil. Repeat to fry the remaining 5 steaks.

YIELD: 6 steaks

WHITE SAUSAGE GRAVY

When we went vegan, we thought rich, peppery, thick breakfast gravy was
a thing of the past. The addition of nondairy sour cream, either
store-bought or homemade (page 211), takes this from good to GRAVY.

INGREDIENTS:

2 tablespoons (28 g) nondairy butter

¼ cup (31 g) all-purpose flour

2 cups (470 ml) vegetable broth

¼ cup (60 g) nondairy sour cream,
store-bought or homemade (page 211)

½ teaspoon freshly ground black pepper

1 piece Breakfast Chicken-Fried Steak (page 32),
cut into tiny chunks

DIRECTIONS:

Melt the butter in a saucepot over medium-high heat.

Add the flour and stir to make a light golden roux (or until
the raw flour smell is gone). Slowly stir in the vegetable
broth and continue to whisk until there are no lumps and
the mixture is thick like gravy, 2 to 3 minutes.

Remove from the heat. Stir in the sour cream, pepper,
and steak pieces. Stir until thick, creamy, and smooth.

YIELD: 2½ cups (590 ml)

RECIPE NOTE

This white gravy is perfect to ladle over the Bacon
Onion Biscuits (page 191) or the Chick' N' Waffles
Party (page 109), and is absolutely essential for the
Breakfast Chicken-Fried Steak (at left).

HAWAIIAN BENEDICT

We all long for vacation time we never seem to get. Might as well escape whichever way we can, like with these stick-to-your-ribs open-faced breakfast sandwiches.

2 tablespoons (30 ml) peanut oil

14 ounces (397 g) extra-firm tofu, drained, pressed, and crumbled

2 tablespoons (20 g) chopped shallot

2 cloves garlic, minced

½ teaspoon fine sea salt

1 teaspoon paprika

2 teaspoons (4 g) curry powder

1 teaspoon turmeric

1 tablespoon (8 g) nutritional yeast

8 slices store-bought vegan Canadian bacon or Tempeh Bacon (page 84)

2 tablespoons (28 g) nondairy butter

8 slices fresh pineapple

4 Avocado Rolls (page 194) or store-bought bread rolls

½ cup (120 ml) Creamy Cheesy Sauce (page 212), made using 2 tablespoons (16 g) cornstarch

¼ cup (15 g) chopped fresh parsley

DIRECTIONS:

Heat the oil in a large skillet over medium heat. Add the tofu, shallot, garlic, and seasonings and cook for 10 minutes, until the tofu turns browns, stirring often. Set aside.

Cook the bacon in a large skillet over medium heat until brown, about 5 minutes. Set aside.

Melt the butter in a large skillet over medium heat. Add the pineapple slices and sauté until heated through, about 6 minutes. Alternatively, use a grill pan to get those visually pleasing grill marks. Set aside.

Toast the rolls. Spread 1 tablespoon (15 ml) sauce on each side of the rolls. Top with 1 slice of bacon. Divide the scrambled tofu among the rolls. Top with 1 slice of pine-apple. Sprinkle the parsley on top, and serve immediately.

YIELD: 4 servings

HEARTY BREAKFAST BOWL

All your breakfast favorites together in one hearty bowlful:
scrambled eggs, potatoes, bacon, and cheesy gravy, oh my!

FOR THE CHEESY GRAVY:

1 cup (235 ml) vegetable broth

2 tablespoons (28 g) nondairy butter

¼ cup (30 g) nutritional yeast

¼ cup (56 g) finely ground raw cashews

½ cup (120 g) nondairy sour cream,
store-bought or homemade (page 211)

Salt and pepper, to taste

FOR THE SCRAMBLED EGGS:

10 ounces (280 g) extra-firm tofu, drained and pressed

2 tablespoons (15 g) nutritional yeast

½ teaspoon garlic powder

½ teaspoon onion powder

¼ teaspoon turmeric

¼ teaspoon black salt

Sea salt and pepper, to taste

2 tablespoons (30 ml) mild-flavored
vegetable oil, for frying

30 tater tots, prepared according to package directions

¼ cup (20 g) imitation bacon bits, store-bought or
homemade (page 216), or crumbled pieces
Hickory-Smoked Breakfast Strips (page 38)

Diced scallion, for serving (optional)

DIRECTIONS:

To make the gravy: To a frying pan, add the vegetable broth and butter, and bring to a boil over medium-high heat. Lower the heat and stir in the nutritional yeast, cashews, and sour cream. Stir until thickened. Season with salt and pepper. Keep warm until ready to serve.

To make the eggs: In a medium-size bowl, crumble the tofu and add the all of the seasonings. Stir together until well incorporated.

Heat the oil in a frying pan over medium-high heat. Add the tofu mixture and cook for about 5 minutes, tossing continuously, until heated through. Divide between 2 bowls and add 15 tater tots to each bowl.

Pour the gravy over the tofu scramble and potatoes, top with the bacon bits and a sprinkling of scallions, and serve.

YIELD: 2 hearty bowls

BACON AND EGG BREAKFAST SANDWICH

Make this sandwich the next time you're craving one of those Mc-things. And if you want it combo style, serve it up with some Breakfast Potatoes O'Brien (page 30). Note that the spread tastes great on all kinds of sandwiches, from Tofurkey and veggie burgers, to tempeh tuna and BLTs.

We use black salt (which is actually pink!) in this recipe to really get that egg-y flavor in the tofu. It can be found in gourmet and specialty shops, and sometimes Indian grocery shops too (where it may be packaged as rock salt).

FOR THE SPREAD:

⅓ cup (80 g) nondairy cream cheese

⅓ cup (75 g) vegan mayonnaise, store-bought or homemade (page 211)

¼ teaspoon liquid smoke

2 tablespoons (13 g) finely chopped scallion or chives

1 tablespoon (3 g) fresh dill or 1 teaspoon dried

Salt and pepper, to taste

FOR THE SANDWICH:

¼ cup (60 ml) vegetable oil

½ teaspoon turmeric

1 teaspoon black salt

1 tablespoon (8 g) nutritional yeast

1 teaspoon Dijon mustard

Sea salt and pepper, to taste

4 slices drained and pressed super-firm tofu about 3 inches (8 cm) square by 1 inch (2.5 cm) thick

¼ cup (20 g) imitation bacon bits, store-bought or homemade (page 216), or crumbled pieces Hickory-Smoked Breakfast Strips (page 38)

4 bagels, English muffins, or rolls, sliced in half, or 8 slices bread, toasted

DIRECTIONS:

To make the spread: Mix all the ingredients together in a small bowl and refrigerate until ready to use.

To make the sandwiches: Mix together the oil, turmeric, black salt, nutritional yeast, mustard, sea salt, and pepper in a shallow dish and set aside.

Make a pocket in each of the tofu slices by inserting a sharp knife into one edge and cutting almost all the way through, leaving it sealed on three sides. Fill each pocket with 1 tablespoon (5 g) bacon bits.

Preheat a nonstick or cast-iron skillet over high heat.

Dip each piece of tofu into the oil and spice mixture to coat on all sides and transfer to the frying pan. Fry until heated through and a slight crust forms.

While the tofu is frying, smear a good amount of spread on both sides of the toasted bread. Place a tofu pocket on each sandwich and serve.

YIELD: 4 sandwiches

HICKORY-SMOKED BREAKFAST STRIPS

These strips are a fun way to add some smoky protein to your breakfast. They also work well in sandwiches, and pretty much anywhere else a bacon strip would be called for.

INGREDIENTS:

1 cup (96 g) TVP granules

1 cup (235 ml) vegetable broth or water

3 tablespoons (45 ml) hickory-flavored liquid smoke

½ cup (72 g) vital wheat gluten flour

2 tablespoons (16 g) tapioca starch or arrowroot powder

½ teaspoon paprika

1½ teaspoons sea salt

¼ teaspoon freshly ground black pepper

½ cup (120 ml) additional water

¼ cup (60 ml) canola or other mild-flavored oil, plus more for frying

2 tablespoons (30 ml) pure maple syrup

1 tablespoon (15 ml) sesame oil

DIRECTIONS:

Reconstitute the TVP one of two ways: 1) Combine with the broth and liquid smoke, cover tightly with plastic wrap, and microwave on High for 5 minutes. Or 2) Combine the liquid smoke with the TVP, bring the broth to a boil, pour over the TVP, stir, cover, and let sit for 10 minutes.

Add the reconstituted TVP, along with the wheat gluten, starch, paprika, salt, pepper, water, ¼ cup (60 ml) canola oil, maple syrup, and sesame oil to a food processor and process until a smooth dough forms with no TVP lumps. If the dough is too wet, add a bit more flour. The dough should be a soft, uniform ball. Let the dough rest for 20 minutes to allow the gluten to develop.

On a smooth, nonstick surface (such as a flexible cutting board or Silpat) break off a handful of dough and roll as thin as possible, trying to get it to at least 1⁄16 inch (1.5 mm). (Use another flexible cutting board or Silpat on top, to prevent the rolling pin from sticking, if you have an extra. A pasta roller would work nicely here, too.)

Pour a thin layer of canola oil into a frying pan and heat over high heat. While the oil is heating, cut the dough into strips about 1 inch (2.5 cm) wide and about 6 inches (15 cm) long. (Cut wavy lines so that it more mimics the look of bacon rather than cutting straight, rectangular strips.)

Place the strips in the hot oil and fry for about 15 to 20 seconds, until crispy and almost blackened. Flip and repeat on the other side. Transfer to a plate lined with paper towels to absorb the excess oil.

Repeat until all the strips are fried. Serve as you would any bacon strip. (These freeze nicely. Store them in layers separated by waxed paper or parchment in an airtight container for up to 1 month.)

YIELD: 1 pound (454 g)

REAL MEN EAT QUICHE LORRAINE

You can make this quiche with or without a crust. (If you opt for a crust, go with the Basic Pie Crust [page 234] for flaky goodness, or opt for a store-bought one to make the task even easier.) You can use a 10-inch (25-cm) cast-iron skillet instead of a pie pan as well. Really, you can make whatever changes you like, as long as you keep your final step the same: devour!

INGREDIENTS:

1 pie crust, store-bought or homemade (page 234), prebaked

14 ounces (397 g) silken tofu, drained but not pressed

¼ cup (30 g) nutritional yeast

¼ cup (30 g) chickpea flour

¼ cup (32 g) cornstarch

¼ cup (60 ml) olive oil

1 teaspoon onion powder

1 teaspoon garlic powder

¼ teaspoon turmeric

1 tablespoon (15 g) Dijon mustard

¼ teaspoon black salt

½ teaspoon cumin

¼ teaspoon paprika

½ teaspoon liquid smoke

1 cup (160 g) diced red or white onion

1¼ cups (140 g) shredded vegan cheese, such as Daiya, divided

10 slices Hickory-Smoked Breakfast Strips (page 38), or store-bought imitation bacon, crumbled

DIRECTIONS:

Preheat the oven to 350°F (180°C, or gas mark 4). Coat a 9-inch (23-cm) pie pan with cooking spray and line with the pie crust. If using a homemade crust, be sure to prebake it at 350°F (180°C, or gas mark 4) for about 16 minutes. Wrap the crust edges in foil to avoid overbaking.

In a blender, combine the tofu, nutritional yeast, chickpea flour, cornstarch, olive oil, onion powder, garlic powder, turmeric, mustard, black salt, cumin, paprika, and liquid smoke. Purée until smooth.

Transfer the mixture to a mixing bowl and stir in the onion, 1 cup (112 g) of the cheese, and bacon. Pour the mixture evenly into the pie crust. Bake, uncovered, for 45 minutes.

Carefully remove the pan from the oven, sprinkle with the remaining ¼ cup (28 g) cheese, and bake for 20 minutes longer, or until the top is golden brown and crispy and the center is firm.

Let cool for at least 10 minutes before slicing and serving.

YIELD: 8 servings

TOFUEVOS RANCHEROS

This spicy breakfast will definitely fill you up until lunchtime, if not dinner!

FOR THE RANCHERO SAUCE:

2 tablespoons (30 g) vegetable oil

4 cloves garlic, minced

1 medium-size yellow onion, diced

1 can (15 ounces, or 425 g) diced tomatoes, with juice

1 can (15 ounces, or 425 g) black beans, rinsed and drained

4 to 6 slices jarred jalapeños, or to taste, diced

1 chipotle pepper in adobo, or to taste, diced

1 tablespoon (15 g) adobo sauce from can, or to taste

Salt and pepper, to taste

FOR THE TOFUEVOS:

20 ounces (560 g) super-firm tofu, drained and pressed

¼ cup (30 g) nutritional yeast

1 tablespoon (8 g) garlic powder

1 tablespoon (8 g) onion powder

1 teaspoon black salt

½ teaspoon turmeric

¼ teaspoon black pepper

2 tablespoons (30 g) vegetable oil

4 teaspoons (4.5 g) nondairy butter

4 corn or flour tortillas

Nondairy sour cream, store-bought or homemade (page 211); avocado, pitted and sliced; and chopped scallion, for serving

DIRECTIONS:

To make the ranchero sauce: Heat the oil in a medium-size pot over medium heat. Add the garlic and onion and sauté until translucent and fragrant, 3 to 5 minutes.

Add the tomatoes, beans, jalapeños, chipotle, and adobo. Stir to mix. Cover, and simmer for 15 minutes.

Remove from the heat and using an immersion blender, pulse the mixture several times until pasty, but still chunky—like really chunky refried beans. Season with salt and pepper. Set aside, but keep warm.

To make the tofuevos: Crumble the tofu and combine with the nutritional yeast, garlic powder, onion powder, salt, turmeric, and pepper in a bowl. Use your hands to make sure everything gets mashed together.

Heat the oil in a pan over medium-high heat. Add the tofu mixture and panfry until heated through and just beginning to brown. Transfer back to the bowl and keep warm while you heat the tortillas.

Using the same pan, melt 1 teaspoon of butter over medium heat. Lightly panfry a tortilla on both sides until warm and soft. Transfer to a plate and cover lightly with a kitchen towel to keep warm. Repeat with the remaining 3 tortillas.

On each plate, divide the Tofuevos evenly on top of each tortilla, then pour the ranchero sauce on top of the tofuevos. Top with the sour cream, avocado, and scallion, and serve.

YIELD: 4 servings

CHORIZO AND EGG FRITTATA

A baked omelet that feeds eight! Don't skimp and skip the crispy onions, because they really make this dish. A 10-inch (25-cm) cast-iron skillet works wonders in this recipe; if you don't have one, go ahead and use a standard pie dish instead. Serve garnished with nondairy sour cream and fresh avocado slices.

INGREDIENTS:

14 ounces (392 g) extra-firm tofu, drained and pressed

6 ounces (168 g) TVP Chorizo (page 216) or store-bought soy chorizo

½ cup (80 g) finely diced yellow or white onion

½ cup (60 g) masa harina flour

¼ cup (32 g) cornstarch or arrowroot powder

¼ cup (30 g) nutritional yeast

1 teaspoon dried cilantro

½ teaspoon black salt

½ teaspoon ground cumin

¼ teaspoon ground coriander

¼ teaspoon turmeric

¼ cup plus 1 tablespoon (75 ml) vegetable oil, divided

¼ cup (60 ml) water

½ cup (56 g) shredded nondairy cheese, such as Daiya, divided

1 cup (96 g) crispy French fried onions

Freshly ground pepper, to taste

Nondairy sour cream, store-bought or homemade (page 211), and sliced avocado, for garnish

DIRECTIONS:

Preheat the oven to 350°F (180°C, or gas mark 4).

In a large mixing bowl, combine the tofu, chorizo, onion, flour, cornstarch, nutritional yeast, spices, ¼ cup (60 ml) of the oil, water, and ¼ cup (28 g) of the cheese, using your hands to get everything uniformly combined and incorporated. The mixture will be like a wet sticky dough, but it shouldn't be runny.

Coat a pan with the remaining 1 tablespoon (15 ml) oil, and spread the mixture evenly in the pan.

Sprinkle the crispy onions evenly over the top. Sprinkle the remaining ¼ cup (28 g) cheese on top of the onions, and season with pepper to taste.

Cover with foil and bake for 45 minutes. Uncover and bake for 20 minutes longer.

Remove from the oven and allow to sit for 10 minutes before slicing. Top with sour cream and avocado upon serving.

YIELD: 8 servings

COCONUT CRÈME BRÛLÉE BAKED OATMEAL

If you were looking for a way to have your first meal of the day be not only nutritious and filling, but deliciously dessertlike and creative too, you can pat yourself on the back for coming across this baked oatmeal recipe. Just be sure to use the hand that doesn't hold the fork when you do.

INGREDIENTS:

2½ cups (200 g) old-fashioned oats

3 tablespoons (36 g) evaporated cane juice or granulated sugar

3 tablespoons (45 ml) pure maple syrup

Juice and zest of 1 large lemon

14 ounces (414 ml) coconut milk

Pinch of salt

1 teaspoon pure vanilla extract

½ cup (120 g) plain or vanilla-flavored coconut yogurt

1 cup (187 g) fresh or frozen raspberries

¼ to ⅓ cup (55 to 73 g) packed light brown sugar

DIRECTIONS:

Combine the oats, sugar, maple syrup, lemon juice and zest, coconut milk, salt, vanilla, and yogurt in a large bowl; you can either let the mixture stand overnight in the refrigerator, covered, to soften the oats or bake it immediately. If choosing the overnight option, stir in the berries just before baking. If baking immediately, stir in the berries now.

Preheat the oven to 350°F (180°C, or gas mark 4). Lightly coat a 9 × 13-inch (23 × 33-cm) pan with nondairy butter. Scrape the mixture into the pan.

Bake for 40 minutes, or until firm and golden brown. Sprinkle the top evenly with the brown sugar to taste. Return the pan to the oven and bake a few minutes longer, until the sugar melts.

Use a kitchen torch or the broiler, and torch/broil until the sugar caramelizes; this should take 2 minutes in the broiler, but keep a careful close eye to make sure it doesn't burn!

YIELD: 6 servings

CINNAMON-Y BREAKFAST CEREAL COOKIES

Still eating your cereal with milk? Bor-ing! Here's a more exciting, over-the-top way to enjoy your morning dose of crunchy goodness.

INGREDIENTS:

2 cups (250 g) all-purpose or whole wheat pastry flour

4½ cups (225 g) vegan shredded wheat cereal, such as Kashi's Cinnamon Harvest, mostly crushed

1 teaspoon baking powder

½ teaspoon fine sea salt

2 teaspoons (4.6 g) ground cinnamon

⅓ cup (80 ml) peanut oil

½ cup (128 g) natural crunchy peanut butter

¼ cup (48 g) Sucanat

½ cup (96 g) raw sugar

¼ cup (60 ml) pure maple syrup

½ cup (80 g) raisins or other dried fruit

⅓ to ½ cup (80 to 120 ml) nondairy milk

2 teaspoons (10 ml) pure vanilla extract

½ teaspoon maple extract

DIRECTIONS:

Preheat the oven to 350°F (180°C, or gas mark 4). Line 2 baking sheets with parchment paper or silicone baking mats.

Combine the flour, shredded wheat, baking powder, salt, and cinnamon in a large bowl.

In a medium-size bowl, stir together the oil, peanut butter, Sucanat, raw sugar, maple syrup, raisins, ⅓ cup (80 ml) of the milk, and extracts.

Combine with the dry ingredients, adding the remaining 2½ tablespoons (40 ml) milk if the mixture is too dry; you want it to hold together when pinched.

Divide the dough into 10 equal portions of ⅓ cup (120 g) per cookie. Place on the prepared baking sheets and flatten the dough, because the cookies won't spread while baking.

Bake for 16 to 18 minutes, or until golden brown at the edges and firm. Let cool on the baking sheet for a few minutes before carefully transferring to a wire rack to cool completely.

YIELD: 10 large breakfast cookies

LEMON—POPPY SEED SCONES

Like most vegans, you know that your local coffee shop has plenty of baked goods, but not a one that a vegan can enjoy. These scones cook up nice and big, just like the ones you'd find at a coffee shop—minus the animal ingredients, of course. The lemon glaze is optional, but it whips up in seconds flat, and adds a bit more of sweet lemony goodness to an otherwise subtly lemony and subtly sweet treat.

FOR THE SCONES:

4 cups (500 g) all-purpose flour

⅓ cup (67 g) evaporated cane juice or granulated sugar

1 teaspoon baking powder

½ teaspoon baking soda

¼ teaspoon salt

1 tablespoon (9 g) poppy seeds

⅔ cup (160 ml) soymilk

2 teaspoons (4 g) lemon zest

⅓ cup (80 ml) freshly squeezed lemon juice

1 teaspoon pure vanilla extract

1 teaspoon pure lemon extract

¼ cup (60 g) nondairy lemon-flavored or plain yogurt

½ cup (112 g) cold nondairy butter, cut into small chunks

FOR THE GLAZE:

½ cup (60 g) powdered sugar, sifted

1 tablespoon (15 ml) freshly squeezed lemon juice

½ teaspoon packed lemon zest

DIRECTIONS:

Preheat the oven to 400°F (200°C, or gas mark 6). Lightly coat a 9-inch (23-cm) pie pan or dish with cooking spray.

To make the scones: In a large mixing bowl, whisk together the flour, sugar, baking powder, baking soda, salt, and poppy seeds.

In a separate small bowl, combine the soymilk, lemon zest, lemon juice, vanilla and lemon extracts, and yogurt. Set aside.

Cut the butter into the flour mixture using an electric mixer on low speed until the mixture is coarse and crumbly. Slowly add the milk mixture, blending until just combined.

Turn the dough out onto a floured surface and gently knead until a soft dough ball forms. Take care not to over-work the dough; you actually want small pieces of butter to be visible (that's what makes them tender and flaky). Press the dough evenly into the pie pan. Using a sharp knife, cut the dough into 8 pie-shaped wedges.

Bake for 30 to 40 minutes, or until golden and a tooth-pick inserted into the center comes out clean.

To make the glaze: Whisk together all the glaze ingredients until smooth.

Remove the scones from the oven and allow to cool to the touch before removing from the pan and cutting apart.

Drizzle on the glaze.

YIELD: 8 giant café-size scones

PB AND OM MUFFINS

Enjoy one or two of these heartily fluffy treats for breakfast, because your appetite is worth the extra time it will take you to actually have something to eat first thing in the morning.

INGREDIENTS:

1 cup (235 ml) soymilk, plus more as needed

1 tablespoon (15 ml) apple cider vinegar

¾ cup (144 g) Sucanat

½ cup (128 g) natural crunchy peanut butter

½ cup (120 g) nondairy plain yogurt

½ teaspoon fine sea salt

1½ teaspoons pure vanilla extract

1½ teaspoons pure orange extract

2 cups (240 g) whole wheat pastry flour

1 cup (80 g) old-fashioned oats

2 teaspoons baking powder

1 teaspoon (9 g) baking soda

¼ cup (80 g) orange marmalade (preferably not bitter) or ¼ cup (24 g) vegan marshmallow creme, such as Ricemellow Creme

DIRECTIONS:

Preheat the oven to 350°F (180°C, or gas mark 4). Line 12 standard muffin cups with paper liners.

In a large bowl, combine the milk, vinegar, Sucanat, peanut butter, yogurt, salt, and extracts until emulsified. Add the flour, oats, baking powder, and baking soda on top. Fold the dry ingredients into the wet, being careful not to overmix. If the batter is too dry (the texture of ingredients will vary), add a little extra milk until it is more manageable.

Place about 2 tablespoons (30 ml) of batter in each paper liner. Make a little well in the center of the batter, and place 1 teaspoon marmalade in each well. Top with the remaining batter, dividing it among the muffins. The batter should reach the top of the liner.

Bake for 22 to 24 minutes, or until golden brown and firm. Remove from the pan and place on a wire rack. Store in an airtight container for up to 2 days.

YIELD: 12 muffins

RECIPE NOTE

Make these with orange marmalade (OM) muffins if you're looking for more traditional breakfast goodies, or use marshmallow creme if you feel there's no wrong time for "fluff" (nix the orange xtract if going for the latter). You can also use a different jam or jelly according to your preferences—we're all about versatility!

SUPER STREUSEL-Y MUFFINS

Who's up for a deliciously sweet topping, combined with a fluffy crumb,
all rolled into a muffin? Everyone, that's who. Grab a couple of these babies
and be on your way to having the day of your life. (Results not typical.)

FOR THE STREUSEL:

½ cup plus 2 tablespoons (76 g) all-purpose flour

¼ cup plus 2 tablespoons (84 g) packed brown sugar

2½ teaspoons (5.5 g) ground cinnamon

¼ cup plus 1 tablespoon (70 g) nondairy butter, softened

FOR THE MUFFINS:

2 teaspoons apple cider vinegar

Scant ½ cup (110 ml) soymilk

8 ounces (227 g) nondairy cream cheese or plain yogurt

½ cup (112 g) nondairy butter

½ teaspoon sea salt

1 tablespoon (8 g) ground cinnamon

1 cup (192 g) light brown sugar, not packed

2 teaspoons pure maple or vanilla extract

2 cups (250 g) all-purpose flour

2 teaspoons (9 g) baking powder

1 teaspoon baking soda

DIRECTIONS:

Preheat the oven to 350°F (180°C, or gas mark 4). Line 16 standard muffin cups with paper liners.

To make the streusel: In a medium-size bowl, combine all the streusel ingredients using your fingertips, until large crumbs form. Set aside.

To make the muffins: Combine the vinegar and soymilk in a medium-size bowl; it will curdle and become like buttermilk.

Using a mixer, combine the cream cheese, butter, salt, cinnamon, brown sugar, and extract. Stir in the buttermilk mixture. Add the flour, baking powder, and baking soda. Mix until combined, being careful not to overmix.

Divide the batter among the muffin liners. Divide the streusel among the muffins, pressing it down a little so it sticks to the batter.

Bake for 25 minutes, or until a toothpick inserted into the center comes out clean. Transfer to a wire rack to cool. Store in an airtight container for up to 2 days.

YIELD: 16 muffins

CHOCOLATE PECAN MUFFINS

The addition of cornmeal and wheat germ makes for a heartier, healthier, bakery-style treat and all-around happier type of breakfast muffin bound to please the most demanding of taste buds.

INGREDIENTS:

1 cup (235 ml) soymilk

½ cup (120 ml) peanut oil

¾ cup (165 g) packed light brown sugar

1 cup plus 1 tablespoon (260 g) pumpkin purée

1 teaspoon pure vanilla extract

2 cups (240 g) whole wheat pastry flour

⅓ cup (38 g) wheat germ

½ cup (70 g) cornmeal

4 teaspoons (16 g) baking powder

½ teaspoon fine sea salt

¼ cup (44 g) chopped dark chocolate

½ cup (50 g) chopped pecans

DIRECTIONS:

Preheat the oven to 375°F (190°C, or gas mark 5). Line 16 standard muffin cups with paper liners, or for 14 standard muffins, lightly coat the muffin cups with nonstick cooking spray without using paper liners.

In a medium-size bowl, combine the milk, oil, brown sugar, pumpkin purée, and vanilla.

In a large bowl, whisk together the flour, wheat germ, cornmeal, baking powder, and salt.

Stir the wet ingredients into the dry, being careful not to overmix. Fold in the chocolate and pecans.

Divide the batter among the prepared cups. Bake for 20 to 24 minutes, or until a toothpick inserted into the center comes out clean. Transfer to a wire rack to cool. Store in an airtight container for up to 2 days.

YIELD: 14 to 16 muffins

BONUS RECIPE

TOP OF THE MUFFIN TO YOU! CHOCOLATE GLAZE

For a variation, don't use chocolate in the muffins themselves (unless you are a real chocolate fiend), but top with chocolate glaze instead.

Ingredients:

½ cup (120 ml) nondairy milk

1 cup (176 g) vegan semisweet chocolate chips

2 tablespoons (30 ml) pure maple syrup

Directions:

Scorch the milk in a medium-size saucepan over medium-high heat. Remove from the heat. Add the chocolate chips, and stir until melted. Stir in the maple syrup. Let cool for 15 minutes before dipping each muffin into the glaze. Let stand at room temperature to set.

CAPPUCCINO MUFFINS

Feeling extra indulgent for breakfast? Enjoy these cakelike muffins with a small scoop of Coffee Bean Ice Cream (page 223) on top for some extra-caffeinated action: hey, the fact that they both contain coffee makes them suitable for breakfast, right? If you'd rather save the exuberance for special occasions such as Valentine's or Mother's Day only, enjoy the muffins by their own lonesome—they're just as lovely solo!

INGREDIENTS:

⅔ cup (160 ml) nondairy milk

¼ cup (60 ml) vegetable oil

½ cup (120 g) nondairy plain or vanilla-flavored yogurt

2 teaspoons (10 ml) white balsamic or apple cider vinegar

½ cup (88 g) vegan semisweet chocolate chips

¼ cup (20 g) unsweetened cocoa powder

1 cup (200 g) evaporated cane juice or granulated sugar

2 tablespoons (6 g) instant coffee

½ teaspoon fine sea salt

2 cups (250 g) all-purpose flour

2 teaspoons (9 g) baking powder

2 teaspoons (9 g) baking soda

DIRECTIONS:

Preheat the oven to 350°F (180°C, or gas mark 4). Line a standard muffin pan with 12 papers liners for larger muffins, or 2 pans with 16 liners for smaller muffins.

Combine the milk, oil, yogurt, vinegar, chocolate chips, cocoa, sugar, coffee, and salt in a large bowl.

Combine the flour, baking powder, and baking soda in a medium-size bowl. Stir the dry ingredients into the wet, being careful not to overmix.

Divide the batter among the muffin liners, filling them two-thirds of the way for smaller muffins, or to the top for larger muffins. Bake for 16 to 20 minutes depending on size, or until a toothpick inserted into the center comes out clean. Let cool on a wire rack. Store in an airtight container for up to 2 days.

YIELD: 12 to 16 muffins

RECIPE NOTE

Make these ultra pretty by dipping the muffin tops into Chocolate Ganache (page 53) and lightly sift powdered sugar on top.

ORANGE CRANBERRY
CREAM CHEESE MUFFINS

These muffins puff up nicely and have a tart and creamy flavor that makes every bite a delight, whether enjoying them at breakfast or anytime for a not too sweet, but yummy treat!

INGREDIENTS:

2 cups (250 g) all-purpose flour

1 teaspoon baking soda

½ teaspoon baking powder

2 tablespoons (16 g) cornstarch

¼ teaspoon salt

1 cup (200 g) evaporated cane juice or granulated sugar

½ cup (120 g) nondairy cream cheese

½ cup (120 ml) orange juice

⅓ cup (80 ml) juice from mandarin orange can

1 teaspoon pure vanilla extract

½ cup (84 g, about 25 segments) mandarin oranges, each segment cut into 3 pieces

1 cup (122 g) dried cranberries

DIRECTIONS:

Preheat the oven to 350°F (180°C, or gas mark 4). Line 12 standard muffin cups with paper liners.

In a large bowl, combine the flour, baking soda, baking powder, cornstarch, and salt.

In a medium-size mixing bowl, beat together the sugar, cream cheese, orange juice, mandarin orange juice, and vanilla. The cream cheese will not cream; rather, it will separate from the juice. This is normal.

Add the wet ingredients to the dry and mix until there are no lumps. Fold in the orange segments and cranberries. Fill the muffin cups three-fourths full.

Bake for 25 to 30 minutes, or until a toothpick inserted into the center comes out clean and the tops are golden. Transfer to a wire rack to cool. Store in an airtight container for up to 2 days.

YIELD: 12 muffins

RECIPE NOTE

We love the flavor of orange and cranberries, but raisins, blueberries, and raspberries taste great in these muffins too.

SWEET YEAST BREAD MUFFINS

A cross between doughnuts and sweet bread rolls, these muffins may take
a bit longer to prepare, but they will keep you chugging all day long.

INGREDIENTS:

½ cup (120 ml) nondairy milk, heated to lukewarm

½ cup (120 ml) coffee-flavored liqueur or nondairy milk, heated to lukewarm

¾ cup (144 g) raw sugar

¼ cup (56 g) nondairy butter, melted

1½ teaspoons active dry yeast

1 teaspoon pure almond extract

3 cups (375 g) all-purpose flour

½ cup (60 g) sliced almonds

2 teaspoons (9 g) baking powder

¾ teaspoon fine sea salt

½ cup (88 g) vegan mini semisweet chocolate chips (optional)

¼ cup plus 2 tablespoons plus 2 teaspoons (101 g) almond butter or marzipan (optional)

DIRECTIONS:

Combine the milk, liqueur, sugar, melted butter, and yeast in a medium-size bowl. Let sit a few minutes until bubbles appear, to ensure the yeast is active. Stir in the extract.

In a large bowl, combine the flour, almonds, baking powder, salt, and chocolate chips.

Stir the wet ingredients into the dry using a rubber spatula, until combined. Cover and let stand for 1 hour at room temperature. Even though the batter won't rise much, this allows the yeast to give these muffins their wonderful texture and flavor.

Lightly coat 10 standard muffin cups with cooking spray. Stir the batter and scrape ¾ inch (1.9 cm) of batter into each muffin cup. The batter will be rather sticky: use a cookie dough scoop or a greased spoon to do it. Add 2 teaspoons almond butter in the center of each muffin. Divide the remaining batter evenly among the muffin cups, being sure to cover the filling completely.

Lightly coat the top of the muffins with cooking spray. Cover with plastic wrap and let stand for 45 minutes to let the flavor of the batter develop further.

Preheat the oven to 375°F (190°C, or gas mark 5). Remove the plastic wrap from the muffins. Bake for 18 minutes, or until golden brown on top. Remove from the pan and let cool on a wire rack. Store in an airtight container for up to 2 days.

YIELD: 10 muffins

RAISIN CORN BREAKFAST BREAD

Raisins and corn for breakfast we say, there's just no better way to start your day.
If you apply a generous layer of nut butter on top of a couple of slices, you're
bound to be kept comfortably full until lunchtime rolls around.

INGREDIENTS:

1¼ cups (295 ml) plain soymilk, divided

2 tablespoons (30 ml) freshly squeezed lemon juice

1 tablespoon (8 g) cornstarch

1 teaspoon pure vanilla extract

1 cup (125 g) all-purpose flour

½ cup (70 g) cornmeal

½ cup (100 g) evaporated cane juice or granulated sugar

2 teaspoons (4.6 g) ground cinnamon

2 teaspoons (9 g) baking powder

1 teaspoon baking soda

½ teaspoon fine sea salt

¼ cup (60 ml) vegetable oil

½ cup (80 g) raisins

DIRECTIONS:

Using a blender, combine 1 cup (235 ml) of the soymilk, lemon juice, and cornstarch. Transfer to a large bowl and heat in the microwave for 2 minutes; keep a close eye on it to make sure the mixture doesn't bubble up too high to make a mess in your microwave. Stir with a fork. Alternatively, use the stove and a medium-size saucepan and cook for about 3 minutes over medium heat, stirring constantly, until thickened. Let cool for at least 1 hour; add the vanilla, stirring with a fork. This will be your yogurtlike mixture.

Preheat the oven to 350°F (180°C, or gas mark 4). Lightly coat an 8 × 4-inch (20 × 10-cm) loaf pan with cooking spray.

In a large bowl, combine the flour, cornmeal, sugar, cinnamon, baking powder, baking soda, and salt.

Stir the remaining ¼ cup (60 ml) soymilk, the oil, and the raisins into the yogurtlike mixture. Fold the wet ingredients into the dry, being careful not to overmix.

Bake for 35 to 40 minutes, or until a toothpick inserted into the center comes out clean.

Let cool on a wire rack, still in the pan, for about 15 minutes before transferring directly to the rack.

YIELD: 10 slices

GO BANANAS BREAD

This recipe yields two standard loaves: one for you, and one to gift. Trust us when we say that you would be really bummed out if you gifted one and didn't have any left for yourself.

Be sure to use metal or aluminum pans when baking these; glass tends to prevent them from rising and baking properly. Also note that the streusel topping sinks down into the bread itself, and gives you nice sweet buttery bites deep within the banana goodness, as well as up on top.

FOR THE STREUSEL TOPPING (OPTIONAL):

⅔ cup (84 g) all-purpose flour

⅔ cup (133 g) evaporated cane juice or granulated sugar

⅔ cup (150 g) cold nondairy butter, cut into chunks

FOR THE BANANA BREAD:

2 cups (250 g) all-purpose flour

1 teaspoon salt

½ teaspoon ground cinnamon

2 teaspoons (9 g) baking soda

1 teaspoon baking powder

¼ cup (32 g) cornstarch

1 cup (200 g) evaporated cane juice or granulated sugar

1 cup (120 g) chopped walnuts or pecans (optional)

½ cup (80 g) raisins (optional)

1 cup (224 g) nondairy butter, softened

1½ cups (338 g) mashed overripe banana

2 teaspoons (10 ml) pure vanilla extract

DIRECTIONS:

Preheat the oven to 350°F (180°C, or gas mark 4). Lightly spray 2 standard 9 × 5-inch (23 × 13-cm) loaf pans with cooking spray.

To make the streusel: Add the flour, sugar, and cold butter to a small mixing bowl and, working with your fingertips, mix and pinch until coarse crumbs form. Place the mixture in the refrigerator to keep cold until ready to use.

To make the bread: In a large mixing bowl, combine the flour, salt, cinnamon, baking soda, baking powder, cornstarch, sugar, nuts, and raisins. In a separate, medium-size mixing bowl, beat together the softened butter, mashed bananas, and vanilla, using an electric mixer. The butter will not cream; rather, it will separate from the banana. That is normal. Add the wet ingredients to the dry and stir to combine, taking care not to overmix.

Fill each loaf pan just under half full. Spread half of the streusel mixture evenly in each pan.

Bake for 60 to 70 minutes, or until a knife inserted into the center of the crown comes out clean. The bread itself will be dark brown, while the streusel stays bright white.

Allow to cool on a wire rack before cutting and serving.

YIELD: 2 loaves

ALTELLA ROLLS

Perfect as a brunch item, these rolls will be even tastier if you drizzle them with the glaze for the Lemon-Poppy Seed Scones (page 46). Just replace the lemon juice with nondairy milk, and the zest with ¼ teaspoon pure almond extract.

INGREDIENTS:

1 recipe Juliette Brioche (page 184) dough, prepared and risen once

1 recipe Altella Spread (page 218)

DIRECTIONS:

On a lightly floured surface, roll out the dough to approximately 18 × 12 inches (46 × 30 cm).

Use an offset spatula to spread the Altella evenly onto the rolled-out dough all the way to the edges. Cut into 6 equal strips 3 inches (7.6 cm) wide.

Lightly coat the cups of a jumbo muffin tin with nonstick cooking spray, or use an 8-inch (20-cm) baking pan, coating it with spray, too.

Roll each cut portion individually and tightly. It is actually less messy to proceed this way rather than cutting the whole loaf up at once. Place in the prepared muffin cups, filling side up. Cover and let rise for another hour.

Preheat the oven to 375°F (190°C, or gas mark 5). Bake for 20 minutes, or until the tops are golden brown. Carefully remove from the pan and transfer to a wire rack to cool.

YIELD: 6 large rolls

RECIPE NOTE

Use vegan puff pastry instead of Juliette Brioche if you're pressed for time. Roll out the puff pastry sheet 1 inch (2.5 cm) larger than its original size on a lightly floured surface. Carefully and evenly apply Altella spread, and cut into 6 strips. Tightly roll each one up. Place each one in the muffin tin. Lightly brush with nondairy milk. Bake for 25 minutes, or until golden brown.

MAPLE BACON DOUGHNUTS

Bacon with chocolate. Bacon in ice cream. Even bacon cupcakes! It's everywhere, and everyone seems to love (or hate) it. So why not let a vegan version join the band?

FOR THE DOUGHNUTS:

½ cup (120 ml) any nondairy milk, heated to lukewarm, divided

2 teaspoons active dry yeast

6 ounces (170 g) plain or vanilla-flavored soy yogurt or nondairy sour cream

¼ cup (56 g) nondairy butter

¼ cup (60 ml) pure maple syrup

¼ cup (50 g) evaporated cane juice or granulated sugar

1 teaspoon pure vanilla extract

1 teaspoon maple extract

3 cups (375 g) all-purpose flour, plus more as needed

½ teaspoon fine sea salt

1½ teaspoons baking powder

FOR THE MAPLE GLAZE:

½ cup (120 ml) pure maple syrup

1½ cups (180 g) powdered sugar, sifted

Vegetable oil, for frying

4 teaspoons (65 g) imitation bacon bits

DIRECTIONS:

To make the doughnuts: Combine ¼ cup (60 ml) of the milk and the yeast in a small bowl. Let sit a few minutes until bubbles appear, to ensure the yeast is active. Set aside.

Combine the remaining ¼ cup (60 ml) milk, yogurt, butter, maple syrup, and sugar in a small saucepan and heat to just lukewarm over low heat. Do not let the temperature rise higher than lukewarm, or it will kill the yeast. Remove from the heat and stir in both extracts. Combine with the yeast mixture.

In a large bowl, combine the flour, salt, and baking powder. Stir the wet ingredients into the dry. Turn the dough out onto a floured surface, add extra flour as needed, and knead for about 5 minutes, just until the dough is smooth and not overly sticky. Return the dough to bowl and lightly coat with oil. Cover with plastic wrap and let rise for 1 hour.

Divide the dough into 8 pieces. Shape into doughnuts by creating a hole in the center with your thumb. Place on a baking sheet lined with parchment paper or a silicone baking mat. Cover loosely with plastic wrap and let rise for another 40 minutes.

To make the glaze: Whisk a small amount of syrup into the powdered sugar at a time, until there are no lumps and the glaze is thick enough to coat the back of a spoon.

Use a deep fryer, or fill a heavy, deep saucepan with 3 inches (7.5 cm) of oil. Heat to 350°F (175°C). Fry 2 doughnuts at a time, flipping each over once, until golden brown on both sides.

Immediately drain on paper towels and repeat with the remaining doughnuts. Let cool on a wire rack before dunking into the glaze and sprinkling with bacon bits.

YIELD: 8 large doughnuts

RECIPE NOTE

If the thought of bacon on top of something sweet doesn't appeal, prepare pecans from the Pecan Peach Gobble-r à La Mode (page 241), chop them up, and sprinkle on the doughnuts in lieu of the bacon bits.

BAKED CINNAMON SUGAR DOUGHNUT HOLES

These are baked in a standard muffin pan, making for 12 doughnut "holes" that are tender and seriously just as good as their fried counterpart. Cross our hearts.

INGREDIENTS:

½ cup (120 ml) nondairy milk, heated to lukewarm, divided

2 teaspoons (8 g) active dry yeast

6 ounces (170 g) vanilla-flavored soy yogurt

¼ cup (56 g) nondairy butter

¾ cup (150 g) evaporated cane juice or granulated sugar, divided

2½ cups (313 g) all-purpose flour

½ teaspoon fine sea salt

1 teaspoon baking powder

1 tablespoon (8 g) ground cinnamon

DIRECTIONS:

Combine ¼ cup (60 ml) of the milk and the yeast in a small bowl. Let sit for a few minutes until bubbles appear, to ensure the yeast is active. Set aside.

Combine the remaining ¼ cup (60 ml) milk, yogurt, butter, and ¼ cup (48 g) of the sugar in a small saucepan. Whisk while heating to lukewarm over low heat. Do not let the temperature rise higher than lukewarm, or it will kill the yeast. Remove from the heat and combine with the yeast mixture.

In a large bowl, combine the flour, salt, and baking powder. Add the wet ingredients to the dry, stirring with a rubber spatula for a couple of minutes until thoroughly combined. Scrape the sides of the bowl with the spatula and gather the dough in the center of the bowl. Cover with plastic wrap and let rise for 60 minutes.

Combine the remaining ½ cup (96 g) sugar with the cinnamon. Set aside.

Coat all the cups in a standard muffin tin with cooking spray. Sprinkle 1 teaspoon of the cinnamon sugar into each cup. Shake the pan so that the sugar coats the bottom and sides of each cup. Using an ice cream scoop, divide the sticky batter among the muffin cups, filling each about three-fourths full. Evenly top with 1 teaspoon of the cinnamon sugar. Cover with plastic wrap and let rise for another 40 minutes.

Preheat the oven to 375°F (190°C, or gas mark 5). Bake for 20 minutes, or until the tops are golden brown. Carefully remove from the pan and transfer to a wire rack to cool.

YIELD: 12 doughnut holes

CHAPTER 3

Mean and Mouthwatering Mains

New favorites, diner classics, and old-fashioned comfort foods—main courses just like grandma used to make (had she been vegan).

If you find yourself daydreaming about your favorite childhood dish or have an extremely reluctant family member who believes vegans eat only shoots and leaves, depriving themselves of the heartiest, meatiest things good food is all about, then you've stumbled upon the perfect chapter that is bound to prove they were wrong all along.

Bring palatable proof to that persnickety uncle/mother-in-law/brother of yours (or even yourself!) that hearty is what it's all about. Vegans can and will do old-fashioned favorites like baked macaroni and cheese, meatloaf sandwiches, pot roasts, casseroles, and other quintessential comfort foods— just in their own (even more flavorful and undoubtedly more animal-friendly) way.

This chapter is guaranteed to provide you with recipes that will not only satisfy even king-size appetites, but also leave you licking your fingers for the leftovers. There's got to be a way to put a lockbox on that lasagna, right?!

ROASTED BROCCOTATO SOUP WITH BACON-FLAVORED CHICKPEAS

A creamy and buttery soup with a chickpea garnish
that you might want to double up on: it's just that good!

FOR THE ROASTED VEGETABLES:

1 shallot, peeled, left whole

1 pound (454 g) potatoes, peeling optional, halved

½ teaspoon fine sea salt, divided

2 tablespoons (30 ml) peanut oil, divided

12 ounces (340 g) broccoli florets

FOR THE CHICKPEA CROUTONS:

1½ to 2 teaspoons liquid smoke

2 tablespoons (30 ml) reduced-sodium soy sauce

1 teaspoon chipotle mustard (or any mustard mixed with ¼ teaspoon chipotle powder)

½ teaspoon paprika

1 teaspoon granulated onion

1½ teaspoons toasted sesame oil

1½ teaspoons pure maple syrup

6 cloves garlic, peeled, left whole

1 can (15 ounces, or 425 g) chickpeas, drained and rinsed

FOR THE SOUP:

4 cups (940 ml) reduced-sodium vegetable broth

½ cup (120 ml) unsweetened nondairy creamer

DIRECTIONS:

Preheat the oven to 400°F (200°C, or gas mark 6).

To make the roasted vegetables: Place the shallot and potato halves in a 9-inch (23-cm) square baking pan. Sprinkle with ¼ teaspoon of the salt. Rub with 1 tablespoon (15 ml) of the oil, using your hands. Bake for 10 minutes.

You now have 10 minutes to prepare the broccoli florets by placing them in another 9-inch (23-cm) square baking pan. Sprinkle with the remaining ¼ teaspoon salt. Rub with the remaining 1 tablespoon (15 ml) oil.

To make the chickpea croutons: Combine all the ingredients in an 8-inch (20-cm) square baking pan.

Place the broccoli and chickpea dishes in the oven with the potatoes. Bake for 10 minutes, checking occasionally to make sure nothing burns. Stir well, and flip the potatoes onto the other side. Bake for 10 minutes longer, or until most of the liquid is gone from the chickpeas and the broccoli and potatoes are fork-tender.

To make the soup: Place the broccoli, potatoes, and half of the chickpeas in a large soup pot. Add the broth and bring to a boil. Reduce the heat and simmer for 10 minutes, uncovered. Using an immersion blender, or transferring to a blender or food processor in batches, blend to the desired consistency. Stir in the creamer and cook for another 2 minutes, until heated through.

Serve sprinkled with the remaining chickpeas.

YIELD: 4 to 6 servings

CREAMY MUSHROOM SOUP

Although this soup is great on its own, the main intention behind this recipe was to create a stock that can be made ahead of time and frozen, then used in recipes for creamy soups. In this book, we call for it in Gramma Jo's Tater Tot Surprise (page 30), but in general, you can use it in any recipe that calls for a creamy condensed-style soup.

INGREDIENTS:

¼ cup (60 ml) vegetable oil

20 ounces (560 g) sliced portobello and button mushrooms

1 medium-size yellow onion, diced

2 stalks celery, chopped

2 tablespoons (30 g) minced garlic

2 cups (470 ml) water

1 cup (235 ml) unsweetened soymilk

1 cup (66 g) instant mashed potato flakes

Salt and pepper, to taste

DIRECTIONS:

Add the oil to a soup pot and heat over medium-low heat. Add the mushrooms, onion, celery, and garlic. Toss to coat, cover, and cook for about 15 minutes.

Uncover, add the water and soymilk, and bring to a boil. Reduce to a simmer and simmer, uncovered, for 20 minutes.

Remove from the heat and stir in the potato flakes a little bit at a time until the desired thickness is reached. If using the soup as an ingredient in other recipes, you will want to add all of the flakes, to get it to the consistency of thick gravy.

Using an immersion blender, or carefully transferring to a tabletop blender, purée until smooth. Season with salt and pepper to taste.

YIELD: 4 cups (1 quart, or 940 ml)

RECIPE NOTE

Other great ways to use this soup: Veganize your grandma's green bean casserole, use it as a sauce over baked tofu, make an easy Stroganoff using this soup poured over boiled pasta and cut up pieces of seitan, and make a quick dinner by adding your favorite vegetables (we like broccoli and carrots) and serving over brown rice.

MULLIGATAWNY SOUP

Creamy and filling deliciousness! We've actually never tried the nonvegan version of this soup, but we don't need to in order to say that this one can be proud of its tasty self.

INGREDIENTS:

2 tablespoons (30 ml) peanut oil

6 ounces (170 g) leeks, white parts only, chopped and thoroughly cleaned

8 ounces (227 g) cremini mushrooms, left whole if small, halved if slightly larger

1 large red bell pepper, cored, seeded, and chopped

1 Granny Smith apple, cored and chopped

¼ cup (40 g) chopped shallot

6 cloves garlic, minced

½ teaspoon fine sea salt

1 tablespoon (6 g) medium curry powder

1 teaspoon ground coriander

½ teaspoon ground cumin

½ teaspoon cayenne pepper

⅔ cup (122 g) uncooked long-grain white rice (or add 2 cups [390 g] cooked long-grain brown rice during the last 5 minutes of simmering)

8 ounces (227 g) chicken-style store-bought or homemade prepared seitan (page 94), chopped

4 cups (940 ml) chicken-flavored broth

6 ounces (170 g) nondairy plain yogurt

1 large lemon, cut into 6 wedges

Freshly ground black pepper, to taste

DIRECTIONS:

Combine the oil, leeks, mushrooms, bell pepper, apple, shallot, garlic, and salt in a large pot. Cook over medium-high heat for 4 minutes, stirring occasionally.

Add the curry, coriander, cumin, cayenne, and rice. Cook for another 2 minutes over medium heat, until fragrant.

Add the seitan and broth. Bring to a boil. Lower the heat, cover, and simmer for 20 minutes, stirring occasionally, until the rice is fully cooked and the veggies are tender. Stir in the yogurt and simmer, uncovered, for 4 minutes longer, until heated through.

Serve each portion with a lemon wedge to be squeezed into the soup, and adjust the seasoning with black pepper and extra salt.

YIELD: 6 servings

LENTIL AND BACON POT O' STEW

We're not ashamed to admit that we danced for joy upon learning this homey and rustic dish got the thumbs-up from the friend of a tester's son. Better yet? The kid in question isn't even vegan.

FOR THE LENTILS:

1 cup (192 g) uncooked green or brown lentils

1½ cups (355 ml) vegetable broth

FOR THE VEGGIES:

1 tablespoon (14 g) nondairy butter

1 tablespoon (15 ml) olive oil

4 cloves garlic, minced

1 shallot, minced

2 carrots, finely diced

2 stalks celery, finely diced

2 large leeks, white and light green parts, cut into ⅓-inch (8-mm) chunks, thoroughly cleaned

½ teaspoon fine sea salt

½ teaspoon ground pepper, or to taste

1 recipe Tempeh Bacon (page 84)

⅓ cup (20 g) chopped fresh parsley

DIRECTIONS:

To make the lentils: Rinse the lentils and pick out any debris. Combine with the broth in a large pot and bring to a boil. Simmer, uncovered, and check for doneness after 20 minutes. If the lentils aren't tender enough for your taste, add extra liquid and cook until adequately tender.

To make the veggies: Place the butter, oil, garlic, shallot, carrots, celery, and leeks in a large pot. Cook over medium-high heat for 10 minutes, or until the flavors develop and the veggies are tender. Season with salt and pepper.

Stir the lentils into the veggies. Simmer for 5 minutes. Crumble the bacon into the stew and heat through. Sprinkle with parsley and extra pepper upon serving.

YIELD: 4 to 6 servings

RECIPE NOTE

For a complete and nourishing meal, consider serving this stew along with a slice of Scalloped Potato Pie (page 122).

HEARTY CHICKEN NOODLE SOUP

There's nothing quite as comforting as a nice hot bowl of chicken noodle soup. And it's even more comforting to know that no chickens were harmed in the making of this soup.

INGREDIENTS:

2 tablespoons (30 ml) olive oil

2 stalks celery, chopped

1 medium carrot, shredded

1 clove garlic, minced

½ cup (80 g) diced white or yellow onion

4 cups (950 ml) chicken-flavored vegetable broth, plus more if you want a brothier soup

1 cup (135 g) corn (fresh, frozen, or canned)

1 cup (135 g) peas (fresh, frozen, or canned)

6 ounces (170 g) large-chunk TVP or Soy Curls

6 ounces (170 g) dry udon, soba, or lo mein noodles

Salt and pepper, to taste

DIRECTIONS:

In a large pot, heat the oil over medium heat. Add the celery, carrot, garlic, and onion and sauté until fragrant and translucent, about 5 minutes.

Add the broth and bring to a boil. Add the corn, peas, and TVP, and return to a boil.

Add the noodles and simmer for 7 to 10 minutes, or until the noodles are tender. Season with salt and pepper to taste.

YIELD: 4 hearty bowls

SLOW COOKER CORN CHOWDER

Slow cookers make life so easy. They don't heat up your house, use less energy than the stove, and allow you to throw everything in and forget about it for hours!

INGREDIENTS:

2 cups (470 ml) vegetable broth

1 cup (235 ml) soy creamer

8 ounces (227 g) nondairy cream cheese

4 cups (544 g) frozen yellow corn kernels

1 pound (454 g) potatoes, peeled and cut into bite-size chunks

1 medium-size yellow onion, diced

1 red bell pepper, cored, seeded, and diced

1 tablespoon (15 g) minced garlic

1 tablespoon (2 g) dried parsley

1 teaspoon ground cumin

½ teaspoon paprika

¼ teaspoon cayenne pepper

Salt and pepper, to taste

DIRECTIONS:

Throw all the ingredients into the slow cooker, stir, and set on High for 3 hours. Dinner is served!

YIELD: 4 servings

ORANGE SEITAN STEW

LOW FAT

Slow-cooking in all its splendor. This thick stew is rich
and filling, while being surprisingly not high in fat.

INGREDIENTS:

1 tablespoon (15 ml) peanut oil

⅓ cup (53 g) chopped shallot

6 cloves garlic, minced

4 medium-size carrots, peeled and
chopped into thin coins

2 large russet potatoes, cubed into ⅓-inch (8-mm) pieces

1 tablespoon (8 g) cornstarch

2 teaspoons (2.8 g) dried thyme

½ teaspoon red pepper flakes (optional)

½ teaspoon celery seed

Freshly ground pepper, to taste

1 cup (260 g) chopped roasted red pepper

½ cup (120 ml) red wine

1 cup (235 ml) fresh orange juice

1 teaspoon packed orange zest

1 tablespoon (15 g) Dijon mustard

1 tablespoon (22 g) regular molasses

2 tablespoons (30 ml) red wine vinegar

1 tablespoon (15 ml) reduced-sodium soy sauce

2 bay leaves

4 Seitan Burgers (page 94), cubed into
½-inch (1.3-cm) pieces

Vegetable broth, as needed

DIRECTIONS:

Combine the oil, shallot, garlic, carrots, and potatoes in
a large pot. Cook for 8 minutes over medium-high heat,
stirring often.

Add the cornstarch, thyme, red pepper flakes, celery
seed, pepper, and roasted red pepper. Stir often and cook
for another 2 minutes.

Add the wine, juice, zest, mustard, molasses, vinegar, soy
sauce, and bay leaves, and bring to a boil; cover, lower the
heat, and simmer for 60 minutes, or until the veggies are
fork-tender. Stir occasionally.

Add the seitan and simmer for 20 minutes longer, adding
a little vegetable broth if the stew is too thick for your
taste. Discard the bay leaves before serving.

YIELD: 4 servings

STEW-TATOUILLE

Celine used to have this all the time as a kid, and loved to add a few squirts of mustard upon eating it, bringing an even greater flavor to the dish. Feel free to switch to different veggies if you prefer: fresh corn, more bell peppers instead of zucchini, summer squash . . . they all make great additions.

INGREDIENTS:

1 tablespoon (15 ml) olive oil

4 cups (400 g) cubed eggplant

¼ cup (60 ml) vegetable broth, plus more as needed

1 medium-size shallot, minced

4 cloves garlic, minced

1 cup (160 g) chopped onion

½ teaspoon fine sea salt, or to taste

Freshly ground pepper, to taste

2¼ cups (340 g) diced bell pepper (any color)

3 cups (360 g) diced zucchini

1 dried bay leaf

2 tablespoons (5 g) chopped fresh basil

1 tablespoon (3 g) chopped fresh thyme

2¼ cups (400 g) diced tomatoes

4 medium-size baked potatoes, cut into bite-size pieces

1 recipe TVP Chorizo (page 216, optional)

1½ tablespoons (5 g) fresh parsley

Dijon mustard, to taste (optional)

DIRECTIONS:

Heat the oil in a large pot over medium heat. Add the eggplant and cook for 5 minutes, or until golden brown, stirring occasionally. If the eggplant or other veggies need more moisture, which will depend on how juicy and ripe they are, add the vegetable broth as needed.

Add the shallot, garlic, onion, salt, and pepper. Cook for 2 minutes. Add the bell pepper and zucchini. Cover and cook for 10 minutes, stirring occasionally.

Add the bay leaf, basil, thyme, tomatoes, and potatoes. Cover and simmer for 15 minutes longer. Once the vegetables are tender, add the TVP.

Spoon into 4 bowls, add a squirt of mustard to each bowl, sprinkle with the parsley, and serve.

YIELD: 4 servings

CHOCOLATE STOUT CHILI

LOW FAT

We've added bold flavors to the quintessential bean-based dish. This is so full of good protein that you will probably not find yourself hungry for your next meal (a rare event, if you're anything like us). For a little added creaminess, top with Tofu Sour Cream (page 211).

INGREDIENTS:

1 tablespoon (15 ml) peanut oil

⅓ cup (53 g) chopped onion

1 red or green bell pepper, cored, seeded, and diced

2 large cloves garlic, minced

1 jalapeño, cored, seeded, and minced

2 tablespoons (10 g) unsweetened cocoa powder

2 tablespoons (16 g) medium chili powder

1½ teaspoons (3.8 g) ground cumin

1½ teaspoons (2 g) dried Mexican oregano

½ teaspoon cayenne pepper, or to taste

1 tablespoon (12 g) Sucanat

2 tablespoons (33 g) tomato paste

1 can (15 ounces, or 425 g) fire-roasted or regular diced tomatoes, with juice

4 ounces (113 g) fire-roasted diced green chiles

12 ounces (355 ml) vegan stout beer (if you can find chocolate stout, more power to you; go to www.barnivore.com to check the vegan-ocity of your beer)

2 Seitan Burgers (page 94), torn into bite-size pieces (the seitan expands a little as it cooks)

2 cans (each 15 ounces, or 425 g) any beans, drained and rinsed

DIRECTIONS:

Heat the oil in a large pot. Add the onion, bell pepper, and garlic. Cook until the veggies just start to get tender, about 4 minutes. Add the jalapeño, seasonings, and Sucanat. Cook for 1 minute. Add the tomato paste, diced tomatoes, chiles, and beer. Bring to a boil. Cook, uncovered, over medium heat for 15 minutes.

Add the seitan and beans. Cook for 15 minutes longer, until thickened.

YIELD: 4 to 6 servings

PANZANELLA SANDWICHES

A sandwich based on the delicious salad made with bread but with the salad . . . in the bread? This recipe is made using large bread rolls, hence the 2 tablespoons (13 g) each tapenade and pesto per side. If you only find smaller rolls, consider using 8 of them and only using 1 tablespoon (7 g) of each spread per side, and adjust the quantity of other ingredients to fit 8 rolls instead of 4.

FOR THE TAPENADE:

1 cup (160 g) olive medley (kalamata, green, etc.), pitted

1 teaspoon capers, drained

1 tablespoon (15 ml) extra-virgin olive oil

1½ teaspoons white balsamic vinegar or other mild vinegar

Pinch of red pepper flakes

¼ cup (15 g) fresh parsley

1 clove garlic, minced

FOR THE SANDWICHES:

4 large fresh and crusty individual artisan breads

½ cup (120 g) Spinach Pesto (page 210)

4 razor-thin slices red onion

4 Beefsteak or large heirloom tomatoes, sliced razor thin (choose tomatoes that aren't overly ripe because you don't want them to soak the bread)

16 thin slices English cucumber

4 leaves fresh basil

¼ cup (25 g) Hemp Almond Parmesan (page 213) or 8 thin slices smoked cheddar Sheese, if available

Freshly ground pepper, to taste

DIRECTIONS:

To make the tapenade: Combine all the ingredients in a food processor and pulse a few times until combined but still chunky.

To assemble the sandwiches: Slice the breads in half. Apply 2 tablespoons (13 g) tapenade on one side, 2 tablespoons (15 g) pesto on the other. Top with 1 slice onion, 1 sliced tomato, 4 slices cucumber, and 1 basil leaf. Sprinkle 1 tablespoon (6 g) parmesan or place 2 slices Sheese over the veggies, grind some pepper over all, and top with the other half of bread. Repeat with the remaining sandwiches. Serve immediately.

YIELD: 4 large sandwiches

THE MONTE CRISTO

Bringing the best of breakfast (French toast!) to lunch in a yummy, crispy sandwich.

FOR THE SPREAD:

¼ cup (56 g) vegan mayonnaise, store-bought or homemade (page 211)

2 tablespoons (34 g) ketchup

1 tablespoon (15 g) sweet pickle relish

1 teaspoon minced garlic

1 teaspoon Dijon mustard

FOR THE FRENCH TOAST:

1 cup (235 ml) unsweetened soy or other nondairy milk

¼ cup (31 g) all-purpose flour

⅛ teaspoon paprika

⅛ teaspoon dried dill

Salt and pepper, to taste

Vegetable oil, for frying

8 slices stale (or firm) sandwich bread

8 slices your favorite vegan deli meat, such as Tofurky or Yves

4 slices your favorite vegan cheese or 4 ounces (113 g) shredded vegan cheese, such as Daiya

Maple syrup, for dipping (optional)

DIRECTIONS:

To make the spread: Whisk all the ingredients together and keep refrigerated until ready to use.

To make the French toast: Mix together the milk, flour, paprika, dill, salt, and pepper in a shallow dish.

In a frying pan or cast-iron skillet, heat about 2 tablespoons (30 ml) oil over high heat.

Dip a piece of bread into the batter and panfry for 2 to 3 minutes per side, or until golden. Repeat with the remaining slices, adding oil as needed.

Preheat the broiler or set the toaster oven on broil. Schmear all 8 slices of the French toast with the spread. Add 2 slices deli meat to each sandwich, followed by either 1 slice or 1 ounce (28 g) cheese. Top with the other slice of French toast and place in the broiler for about 5 minutes to heat through and melt the cheese. Alternatively, you can use a panini press.

Serve hot with the maple syrup for dipping.

YIELD: 4 sandwiches

EAT YOUR VEGGIES!

This sandwich tastes great served up alongside a nice salad of raw torn kale tossed with olive oil, dried cranberries, pine nuts, and cherry tomatoes cut in half.

TEMPEH, PEPPER, AND SPINACH-PESTO SANDWICH

A spin on a traditional BLT, this sandwich is particularly exceptional served alongside a generous helping of German Potato Salad (page 168).

FOR THE TEMPEH BACON:

8 ounces (227 g) tempeh, sliced into 16 strips (cut in half lengthwise, each half cut into 8 thin strips)

1½ tablespoons (23 ml) reduced-sodium soy sauce

2 teaspoons (10 ml) liquid smoke

1 teaspoon Dijon mustard

1½ teaspoons toasted sesame oil

1 teaspoon granulated onion

½ teaspoon paprika

¼ teaspoon chipotle chile powder (optional)

2 cloves garlic, quartered

1½ teaspoons (7.5 g) light brown sugar

FOR THE SANDWICHES:

¼ cup (56 g) vegan mayonnaise, store-bought or homemade (page 211)

¼ cup (60 g) Spinach Pesto (page 210)

8 slices whole-grain sandwich bread, toasted

2 whole roasted red peppers, patted dry and halved

3¾ cups (113 g) fresh baby spinach leaves or (75 g) baby arugula

DIRECTIONS:

Preheat the oven to 400°F (200°C, or gas mark 6). Line a baking sheet with parchment paper or a silicone baking mat.

To make the bacon: Place the tempeh slices in a shallow dish. Combine the soy sauce, liquid smoke, mustard, oil, onion, paprika, chile powder, garlic, and brown sugar in a small bowl. Pour on top of the tempeh slices, carefully brushing it all over on both sides. Spread on the prepared baking sheet. Lightly coat the top of the tempeh with cooking spray.

Bake for 10 minutes, flip over, lightly coat with spray again, and bake for 10 minutes longer, or until golden brown. Transfer to a wire rack. (The bacon is at its crispiest right out of the oven.)

To assemble the sandwiches: Combine the mayonnaise and pesto in a small bowl. Apply 1 tablespoon (15 g) on every slice of bread. Place 4 slices of bacon on 4 slices of bread. Top each sandwich with half a roasted red pepper, 1 scant cup (28 g) spinach or (19 g) arugula, and the remaining slice of bread.

YIELD: 4 sandwiches

SWEET POTATO PO' BOYS

Now a true Po' Boy would be a foot long, so these are considered "shorties,"
and if you decide to use the highly recommended pile of Sweet Peppercorn Coleslaw (page 172),
well, then, you can consider your Po' Boy "dressed." As always, a deep fryer works best here,
but if you don't have one, a pot filled with about 1 inch (2.5 cm) of oil will work just fine.

INGREDIENTS:

1 large sweet potato

FOR THE FENNEL MARMALADE:

2 tablespoons (30 ml) olive oil

1 bulb fennel, julienned, leaves reserved

2 cloves garlic, thinly sliced

2 shallots, thinly sliced

Pinch of salt

2 tablespoons (42 g) agave nectar

FOR THE AIOLI:

⅓ cup (75 g) vegan mayonnaise,
store-bought or homemade (page 211)

½ teaspoon Old Bay seasoning

1 tablespoon (2 g) chopped fennel leaves
(reserved from the bulb above)

1 teaspoon minced garlic

Vegetable oil, for frying

½ cup (120 ml) plain soymilk or other nondairy milk

½ cup (62 g) all-purpose flour

½ cup (14 g) cornflakes, crushed

1 teaspoon Old Bay seasoning

¼ teaspoon cayenne pepper

4 (6-inch, or 15-cm) French rolls

1 recipe Sweet Peppercorn Coleslaw
(page 172, optional but highly recommended)

DIRECTIONS:

Preheat the oven to 400°F (200°C, or gas mark 6).
Line a baking sheet with parchment paper or a silicone
baking mat.

Slice the sweet potato into thin rounds, about ¼ inch
(6 mm) thick. You can peel them if you choose, but we
like ours with the skin on. Spread on the prepared
baking sheet.

Bake for 20 minutes. Remove from the oven and allow
to cool.

To make the fennel marmalade: While the potatoes are
cooking, add the olive oil to a pan and heat over low heat.
Add the fennel, garlic, shallots, and salt. Slowly cook until
very soft and tender, and just beginning to caramelize,
about 15 minutes, stirring occasionally. Add the agave
and toss to coat. Crank up the heat and cook for about
5 more minutes, stirring constantly, until caramelized,
sticky, and browned. Remove from the heat and set aside.

To make the aioli: Whisk all the ingredients together.
Keep refrigerated until ready to use.

Preheat the oil to 350°F (180°C).

Place the milk in a shallow dish. Add the flour, cornflakes,
Old Bay, and cayenne to a resealable plastic bag and
shake to combine.

Dip 1 sweet potato round into the milk to coat and then
add it to the bag. Repeat until you have about 5 rounds
in the bag. Shake to coat the potatoes with the flour
mixture. Carefully add the coated potatoes to the hot oil
and cook for 2 to 3 minutes, flipping halfway through,
until golden and crispy. Transfer to a plate lined with
paper towels to absorb the excess oil. Repeat until all the
potatoes are fried.

Spread a layer of aioli on each half of the French roll. Pile
one-fourth of the sweet potatoes on the bottom half of
the roll, top with one-fourth of the marmalade, and add a
heaping pile of the coleslaw. Repeat with the remaining
3 rolls. Serve immediately.

YIELD: 4 sandwiches

WALDORF SALAD WRAPS

This is what we like to call a treasure hunt salad. With every bite, your mouth finds a little treasure! This salad works perfectly to make wraps or even stuff in pitas, but we'll let you in on a little secret. It tastes really good right out of the bowl, too. Find the largest, freshest, most pliable tortillas you can, because they work best for wraps.

FOR THE DRESSING:

1 cup (224 g) vegan mayonnaise, store-bought or homemade (page 211)

½ cup (120 g) nondairy sour cream, store-bought or homemade (page 211)

½ cup (120 ml) orange juice

1 tablespoon (9 g) poppy seeds

Salt and pepper, to taste

FOR THE SALAD:

3 hearts (12 ounces, or 340 g) romaine lettuce, chopped

2 medium-size Granny Smith apples, cored and cubed

3 stalks celery, chopped

1 cup (160 g) diced red onion

1 cup (109 g) pecan pieces

1 cup (160 g) raisins

6 large burrito-size tortillas

DIRECTIONS:

To make the dressing: Whisk together all the ingredients in a medium-size bowl. Set aside.

To make the salad: Toss all the ingredients together in a large mixing bowl, add the dressing, and toss to coat. Refrigerate until ready to use.

Cut 6 pieces of parchment paper into squares just larger than the tortillas. Lay 1 piece of parchment on a flat surface. Place a tortilla in the center of the parchment. Place 2 to 3 cups (340 g to 510 g), depending on the size of your tortilla, of prepared salad in the tortilla, spread out across the half of the tortilla closest to you. It will seem like a lot, but that's the magic of making a tight deli-style wrap. Using the parchment to help keep the tortilla from tearing, begin to roll it up like a burrito, folding in the edges halfway through. Roll as tightly as possible. Tape the parchment to keep it tightly closed. Use a sharp knife to cut the wrap in half on the bias. Repeat with the remaining 5 tortillas.

YIELD: 6 wraps or a large bowl of salad (about 15 cups [2.6 kg])

RECIPE NOTE

Cubed tofu and cubed avocado make a wonderful addition to this salad.

COBB SANDWICH

This sandwich is a spin on a classic American salad made famous at the Brown Derby in Hollywood in the 1930s. The crumbled tofu stands in for the Roquefort cheese in the original dressing, so don't blend it in, or you'll miss out on the texture. You can also take a shortcut and buy mixed baby greens to stand in for the mixed greens in the recipe. We won't tell anybody.

FOR THE SPREAD:

6 ounces (170 g) plain soy yogurt

2 tablespoons (30 ml) white balsamic or other light-colored vinegar

1 tablespoon (15 g) whole-grain brown mustard

1 teaspoon dried dill

4 ounces (113 g) extra- or super-firm tofu, drained, pressed, and crumbled

FOR THE MIXED GREENS:

4 leaves romaine lettuce, chopped

4 leaves iceberg lettuce, chopped

1 cup (30 g) baby spinach

1 cup (30 g) wild or baby arugula

FOR THE CHICKEN:

4 ounces (113 g) large-chunk TVP or Soy Curls

2 cups (470 ml) boiling water

1 teaspoon Old Bay seasoning

FOR THE SANDWICHES:

4 ciabatta rolls, lightly grilled or toasted

1 large ripe avocado, sliced

1 large ripe tomato, sliced into 8 thin slices

8 slices vegan bacon, store-bought or homemade (page 84)

DIRECTIONS:

To make the spread: Whisk together the yogurt, vinegar, mustard, and dill until smooth. Fold in the crumbled tofu. Refrigerate until ready to use.

To prepare the greens: Toss together the greens, and set aside.

To make the chicken: Reconstitute the TVP by placing it in a bowl and pouring the boiling water over it. Cover and let sit for 10 minutes. Drain any excess liquid. Sprinkle with the Old Bay, toss to coat, and set aside.

To assemble the sandwiches: Slather each side of the ciabatta roll with the spread. Starting on the bottom place one-fourth of the greens, then pile on one-fourth of the chicken, then one-fourth of the avocado, then 2 slices tomato, then 2 slices bacon. Top with the other half of the bun. Repeat with the remaining 3 rolls, and serve.

YIELD: 4 sandwiches

THE DOUBLE TAKE

It's a sandwich that uses the chicken as the bread! Inspired by the ultra artery-clogging sandwich from the ultra disgusting KFC. Made with our own blend of seven herbs and spices. Thanks to Gardein, the realistic chicken part is easy. We like to make 4 little slider-size sammies, but you can make 2 large ones instead—just don't cut the breasts in half.

INGREDIENTS:

4 Gardein chicken breasts (or chicken-style seitan cutlets)

Vegetable oil, for frying

FOR THE FLOUR MIXTURE:

1 cup (125 g) all-purpose flour

1 teaspoon dried parsley

½ teaspoon garlic powder

½ teaspoon onion powder

½ teaspoon dried mustard

¼ teaspoon smoked paprika

¼ teaspoon salt

¼ teaspoon black pepper

1 cup (235 ml) soymilk

2 tablespoons (30 ml) freshly squeezed lemon juice

FOR THE SPECIAL SAUCE:

¼ cup (56 g) vegan mayonnaise, store-bought or homemade (page 211)

1 tablespoon (15 g) ketchup

1 tablespoon (15 g) Sriracha

½ teaspoon dried chives or parsley

4 slices vegan bacon, store-bought or homemade (page 84), prepared

¼ cup (56 g) Smoky Pub Cheese (page 213)

DIRECTIONS:

Defrost the chicken breasts. Cut each breast in half so you have 8 pieces.

Preheat the oil in a deep fryer, or fill a frying pan with about 1 inch (2.5 cm) of oil, and heat over high heat to 350°F (180°C).

To make the flour mixture: Combine the flour, parsley, garlic powder, onion powder, dried mustard, paprika, salt, and pepper in a shallow dish. Combine the soymilk and lemon juice in a separate small bowl. It will curdle and become like buttermilk.

Dip one chicken piece in the flour mixture to lightly coat, then dip in the buttermilk mixture, then back into the flour mixture for a thicker coat.

Carefully place in the oil and fry for 2 to 3 minutes, or until golden and crispy. (If you are using the frying pan method, you will need to flip after about 2 minutes and repeat on the other side.) Transfer to a plate lined with paper towels to absorb the excess oil. Repeat with the remaining 7 chicken pieces.

To make the sauce: Whisk ingredients in a small bowl.

Spread a layer of sauce on 1 piece of fried chicken, then top with 1 piece of bacon, broken in half, then a schmear of pub cheese, then spread with more sauce. Top it off with another piece of fried chicken. Serve immediately.

YIELD: 4 sliders or 2 sandwiches

RECIPE NOTE

To make your own chicken-style seitan cutlets, try using the recipe for the Slow Cooker Russian Chicken (page 108), but instead of cooking them in the Russian broth in a slow cooker, simply simmer them, covered, for an hour in a pot filled with chicken-flavored vegetable broth.

TEMPEHITAN BURGERS

These quirky, protein-filled patties contain both tempeh and seitan to join forces in keeping your muscles well nourished and your taste buds doing a tap dance. If you want them larger, divide the preparation into 4 or 6 instead of 8. In this case, consider baking them in a 350°F (180°C, or gas mark 4) oven for 15 minutes to make sure they are fully cooked. Flip them halfway through, and then panfry them until golden brown.

INGREDIENTS:

8 ounces (227 g) tempeh

¼ cup (64 g) tahini

¼ cup (80 g) orange marmalade (preferably not bitter) or mango chutney

2 tablespoons (30 ml) peanut oil

2 teaspoons (4.8 g) granulated onion

1 clove garlic, minced

2 teaspoons garam masala

1 teaspoon ground coriander

½ teaspoon red pepper flakes

½ teaspoon fine sea salt

½ cup (72 g) vital wheat gluten flour

¼ cup (60 ml) vegetable broth

6 tablespoons (47 g) all-purpose flour, as needed

Vegetable oil, for panfrying

DIRECTIONS:

Crumble the tempeh into small pieces and place in a large bowl. Stir in the tahini, marmalade, oil, onion, garlic, garam masala, coriander, red pepper flakes, and salt.

Stir in the wheat gluten. Add the broth and knead in as much all-purpose flour as needed just so that the preparation isn't overly sticky; it depends on the consistency of both the tahini paste and the marmalade. Let stand for 15 minutes to let the gluten develop.

Divide the mixture into 8 equal portions of approximately ¼ cup (70 g) each.

Coat a skillet with oil and panfry for 6 minutes on each side over medium-low heat, or until golden brown and fully cooked.

YIELD: 8 slider-size burgers

EAT YOUR VEGGIES!

Toast an Avocado Roll (page 194), top it with crunchy coleslaw and cucumber slices tossed with some of the tahini sauce from the Falafel (page 114) recipe, with a little extra lemon juice or seasoned rice vinegar sprinkled on it for extra zing, and crown with 1 or 2 burgers.

SEITAN BURGERS FOR STEWS AND CHILIS

LOW FAT

You know how some seitan recipes make for a spongy texture once added to stews?
This one holds up great in any recipe involving a long simmering time.

INGREDIENTS:

12 ounces (355 ml) vegan beer or vegetable broth (go to www.barnivore.com to check the vegan-ocity of your beer)

2 tablespoons (30 ml) reduced-sodium soy sauce

1 tablespoon (15 g) whole-grain mustard

1 tablespoon (7 g) granulated onion

1 teaspoon liquid smoke

¼ cup (30 g) nutritional yeast

Freshly ground pepper, to taste

1 tablespoon (21 g) agave nectar

¾ cup (90 g) garbanzo fava bean flour

1½ cups (216 g) vital wheat gluten flour

DIRECTIONS:

Preheat the oven to 350°F (180°C, or gas mark 4). Line a baking sheet with parchment paper or a silicone baking mat. Have handy an extra baking sheet and an extra piece of parchment or silicone baking mat.

Combine the beer, soy sauce, mustard, onion, liquid smoke, nutritional yeast, pepper, and agave in a large bowl. Add the flour and wheat gluten, and work the dough until perfectly combined, using your hands. Knead directly in the bowl for a couple of minutes. Let rest for 15 minutes to let the gluten develop.

Divide the dough into 6 burgers using ½ cup (140 g) each. Shape into balls. Place on the prepared baking sheet and press down gently. Add the extra piece of parchment on top, along with an upside-down extra baking sheet.

Bake for 20 minutes. Carefully remove the top baking sheet and parchment, flip the burgers over, and cover again with the parchment and baking sheet. Bake for 15 minutes longer, or until golden brown on both sides. Place on a wire rack to cool.

YIELD: 6 burgers

RECIPE NOTE

Give a test run to these seitan burgers by making Orange Seitan Stew (page 77) or Chocolate Stout Chili (page 81).

ULTIMATE PATTY MELT

Crispy grilled sourdough, slathered with tangy Garlic Onion Mayo Sauce and smothered in sharp Smoky Pub Cheese (page 213). Those greasy spoons have nothing on us!

FOR THE SAUCE:

½ cup (112 g) vegan mayonnaise, store-bought or homemade (page 211)

½ teaspoon Dijon mustard

½ teaspoon garlic powder

½ teaspoon onion powder

Freshly ground pepper, to taste

FOR THE PATTIES:

1 cup (96 g) TVP granules

1 cup (235 ml) vegetable broth

1 cup (144 g) vital wheat gluten flour

¼ cup (30 g) nutritional yeast

1 tablespoon (8 g) garlic powder

1 tablespoon (8 g) onion powder

1 teaspoon smoked paprika

½ teaspoon black pepper

2 tablespoons (1 g) dried chives

¼ cup (60 ml) steak sauce

¼ cup (60 g) ketchup

2 tablespoons (32 g) creamy no-stir peanut butter

1 tablespoon (15 ml) liquid smoke

Vegetable oil, if panfrying or grilling

8 slices sourdough bread

Nondairy butter, for toasting

1 recipe Smoky Pub Cheese (page 213)

DIRECTIONS:

To make the sauce: Whisk together all the ingredients in a small bowl and refrigerate until ready to use.

To make the patties: Reconstitute the TVP in the broth. To do this, either place the TVP and broth in a microwave-safe bowl, cover tightly with plastic wrap, and microwave on High for 5 to 6 minutes, or pour the boiling broth over the TVP, cover, and let stand for 10 minutes. The TVP will absorb all of the liquid.

Meanwhile, mix together the wheat gluten, nutritional yeast, and dry spices.

Once the rehydrated TVP is cool enough to handle, combine it with the steak sauce, ketchup, peanut butter, and liquid smoke. Add to the gluten and spice mixture and, using your hands, mix everything together until a sticky dough forms. Allow to sit for about 15 minutes for the gluten to develop.

Form the mixture into 4 patties and cook one of three ways:

1. Cover loosely with foil and bake on a baking sheet lined with parchment paper or a silicone mat at 350°F (180°C, or gas mark 4) for 15 minutes. Flip, re-cover, and bake for 15 minutes longer.

2. Panfry in oil over medium heat for 5 to 7 minutes per side. This preparation makes for a burger with a much crispier outside, while leaving a soft, juicy center.

3. Grill! These patties are hearty and do well on the grill, just be sure to oil either the patties or the grill to prevent sticking. Grill over a medium-low flame for about 7 to 10 minutes per side.

To serve: Spread the bread slices with a little nondairy butter and panfry until toasty. Layer bread with mayo, patty, pub cheese, and top bread slice.

YIELD: 4 sandwiches

SLOPPY JO-NIS

Weeknight meals made easy, thanks to the use of the versatile TVP and everybody's favorite condiment . . . KETCHUP! You can replace the ketchup with barbecue sauce for a tangy twist.

Note that if using certified gluten-free ingredients this dish is indeed gluten free.

INGREDIENTS:

1 cup (96 g) TVP granules

1 cup (235 ml) vegetable broth
(Not-Beef broth works best here, but any will do)

¼ cup (60 ml) vegetable oil

¼ cup (40 g) finely diced onion

¼ cup (40 g) finely diced green bell pepper

4 cloves garlic, minced

1 tablespoon (15 g) prepared yellow mustard

¾ cup (204 g) ketchup

1 tablespoon (15 g) steak sauce

1 tablespoon (14 g) packed brown sugar (optional)

Salt and pepper, to taste

4 hamburger buns

DIRECTIONS:

Reconstitute the TVP in the broth. To do this, either place the TVP and broth in a microwave-safe bowl, cover tightly with plastic wrap, and microwave on High for 5 to 6 minutes or pour the boiling broth over the TVP, cover, and let stand for 10 minutes. The TVP will absorb all of the liquid.

In a frying pan, heat the oil over medium-high heat. Add the onion and bell pepper. Sauté for about 3 minutes. Add the garlic and sauté for about 2 minutes longer.

Reduce the heat to low and add the reconstituted TVP, mustard, ketchup, steak sauce, and brown sugar. Stir to coat, and heat through. Season with salt and pepper to taste.

Serve piled sloppily onto the hamburger buns.

YIELD: 4 servings

EAT YOUR VEGGIES!

Serve with corn on the cob and Mexican-Style Dipping Sauce for Corn (page 207). Oh, and don't forget extra napkins—this is the type of meal that *requires* them!

HAUTE POCKETS

You may recognize these ready-in-moments frozen savory pockets from your days as a hungry college student. Rejoice, for here is a delicious vegan alternative which makes sure there will be no more starving for you, fellow compassionate co-ed.

INGREDIENTS:

¼ cup (56 g) nondairy butter, softened

¼ cup (60 g) ketchup

1 tablespoon (15 ml) hot sauce, or to taste

2 large cloves garlic, minced

1 teaspoon dried thyme

½ teaspoon paprika

1 cup (235 ml) unsweetened soymilk

1 tablespoon (8 g) cornstarch

2 teaspoons (10 ml) freshly squeezed lemon juice

½ teaspoon fine sea salt

4 Ham-ish Saucisses (page 156), cubed small

2 frozen sheets vegan puff pastry, thawed for at least 40 minutes prior to rolling out

1 cup (156 g) chopped broccoli florets, steamed

DIRECTIONS:

Preheat the oven to 375°F (190°C, or gas mark 5). Line a baking sheet with parchment paper or a silicone baking mat.

In a medium-size microwave-safe bowl, combine the butter, ketchup, hot sauce, garlic, thyme, paprika, soymilk, cornstarch, lemon juice, and salt. Microwave for 2 minutes, keeping a close eye so that it doesn't boil over. Add the cubed saucisses to the sauce and set aside.

Roll out the puff pastry to about 2 inches (5 cm) larger than its original size on a lightly floured counter. Cut each sheet into 6 equal rectangular portions. Place a little under ¼ cup (55 ml) filling in the center of 6 of them. Top with 2½ tablespoons (26 g) broccoli. Cover with a second piece of puff pastry, using the tines of a fork to seal. Cut a couple of air vents on top of the pastry for ventilation purposes. Repeat with the remaining pastries.

Bake for 25 minutes, or until golden brown. Let cool on a wire rack.

YIELD: 6 pastries

RECIPE NOTE

This homemade, preservative-free, Buffalo-style version yields pastries large and filling enough to cover for a meal, especially when served with a portion of any deli-style salad (try the filling for Waldorf Salad Wraps [page 89]) or a piping hot bowl of soup (such as Pesto Pea-damame [page 150]).

COLCANNON PATTIES

Colcannon is a traditional and affordable Irish dish composed mainly of mashed potatoes and kale or cabbage. These all-in-one patties combine all the colcannon flavors in one fell swoop and are meant to be enjoyed alongside Irish Soda Bread (page 190) slathered with nondairy butter and maybe Marmite (if you like it), pickles, and a cold brew.

FOR THE POTATOES:

2 tablespoons (28 g) nondairy butter

3 medium-size russet potatoes (658 g), peeling optional, sliced ¼ inch (6 mm) thick

Pinch of fine sea salt

2 teaspoons granulated onion

1 cup (235 ml) vegan stout beer (go to www.barnivore.com to check the vegan-ocity of your beer)

FOR THE CABBAGE:

2 tablespoons (28 g) nondairy butter

14 ounces (397 g) shredded coleslaw

3 cloves garlic, minced

2 teaspoons granulated onion

Salt and pepper, to taste

½ cup (40 g) bread crumbs

¼ cup (20 g) imitation bacon bits, store-bought or homemade (page 216)

½ cup (63 g) all-purpose flour, plus more as needed

Vegetable oil, for panfrying

DIRECTIONS:

To make the potatoes: Place the butter, potatoes, salt, and onion in a pot. Brown for 8 minutes over medium heat, stirring often. Add the beer, cover, and bring to a boil. Lower the heat to medium and cook for 20 minutes, or until tender enough to mash. Transfer to a large bowl.

To make the cabbage: Using the same pot, combine the butter, coleslaw, garlic, and onion. Season with salt and pepper to taste. Cook over medium heat until tender, about 8 minutes.

Place the cabbage, potatoes, and bread crumbs in a food processor and pulse a few times to combine. Depending on the size of your food processor, you might want to do this in several batches. Stir in the bacon bits, along with as much flour as needed to get the preparation to bind. Chill for 1 hour.

Shape the mixture into 8 burgers using ½ cup (130 g) each.

Coat a skillet with oil, and fry the burgers over medium heat for about 6 minutes on each side. Do not overcrowd the skillet: Cook 2 to 4 burgers at a time, depending on the size of the skillet.

YIELD: 8 burgers

I WOULD DO ANYTHING FOR (MEAT)LOAF

Drop the idea that your tender meatloaf drenched in good gravy days are over, because it's all here at your fingertips. Reach out and touch faith! Serve with Baked Asparagus with Mushroom Sauce (page 166).

INGREDIENTS:

8 ounces (227 g) firm tofu, crumbled and drained of extra liquid in a fine-mesh sieve

2 carrots, finely grated

3 cloves garlic, minced

1 tablespoon (7 g) granulated onion

2 teaspoons (1.4 g) dried basil

½ to 1 teaspoon dried thyme, or to taste

1 teaspoon dried oregano

½ teaspoon fine sea salt

½ teaspoon ground pepper, or to taste

½ cup (72 g) vital wheat gluten flour

¼ cup (25 g) Hemp Almond Parmesan (page 213)

½ cup (120 ml) vegetable broth

1 to 1½ cups (80 to 120 g) panko or regular bread crumbs, as needed

DIRECTIONS:

Preheat the oven to 375°F (190°C, or gas mark 5). Have an 8 × 4-inch (20 × 10-cm) loaf pan and a piece of parchment paper handy.

In a large bowl, combine the tofu, carrots, garlic, onion, basil, thyme, oregano, salt, and pepper by mashing together with your hands. Add the wheat gluten and parmesan, still mashing with your hands. Add the broth and mash to combine. Add the bread crumbs, a ½ cup (40 g) at a time, until the mixture holds together well.

Shape into an approximately 7 × 3-inch (18 × 8-cm) loaf. Place on the parchment paper. Fold the paper over the loaf. Place the wrapped loaf in the pan, folded side down.

Bake for 1 hour. Let stand for 30 minutes before unfolding from the parchment, slicing, and placing on a wire rack.

YIELD: 4 servings

BONUS RECIPE

HEARTY MEATLOAF SANDWICH

Give those leftovers some love by turning them into one fabulous sandwich. Repeat as necessary!

Directions:
Cut 2 thick slices of crusty bread such as bruschetta or sourdough, toast them up, and rub a clove of garlic on each side.

Brown two ½-inch (1.27-cm) thick slices of meatloaf in 2 teaspoons olive oil.

Coat the bread with 2 teaspoons vegan mayo on one side, and 2 teaspoons Dijon mustard on the other. Place the slices of meatloaf between the slices.

This is delicious with heirloom tomato slices, baby spinach, a couple leaves of fresh basil, dandelion or any leafy green, and red onion, too.

BAKED BBQ BUNS

If you prefer your sandwiches to be hot (just like you!), try these tasty buns that come packed with a spicy and meaty filling.

FOR THE DOUGH:

14 ounces (414 ml) light coconut milk, heated to lukewarm

2 teaspoons (8 g) active dry yeast

1 tablespoon (14 g) packed light brown sugar

2 cups (240 g) white whole wheat flour

2 cups (240 g) whole wheat pastry flour

1 tablespoon (9 g) vital wheat gluten flour

1 teaspoon fine sea salt

FOR THE FILLING:

2 teaspoons (10 ml) peanut oil

½ cup (80 g) finely chopped onion

2 cloves garlic, minced

10 ounces (283 g) orange marmalade (preferably not bitter)

2 tablespoons (30 ml) apple cider vinegar

½ cup plus 2 tablespoons (170 g) brown sauce, such as HP

1 tablespoon (15 ml) blended chipotle and adobo sauce

8 ounces (227 g) tomato sauce

Salt, to taste

1 pound (454 g) any seitan steak, cubed in bite-size pieces

FOR THE BUN WASH:

½ cup (120 ml) boiling water

¼ cup (55 g) baking soda

8 teaspoons (24 g) sesame seeds

DIRECTIONS:

To make the dough: Combine the milk, yeast, and brown sugar in a large bowl. Let sit for a few minutes until bubbles appear, to ensure the yeast is active.

Stir in the flours, wheat gluten, and salt. Turn out onto a lightly floured surface to knead until the dough is smooth and pliable, about 8 minutes. Place in a lightly oiled large bowl, cover with a lid or plastic wrap, and let rise until doubled in size, 60 to 90 minutes.

To make the filling: Heat the oil in a medium-size saucepan. Add the chopped onion and garlic, and cook over medium heat for 2 minutes. Add all remaining ingredients except the seitan. Bring to a boil. Lower the heat and simmer for 30 minutes. Adjust the seasoning, if needed. Add the seitan and simmer for 10 minutes longer, or until the sauce thickens up. Set aside.

Gently deflate the dough and divide into 8 equal portions. Roll out each portion into a 7-inch (18-cm) square. Place ½ cup (120 g) of the BBQ filling in the center of each portion. Carefully lift all corners of the dough and place them on top of the filling, pinching a little to seal (the dough should cooperate here). Carefully transfer buns to baking sheets lined with parchment paper or silicone baking mats and let rest for about 15 minutes while you preheat the oven to 375°F (190°C, or gas mark 5).

Meanwhile, to make the bun wash: Combine the water and baking soda in a medium-size bowl. Lightly brush each bun with the preparation and sprinkle 1 teaspoon sesame seeds on top.

Bake for 18 minutes, or until golden brown. Transfer to a wire rack until ready to serve.

YIELD: 8 buns

BARBECUE RIBS

Yes! Even vegans can enjoy a big ol' rack of barbecue ribs. Wow the skeptics with these remarkably realistic ribs complete with bones!

INGREDIENTS:

3 cups (432 g) vital wheat gluten flour

1 cup (120 g) whole wheat flour

¼ cup (30 g) nutritional yeast

2 tablespoons (16 g) onion powder

1 tablespoon (8 g) garlic powder

1 teaspoon smoked paprika

½ teaspoon salt

½ teaspoon black pepper

2 cups (470 ml) water

2½ cups (580 ml) Whiskey Barbecue Sauce (page 210) or store-bought barbecue sauce, divided

¼ cup (60 ml) steak sauce

2 tablespoons (30 ml) soy sauce

2 tablespoons (30 ml) liquid smoke

2 tablespoons (30 ml) olive oil

6 bones (see note)

DIRECTIONS:

Preheat the oven to 350°F (180°C, or gas mark 4). Line a 9 × 13-inch (23 × 33-cm) baking pan with foil or parchment paper.

In a large mixing bowl, combine the wheat gluten, flour, nutritional yeast, onion powder, garlic powder, paprika, salt, and pepper.

In a separate bowl, combine the water, ½ cup (118 ml) of the barbecue sauce, steak sauce, soy sauce, liquid smoke, and oil. Add the wet ingredients to the dry and knead for 5 minutes. Let the mixture rest for 20 minutes to allow the gluten to develop.

Shape the mixture into a large rectangle, to fit in the pan, with at least 1 inch (2.5 cm) of space around the edges. Push the bones through the mixture, at equal distances from each other.

Pour ¾ cup (180 ml) of the remaining barbecue sauce into the bottom of the baking pan. Place the rack of ribs in the pan. Spread ¾ cup (180 ml) of the remaining barbecue sauce over the top. Cover the pan tightly with foil and bake for 90 minutes.

You can enjoy these as is, brushed with the remaining ½ cup (118 ml) barbecue sauce and sliced apart, or refrigerate for later use. To reheat, fire up the grill to give the ribs an extra smoky flavor and grill marks. Brush with the remaining ½ cup (118 ml) barbecue sauce while grilling, and slice apart before serving.

YIELD: 6 servings

RECIPE NOTE

Disposable bamboo chopsticks or even Popsicle sticks work wonders as "bones" here, but if you want to kick it up a notch, try food-grade cedar cut into ½ × 6-inch (1.3 × 15-cm) bones, being sure to sand down any rough edges. Whichever you choose, start by soaking them in a mixture of 2 cups (470 ml) warm water mixed with 2 tablespoons (30 ml) liquid smoke to add some smoky flavor to the ribs. For an edible set of bones, try taro root. Although this method will yield edible bones, they will be more flimsy after cooking, thus requiring a fork and knife for eating.

SWEET AND SOUR MEATBALLS

These balls work well in many applications. Simply serve them alone as appetizers. Double the sauce recipe, and serve them over rice or noodles. Make lettuce wraps with rice noodles and balls. Even try them in a Vietnamese-style sandwich by adding 4 or 5 balls to a hollowed-out baguette dressed with pickled carrots, cucumber, cilantro, and vegan mayo.

FOR THE SAUCE:

¾ cup (180 ml) pineapple juice

2 tablespoons (30 ml) rice wine vinegar

2 tablespoons (25 g) evaporated cane juice or granulated sugar

2 tablespoons (34 g) ketchup

2 tablespoons (30 ml) soy sauce

¼ teaspoon salt

1 teaspoon red pepper flakes (optional)

1 tablespoon (8 g) cornstarch dissolved in ¼ cup (60 ml) water to make a slurry

FOR THE MEATBALLS:

2 cups (192 g) TVP granules

1¾ cups (415 ml) vegetable broth

2 tablespoons (30 ml) olive oil, plus more for frying

1 medium-size yellow onion, finely diced

2 cloves garlic, minced

½ cup (72 g) vital wheat gluten flour

1 tablespoon (15 ml) tamari or soy sauce

½ teaspoon freshly cracked black pepper

½ teaspoon oregano

½ teaspoon chili powder

½ teaspoon garlic powder

½ teaspoon onion powder

¼ cup (32 g) cornstarch dissolved in ½ cup (120 ml) vegetable broth to make a slurry

DIRECTIONS:

To make the sauce: Place the juice, vinegar, sugar, ketchup, soy sauce, salt, and pepper flakes into a pot and bring to a boil. Reduce to a simmer and simmer for 5 to 10 minutes. Stir in the slurry and remove from the heat. Set aside, or keep warm over very low heat until the meatballs are ready.

To make the meatballs: Reconstitute the TVP in the broth. To do this, either place the TVP and broth in a microwave-safe bowl, cover tightly with plastic wrap, and microwave on High for 5 to 6 minutes or pour the boiling broth over the TVP, cover, and let stand for 10 minutes. The TVP will absorb all of the liquid.

In a skillet, heat the 2 tablespoons (30 ml) oil and sauté the onion and garlic until translucent and fragrant, about 5 minutes. Remove from the heat and mix in the wheat gluten, tamari, the spices, and the cornstarch slurry. Let sit for about 15 minutes to let the gluten develop.

With your hands, form the dough into 20 balls about 1½ inches (3.8 cm) in diameter. Use a lot of pressure when forming the balls so they won't fall apart.

Heat a small amount of the remaining oil in a skillet over medium-high heat and lightly fry the meatballs, gently rolling them around in the pan to brown all sides. Transfer the meatballs to the sauce and gently toss to coat.

YIELD: 20 meatballs

POLISH SAUSAGE

For a true Polish sausage experience, slice your sausage in half lengthwise, panfry or grill until crispy and hot, then place in between 2 slices of strong rye bread schmeared with mustard and topped with diced onion and a dill pickle spear.

INGREDIENTS:

1 cup (96 g) TVP granules

1 cup (235 ml) vegetable broth

1 cup (144 g) vital wheat gluten flour

½ cup (60 g) whole wheat pastry flour

2 teaspoons (12 g) salt

½ teaspoon freshly ground black pepper

1½ teaspoons evaporated cane juice or granulated sugar

½ teaspoon dried thyme

½ teaspoon ground mustard

½ teaspoon dried marjoram

¼ teaspoon dried basil

¼ teaspoon garlic powder

1 cup (235 ml) water

2 tablespoons (30 ml) vegetable oil

½ teaspoon liquid smoke

DIRECTIONS:

Reconstitute the TVP in the broth. To do this, either place the TVP and broth in a microwave-safe bowl, cover tightly with plastic wrap, and microwave on High for 5 to 6 minutes or pour the boiling broth over the TVP, cover, and let stand for 10 minutes. The TVP will absorb all of the liquid. Let sit until cool enough to handle.

In a food processor, place the flours and seasonings. Process to combine.

Once the TVP mixture has cooled, add to the flour mixture in the processor. Process to combine.

Slowly add the water, oil, and liquid smoke, while the processor is running, until a dough ball forms. Let rest for 20 minutes to allow the gluten to develop.

Divide the dough into 6 to 8 pieces and form into a sausage shape. Wrap tightly in either foil or parchment, and cook one of three ways:

1. In the oven: Seam side down on a baking sheet at 350°F (180°C, or gas mark 4) for 20 minutes, flip seam side up and cook for 20 minutes longer, or until firm.

2. On the barbecue: Place over a low heat section of the grill and cook for about 45 minutes, rotating often.

3. Steam: Place in a steamer (works best with foil) and steam for 35 to 40 minutes, or until firm.

YIELD: 6 to 8 sausages

EAT YOUR VEGGIES!

We love serving these tasty sausages with sautéed kale and baked beans, as shown.

SLOW COOKER RUSSIAN CHICKEN

This rich and filling dish boasts the creamy and tangy flavors of Russian dressing, usually reserved for salads. It tastes great over rice with lots of the remaining broth ladled on top.

FOR THE RUSSIAN BROTH:

2 cups (470 ml) vegetable broth

1 cup (272 g) ketchup

1 cup (224 g) vegan mayonnaise
(Vegenaise is recommended here)

2 tablespoons (30 g) Dijon mustard

2 tablespoons (30 g) horseradish

1 tablespoon (15 g) minced garlic

1 teaspoon celery seed

2 tablespoons (30 g) pickle relish

1 tablespoon (16 g) capers

½ cup (80 g) finely diced white onion

Salt and pepper, to taste

FOR THE CHICKEN:

2 cups (288 g) vital wheat gluten flour

3 tablespoons (24 g) cornstarch

1 teaspoon paprika

1 teaspoon onion powder

1 teaspoon garlic powder

¼ teaspoon salt

¼ teaspoon ground black pepper

1¼ cups (295 ml) water

2 tablespoons (30 ml) soy sauce

2 tablespoons (30 ml) olive oil

1 tablespoon (15 ml) liquid smoke

DIRECTIONS:

To make the Russian broth: In a medium-size bowl, blend together the vegetable broth, ketchup, mayonnaise, mustard, horseradish, garlic, and celery seed until smooth. Stir in the relish, capers, and onion. Season with salt and pepper. Pour into the bottom of your slow cooker.

To make the chicken: In a medium-size bowl, combine the wheat gluten, cornstarch, paprika, onion powder, garlic powder, salt, and pepper.

In a separate small bowl, mix together the water, soy sauce, oil, and liquid smoke. Add the wet ingredients to the dry and knead together until well incorporated. The dough will be very stiff, but very elastic and stringy. Cover and let rest for 20 minutes to let the gluten develop.

Divide the dough into 6 equal pieces and form into unevenly shaped cutlets. Press them as flat as possible (this is difficult due to the elasticity of the dough, so just do your best). Place in a single layer in the broth, cover, and set the slow cooker on High for 3 hours.

Serve over a bed of steamed rice, with the broth from the slow cooker ladled over the top.

YIELD: 6 servings

EAT YOUR VEGGIES!

Serve with steamed broccoli florets, tossed with a little olive oil, whole roasted garlic cloves, and a sprinkle of sea salt.

CHICK' N' WAFFLES PARTY

Here's a meal that would make Paula Deen proud! Combining the savory crispness of the waffles with the meaty goodness of the chicken and the richness of either one of the sauces makes for a perfectly decadent triple threat that will satisfy the hungriest among us.

INGREDIANTS:

1 recipe fried chicken from The Double Take (page 91) or 1 recipe Breakfast Chicken-Fried Steak (page 32)

1 cup (235 ml) Creamy Cheesy Sauce (page 212) or White Sausage Gravy (page 33)

FOR THE WAFFLES:

2 cups (470 ml) unsweetened soymilk

2 tablespoons (30 ml) white balsamic vinegar

6 tablespoons (84 g) nondairy butter, melted

Few grinds salt and pepper, to taste

2 cups (250 g) all-purpose flour

2 teaspoons (9 g) baking powder

2 teaspoons (9 g) baking soda

DIRECTIONS:

Prepare your friend chicken and desired sauce and set aside.

To make the waffles: Combine the soymilk and vinegar; it will curdle and become like buttermilk. Let stand for 2 minutes. Add the butter, salt, and pepper to the buttermilk mixture. Add the flour, baking powder, and baking soda and stir until just combined. Following the manufacturer's instructions, coat the waffle iron with cooking spray in between each waffle, when the machine has been sufficiently preheated. Add about ¾ cup (180 ml) batter per waffle in a Belgian-style waffle iron, ½ cup (120 ml) per standard waffle iron. For extra crispness, toast the waffles before enjoying.

Place 2 pieces of fried chicken on top of 1 Belgian waffle, or 1 piece per standard waffle. Top with as much sauce as desired.

YIELD: 4 servings (4 Belgian waffles or 6 to 8 standard waffles)

RECIPE NOTE

This unusual, soul food-type of dish is often served simply with (nondairy) butter and pure maple syrup. Consider trying this version instead of using the sauce or gravy.

JALAPEÑO HOT DOGS

These sausages have TVP in them, to really give them those toothy bits you might remember from your bratwurst-eating days. With or without the optional cheese filling, they taste yummy topped with diced onion and nacho cheese sauce.

INGREDIENTS:

1 cup (96 g) TVP granules

1 cup (235 ml) vegetable broth

1 teaspoon liquid smoke

1 cup (144 g) vital wheat gluten flour

1 teaspoon paprika

1 teaspoon onion powder

¼ cup (30 g) nutritional yeast

12 slices jarred jalapeños, diced, or to taste

2 tablespoons (30 ml) juice from the jar of jalapeños

¼ cup (60 g) nondairy cream cheese

2 tablespoons (36 g) white or yellow miso

Salt and pepper, to taste

½ cup (56 g) shredded vegan cheese, such as Daiya (optional)

DIRECTIONS:

Preheat the oven to 375°F (190°C, or gas mark 5).

Reconstitute the TVP by mixing together the TVP, vegetable broth, and liquid smoke in a microwave-safe bowl, covering tightly with plastic wrap, and microwaving on High for 5 to 6 minutes. Alternatively, bring the vegetable broth to a boil, pour over the TVP mixed with the liquid smoke, stir, cover, and let sit for 10 minutes. Let the TVP rest until cool enough to handle.

Transfer the reconstituted TVP to a mixing bowl, and add the wheat gluten, paprika, onion powder, nutritional yeast, jalapeños, jalapeño juice, cream cheese, salt, and pepper. Using your hands, knead everything together until very well incorporated and uniform. Divide into 8 equal pieces. Let rest for 20 minutes to allow the gluten to develop.

Place a sheet of foil, about 12 × 6 inches (30 cm × 15 cm), on the counter. Place 1 piece of dough in the center of the foil and flatten into an oblong shape. Place about 1 tablespoon (7 g) of the cheese in the center of the dough and wrap the dough around the cheese to form a hot dog shape. (Or you can omit the cheese and just form into a hot dog shape.) Roll the foil around the sausage and tightly twist the ends to form a casing. Repeat with the remaining 7 pieces of dough.

Bake the hot dogs, seam side down on a baking sheet, for 30 minutes. Let rest until cool enough to handle before unwrapping.

YIELD: 8 sausages

RECIPE NOTE

Turn these hot dogs into pigs in a blanket, taquito style! Put a thin layer of nacho cheese sauce or salsa verde on 8 corn tortillas. Tightly wrap each sausage into the tortilla, closing it with a toothpick. Follow the instructions in Chorizo Flautas (page 164) to fry or bake. Dip into more nacho cheese sauce or salsa verde, store-bought or homemade (page 206), and serve.

PIGGIES IN A BLANKET

For a weeknight meal in minutes, you can make these entirely with store-bought ingredients.
If you have a bit more time on your hands, you can make most of the ingredients from scratch.
Semi-homemade or totally homemade, these little piggies are fun and tasty!

INGREDIENTS:

Four 5-inch (12.5-cm) square vegan puff pastry pieces,
thawed according to package directions

¼ cup (56 g) vegan mayonnaise,
store-bought or homemade (page 211)

8 slices your favorite vegan cheese

8 slices vegan bacon,
store-bought or homemade (page 84)

8 vegan hot dogs,
store-bought or homemade (page 157)

¼ cup (56 g) nondairy butter, melted

DIRECTIONS:

Preheat the oven to 400ºF (200ºC, or gas mark 6).
Line a baking sheet with parchment paper or a silicone
baking mat.

Cut each pastry square on the diagonal to make 8
triangles. Spread each triangle with mayonnaise, then
lay down a slice of cheese. Lay the bacon along the side
of the hot dog. Starting at one corner, roll the hot dog
and bacon up in the triangle of puff pastry. Secure with a
toothpick. Repeat with the remaining 7 triangles.

Place all 8 piggies on the prepared baking sheet. Brush
with the melted butter. Bake for 12 to 15 minutes, or until
golden and crispy.

YIELD: 8 piggies

RECIPE NOTE

Instead of store-bought hot dogs, try making the Slow
Cooker Cocktail Weenies (page 157), sauce and all—but as
full-size hot dogs—then use those! Mmmm, saucy piggies!

SESAME UDON STIR-FRY

This dish is perfect for quick weeknight dinners, and makes enough for leftovers so you can pack up easy lunches the rest of the week. Plus, it tastes great hot or cold.

INGREDIENTS:

1 package (16 ounces, or 454 g) udon noodles, prepared according to package directions

¼ cup (60 ml) sesame oil (not toasted)

2 tablespoons (30 ml) peanut or other vegetable oil

1 red bell pepper, seeded, cored, and diced

½ cup (80 g) finely diced red onion

½ cup (65 g) cashews (raw or roasted is fine)

2 cloves garlic, minced

1 bunch (8 ounces, or 227 g) bok choy, roughly chopped

1 cup (136 g) yellow corn

1 cup (134 g) green peas

8 ounces (227 g) sugar snap peas

2 tablespoons (30 ml) soy sauce

1 teaspoon red pepper flakes (optional)

Salt and pepper, to taste

DIRECTIONS:

When the noodles are done cooking, drain and return to the pot. Add the sesame oil and toss to coat. Set aside.

In a large wok, heat the peanut oil over medium-high heat. Add the bell pepper, onion, and cashews. Cook for about 3 minutes, tossing regularly. Add the garlic, bok choy, corn, peas, and snap peas and continue to cook for about 5 more minutes, tossing regularly, until the bok choy is wilted and all the vegetables are cooked, but still bright and crisp.

Add the soy sauce and red pepper flakes; toss to coat. Add the udon noodles and toss to combine. Continue to cook for about 3 more minutes, tossing constantly. Season with salt and pepper to taste. Serve hot or cold.

YIELD: 8 main dish servings

RECIPE NOTE

Add a punch of protein by throwing in some cubed super firm tofu, soy curls, or sliced seitan into the mix when you add the vegetables.

FALAFEL AND TAHINI SAUCE

You can eat them as is or fill half a pita bread with slices of tomato and cucumber,
a small handful lettuce, and as many falafel as will fit, and then top with sauce.

FOR THE SAUCE:

¼ cup (64 g) tahini

Juice of 1 lemon (about 3 tablespoons [45 ml])

¼ teaspoon fine sea salt

¼ teaspoon red pepper flakes

1 tablespoon (8 g) cornstarch

1 clove garlic, minced

¾ cup (180 ml) unsweetened soymilk

½ teaspoon ground cumin

FOR THE FALAFEL:

1 can (15 ounces, or 425 g) chickpeas, drained and rinsed

Juice of 1 small lemon (about 3 tablespoons [45 ml])

2 cloves garlic, minced

1 teaspoon granulated onion

1 teaspoon ground cumin

2 teaspoons (4 g) ground coriander

2 teaspoons (1.2 g) dried cilantro

¼ teaspoon red pepper flakes

¼ teaspoon fine sea salt

6 tablespoons (30 g) panko bread crumbs

2 tablespoons (18 g) vital wheat gluten flour

1 tablespoon (16 g) tahini

1 small roasted red pepper, chopped

Vegetable oil, for frying

DIRECTIONS:

To make the sauce: Using a blender, combine all the ingredients. Heat over medium-high heat in a medium-size saucepan, whisking constantly, until slightly thickened, about 3 minutes. Set aside.

To make the falafel: Using a food processor, pulse the chickpeas a few times just until none are left whole. Add the remaining ingredients and pulse until combined: you want the batter to hold together when pinched, but not be completely smooth because you want some texture left. Gather 2 generously packed tablespoons (40 g) per falafel, and shape into a ball. You will get 10 falafel in all.

Use a deep fryer, or fill a heavy, deep saucepan with 3 inches (7.5 cm) of oil. Heat to 350°F (180°C). Do not overcrowd! Fry the falafel in batches until golden brown, flipping them once, about 2 minutes. Remove from the oil with a heat-proof slotted spoon. Drain on paper towels. Repeat with the remaining falafel.

YIELD: 10 falafel, 2 to 4 servings, with 1½ cups (455 ml) sauce

RECIPE NOTE

If you're not fond of deep-frying foods, try baking these instead: Preheat the oven to 375°F (190°C, or gas mark 5). Lightly coat the falafel with cooking spray. Bake for 10 minutes, covered with foil. Remove the foil and bake for another 10 minutes, or until the falafel are golden brown and firm.

BBQ SLAW TACOS

Sweet and smoky flavors combine to make these unusual tacos reminiscent of barbecue pulled pork and slaw. Don't mind if we do.

FOR THE SLAW:

1 cup (245 g) sweet pickle relish

6 tablespoons (96 g) natural crunchy peanut butter

1 tablespoon (8 g) capers

2 tablespoons (30 ml) brine from capers

Pinch of red pepper flakes

1 tablespoon (15 g) stone-ground mustard

10 ounces (283 g) shredded coleslaw

FOR THE FILLING:

1 tablespoon (15 ml) peanut oil

1 pound (454 g) store-bought vegan chicken-style strips or Chi-fu (recipe below)

⅔ cup (160 ml) Whiskey Barbecue Sauce (page 210; substitute vegetable broth for whiskey, if desired)

8 flour tortillas

DIRECTIONS:

To make the slaw: In a large bowl, combine the relish, peanut butter, capers, brine, red pepper flakes, and mustard until emulsified. Add the coleslaw and toss to combine. The salad will look dry, but as the slaw chills it will release moisture. Cover and chill for 2 hours.

To make the filling: Heat the oil in a large skillet. Add the chicken strips and sauté until light golden brown, about 8 minutes. Remove from the heat to add the barbecue sauce, to avoid splatters. Cook for 2 minutes longer, until heated through. Set aside.

Grab a tortilla, add a scoop of slaw, and top with the filling. Repeat with the remaining tortillas, and serve.

YIELD: 8 servings

BONUS RECIPE

HOMEADE CHI-FU!

If you'd rather go homemade then storebought, try this fabulous recipe for tofu chicken. It's super simple!

Ingredients:
   1 tablespoon (15 ml) peanut oil
   1 pound (454 g) super-firm tofu, torn into
      bite-size pieces
   ½ teaspoon fine sea salt
   1 tablespoon (8 g) nutritional yeast

Directions:
In a large skillet, heat the oil and sauté the tofu over medium-high heat for 5 minutes. Add the salt and nutritional yeast, and cook for 5 minutes longer, or until browned.

Yield: 1 pound (454 g)

CRISPY BURRITOS CON CARNE

These burritos are reminiscent of the ones that can be bought from the Mexican food carts and trucks here in Southern California. No beans! No rice! Just meaty, gooey goodness that goes great with some guacamole for dipping.

INGREDIENTS:

1 cup (96 g) TVP granules

1 teaspoon evaporated cane juice or granulated sugar

2 tablespoons (14 g) paprika

1 teaspoon ground cumin

1 teaspoon garlic powder

1 teaspoon onion powder

½ teaspoon chili powder

¼ to ½ teaspoon chipotle chile powder, or to taste

½ teaspoon salt

6 to 8 slices jarred jalapeños, finely diced

1 medium-size yellow onion, finely diced

1 cup (235 ml) water or vegetable broth

¼ cup (60 ml) canola oil

1 cup (240 g) nondairy sour cream, store-bought or homemade (page 211)

¼ cup (30 g) nutritional yeast

4 burrito-size flour tortillas

Vegetable oil, for frying

DIRECTIONS:

In a microwave-safe bowl, mix together the TVP, sugar, spices, jalapeño peppers, and onion. Stir in the water and canola oil. Cover tightly with plastic wrap, and microwave on High for 5 minutes. Alternatively, sauté the onions in a little canola oil until translucent, 3 to 5 minutes, and then add the TVP, sugar, spices, and jalapeño peppers. Bring the water to a boil. Pour over the mixture, cover tightly, and let sit for 10 minutes.

Mix in the sour cream and nutritional yeast.

Divide the mixture evenly among the 4 tortillas and roll by first tucking in the ends, then rolling up.

Heat about 1 inch (2.5 cm) of vegetable oil in a cast-iron skillet or frying pan over high heat. Place 1 burrito, seam side down, in the oil and fry for 10 to 20 seconds, until golden and crispy, then flip and repeat on the other side. Place on a paper towel lined-plate to absorb the excess oil. Serve immediately.

YIELD: 4 burritos

EAT YOUR VEGGIES!

We beg you to *please* eat a side of leafy greens with these! The Kale with a Kick (page 172) is an excellent choice.

TACO SALAD

Ever since Joni was wee, she loved the salad that came in a bowl you could eat!
Don't want to bother with tortilla bowls? No worries . . . throw a handful of
tortilla chips in the bottom of a regular bowl before tossing in your salad!

FOR THE DRESSING:

½ cup (112 g) vegan mayonnaise,
store-bought or homemade (page 211)

1 ripe avocado

¼ cup (60 ml) fresh lime juice

½ teaspoon ground cumin

¼ teaspoon cayenne pepper, or to taste

Salt and pepper, to taste

FOR THE SALAD:

½ head green cabbage, shredded

1 recipe TVP Chorizo (page 216)

1 can (14 ounces, or 392 g) pinto or black beans,
drained and rinsed

½ cup (68 g) corn kernels

½ cup (130 g) prepared salsa

1 ripe avocado, cubed

DIRECTIONS:

To make the dressing: Add all of the ingredients to a
blender and blend until smooth.

To make the salad: In a large mixing bowl, toss together
all of the ingredients. Divide the salad among 4 bowls.
Drizzle with the dressing and serve.

YIELD: 4 servings

RECIPE NOTE

Make your own tortilla bowls by using 2 small stainless
steel nesting bowls. Preheat the oven to 450°F (230°C,
or gas mark 8). Place the smaller of the 2 nesting bowls
upside down on a baking sheet. Spray a burrito-size flour
tortilla liberally on both sides with cooking spray. Drape
the tortilla over the smaller bowl and then place the
larger bowl over the tortilla to keep its shape. Bake for
15 to 20 minutes. Remove from the oven and carefully
remove the top bowl. Allow the bowl to cool while still
on the smaller bowl to stiffen up.

BLACK AND BRAISED TOFU

Here we use an old-school cooking technique (originally intended for tough cuts of meat) to create a spicy and savory tofu steak. After cooking, spoon the braising veggies on top of the steaks as a garnish; they hold lots of yummy flavor. As an FYI, this dry rub also works well when grilling or smoking tofu.

FOR THE DRY RUB:

1 to 2 tablespoons (15 to 30 g) red pepper flakes, or to taste

1 tablespoon (8 g) garlic powder

1 tablespoon (8 g) onion powder

1 tablespoon (7 g) paprika

1 teaspoon salt

1 teaspoon ground black pepper

¼ teaspoon cayenne pepper, or to taste

24 ounces (680 g) extra- or super-firm tofu, drained and pressed

FOR THE BRAISING LIQUID:

2 tablespoons (30 ml) vegetable oil

1 cup (160 g) finely diced white onion

½ cup (54 g) diced or shredded carrot

½ cup (51 g) finely chopped celery

2 tablespoons (30 g) minced garlic

2 cups (470 ml) water

DIRECTIONS:

To make the dry rub: Place all the ingredients in a small airtight container and shake to combine.

Cut the tofu into 4 steaks. Liberally coat the steaks on all sides with the rub. Set aside.

To make the braising liquid: Add the oil to a large pan with a tight-fitting lid and heat over medium-high heat. Add the onion, carrot, celery, and garlic and cook until translucent and fragrant, turning occasionally to prevent scorching, 5 to 7 minutes. Add the water, bring to a boil, reduce to a low simmer, and cover.

In a dry pan over high heat, fry the tofu to blacken the spices, about 4 to 5 minutes per side. Lay the blackened tofu on top of the braising liquid, cover, and cook for 20 minutes. Transfer the tofu to serving plates and spoon the vegetables on top of the tofu.

YIELD: 4 steaks

EAT YOUR VEGGIES!

Serve with a side of Baked Asparagus with Mushroom Sauce (page 166) for a complete meal.

SAVORY CHEESECAKE

Make this quiche-like cheesecake ahead of time so it will slice easily.

INGREDIENTS:

1 cup (235 ml) unsweetened soymilk

¼ cup (56 g) nondairy butter, melted

3 tablespoons (24 g) cornstarch

½ cup (50 g) Hemp Almond Parmesan (page 213)

½ recipe Skillet Cornbread (page 200)

14 ounces (397 g) nondairy cream cheese

8 ounces (227 g) extra-firm tofu, drained and crumbled

1 tablespoon (8 g) granulated onion

2 tablespoons (2 g) chopped fresh cilantro

2 tablespoons (8 g) chopped fresh parsley

2 cloves garlic, minced

½ teaspoon fine sea salt

½ teaspoon ground pepper

⅛ teaspoon ground nutmeg

1 pound (454 g) frozen green peas, thawed

DIRECTIONS:

Using a blender, combine the soymilk, butter, cornstarch, and parmesan. Place in a 4-cup (940-ml) glass measuring cup, place in the microwave, and bring to a boil on High for 2 minutes, or until thickened. Stir with a fork or use the blender again, to eliminate lumps. Alternatively, bring the mixture to a boil in a medium-size saucepan, lower the heat to medium, and cook for 3 minutes, or until thickened, stirring constantly. Set aside to cool.

Preheat the oven to 375°F (190°C, or gas mark 5). Lightly coat a 9-inch (23-cm) round pan with cooking spray.

Using a food processor, crumble the cornbread. If the cornbread is dry, add 1 to 2 tablespoons (15 to 30 ml) olive oil so that it holds together when pinched. Press down into the bottom of the prepared pan.

Bake for 10 minutes, or until golden brown. Place the pan on a wire rack to cool before adding the filling. Turn down the oven to 350°F (180°C, or gas mark 4).

Using a food processor, combine the soymilk mixture, cream cheese, tofu, onion, cilantro, parsley, garlic, salt, pepper, and nutmeg. You may need to do this in a couple of batches, depending on the size of the food processor. Add the peas and pulse just to combine. Pour the filling evenly into the cooled crust.

Bake for 45 minutes, or until golden brown and firm. Place the pan on a wire rack to cool. Chill overnight. Reheat in a 350°F (180°C, or gas mark 4) oven for 10 minutes, or enjoy at room temperature.

YIELD: 8 servings

EAT YOUR VEGGIES!

Serve with a mix of spring greens, radicchio, and fresh herbs drizzled with Mamou's Magical Vinaigrette (page 209).

RECIPE NOTE

If you'd rather use nondairy yogurt instead of cream cheese, replace the cream cheese with 2 containers (each 6 ounces, or 170 g) unsweetened nondairy yogurt, and increase the amount of cornstarch to ¼ cup (32 g) in the soymilk mixture, then pulse in another 2 tablespoons (16 g) cornstarch at the same time you add the herbs and seasoning to the food processor.

SCALLOPED POTATO PIE

If piling up thinly sliced and delicately spiced potatoes in crispy and buttery
puff pastry—adding creamy sauce and caramelized onions to the mix—is wrong,
then we don't want to be right. Enjoy with a crunchy salad composed of diced yellow
bell pepper, baby tomatoes, and baby spinach, drizzled with your favorite dressing.

INGREDIENTS:

1 sheet (245 g) frozen vegan puff pastry

22 ounces (615 g) russet potatoes, thinly sliced

2 teaspoons fine sea salt

½ cup (80 g) caramelized chopped onion (see note)

FOR THE BÉCHAMEL:

1 cup (235 ml) unsweetened nondairy milk

4 ounces (113 g) nondairy cream cheese

2 large cloves garlic

1 medium-size shallot

½ teaspoon dried thyme

1 teaspoon fine sea salt

¼ teaspoon ground pepper, plus extra to season layers

¼ teaspoon freshly grated nutmeg

1 tablespoon (8 g) cornstarch

2 teaspoons (10 ml) freshly squeezed lemon juice

DIRECTIONS:

Thaw the puff pastry for 40 minutes prior to rolling it out.

In the meantime, cover the potatoes with water in a large pot. Add the salt. Cook for 10 minutes, or until barely tender. Drain and set aside.

To make the béchamel: Combine all the ingredients in a microwave-safe measuring cup. Blend, using an immersion blender. Microwave for 2 minutes. Blend again and set aside.

Preheat the oven to 375°F (190°C, or gas mark 5). Lightly coat a 9-inch (23-cm) round baking pan with cooking spray.

Roll out the puff pastry to ⅛ inch (3 mm) on a lightly floured surface. Place in the prepared pan and lightly prick with a fork. Tuck the overhanging dough into the pan to make croissant-like crust edges.

Evenly arrange half of the potatoes on top of the pastry dough, layering them as necessary layer. Top with a pinch of pepper and an even layer of béchamel. Top with an even layer of the caramelized onions. Repeat a second time, topping the second layer of potatoes with a generous amount of béchamel.

Bake for 45 minutes, or until golden brown. Let cool for 20 minutes, then remove from the pan, slice, and serve.

YIELD: 8 servings

RECIPE NOTE

To caramelize onions: Add ½ cup (80 g) chopped onion and ¼ teaspoon fine sea salt to a skillet coated with olive oil. Sauté for 20 minutes over medium heat, or until caramelized.

POT PIE EXPLOSION

QUICK AND EASY

If you don't want to commit to making a crust and happen to have biscuits lying around, this will be a quick and easy meal to make and guaranteed to bring comfort as much as a more involved pot pie would.

INGREDIENTS:

2 tablespoons (28 g) nondairy butter

4 cups (496 g) steamed finely chopped cauliflower

8 ounces (227 g) sliced button mushrooms

2 tablespoons (20 g) chopped shallot

6 cloves garlic, minced

½ teaspoon fine sea salt, or to taste

½ teaspoon ground pepper, or to taste

½ teaspoon dried basil

2 tablespoons (16 g) cornstarch or any flour

1 tablespoon (15 g) maca powder or 2 tablespoons (15 g) nutritional yeast

1 cup (235 ml) vegetable broth

⅔ cup (160 ml) coconut milk or nondairy creamer

1 recipe Bacon Onion Biscuits (page 191)

⅓ cup (20 g) chopped fresh parsley (optional)

DIRECTIONS:

Combine the butter, cauliflower, mushrooms, shallot, and garlic in a large pot. Cook for 6 minutes over medium heat, or until the mushrooms brown up a little.

Add the salt, pepper, and basil. Cook for 4 minutes longer, or until the mushrooms have rendered their water.

Add the cornstarch and maca powder. Cook for 2 minutes longer.

Add the broth and coconut milk and cook for 4 minutes longer, or until thickened.

Split the biscuits in half and serve with gravy, garnished with a sprinkling of parsley.

YIELD: 4 servings (3 biscuit halves per person, with gravy)

EAT YOUR VEGGIES!

Serve with Pesto Pea-damame Soup (page 150) or Roasted Broccotato Soup with Bacon-Flavored Chickpeas (page 70).

RECIPE NOTE

To make this into an even more substantial meal, make tofu cubes following the instructions in Creamy All-in-One Bowl (page 130) , replacing the ground ginger with freshly ground pepper to taste.

BRUSSELS SPROUT AND CHESTNUT POT PIE

Make this hearty pie even more delectable by pouring some White Sausage Gravy (page 33) or extra Creamy Cheesy Sauce (page 212) on top upon serving. You can also prepare 4 individual pot pies by dividing the crust into four 4-inch (10-cm) pie plates. The baking time will decrease to about 1 hour.

INGREDIENTS:

2 tablespoons (30 ml) olive oil

¼ cup (40 g) minced shallot

4 cloves garlic, minced

1 pound (454 g) brussels sprouts, trimmed and quartered

1 package (3½ ounces, or 100 g) prepared roasted chestnuts, crumbled

½ teaspoon fine sea salt

¼ teaspoon ground black pepper

2½ teaspoons (.17 g) dried sage

½ cup (114 g) store-bought tempeh bacon strips (about 6 strips), pan-fried until browned, chopped

1 cup (235 ml) Creamy Cheesy Sauce (page 212), made with 1 tablespoon (8 g) cornstarch

1 recipe Basic Pie Crust (page 234), chilled

1 tablespoon (15 ml) nondairy milk

DIRECTIONS:

Preheat the oven to 375°F (190°C, or gas mark 5). Combine the oil, shallot, garlic, sprouts, chestnuts, salt, pepper, and sage in a 9-inch (23-cm) baking dish. Roast for 24 minutes, or until the sprouts are just al dente. This will depend on the size of your sprouts.

Remove from the oven and stir in the chopped bacon and cheese sauce.

Lightly coat an 8-inch (20-cm) round baking pan with cooking spray.

Divide the pie crust in two, with one portion slightly larger than the other. Roll out the larger portion on a lightly floured surface into a 10 ½-inch (27-cm) circle. Fit into the baking pan, leaving the overhanging crust as is. Using a fork, prick the bottom and sides of the crust to prevent puffing up.

Roll out the smaller portion of pie crust on a lightly floured surface into an 8 ½-inch (22-cm) circle.

Place the filling evenly over the pie crust. Cover with the smaller crust. Bring the overhanging crust up to meet the top crust and crimp both crusts together at the edges. Using a pair of clean kitchen scissors, cut out a couple of small air vents in the center of the top crust. Lightly brush the top crust with the milk.

Bake for 75 minutes, or until the top of the crust is golden brown all over. Let stand for 15 minutes before slicing and serving.

YIELD: 6 servings

BETTER LOVE YOUR BEANS BAKE

Your ravenous family is bound to join you in the kitchen to enjoy the wonderful fragrance of this creamy mock meat-free dish while it bakes, in anticipation of official dinnertime. Be prepared!

FOR THE TOPPING:

1 can (15 ounces, or 425 g) chickpeas, drained and rinsed

¼ cup (30 g) nutritional yeast

1 clove garlic, minced

1 teaspoon granulated onion

½ cup (120 g) nondairy sour cream, store-bought or homemade (page 211)

½ cup (120 ml) unsweetened nondairy milk

¼ teaspoon paprika

Freshly ground pepper, to taste

FOR THE FILLING:

2 teaspoons (10 ml) olive oil

¼ cup (40 g) chopped onion

4 cloves garlic, minced

1 red bell pepper, cored, seeded, and diced

12 ounces (340 g) uncooked whole wheat macaroni pasta

1 can (15 ounces, or 425 g) black beans, drained, rinsed, and coarsely mashed

¾ cup plus 2 tablespoons (210 g) salsa verde, store-bought or homemade (page 206), or regular salsa

6 tablespoons (90 g) prepared guacamole

Juice of 1 lemon

2 teaspoons hot sauce, or to taste

1 tablespoon (7 g) taco seasoning

DIRECTIONS:

To make the topping: Combine all the ingredients in a blender, and purée until smooth.

To make the filling: Heat the oil in a medium-size skillet over medium heat. Add the onion, garlic, and bell pepper. Cook for 4 minutes, stirring occasionally, until the onion is translucent.

Cook the pasta in a pot of boiling water until short of al dente, then drain; the pasta will keep cooking in the oven.

Preheat the oven to 375°F (190°C, or gas mark 5). Lightly grease a 9-inch (23-cm) square baking dish.

Combine the beans, salsa, guacamole, lemon juice, hot sauce, and taco seasoning in a large bowl, stirring well. Stir in the cooked onion mixture and the pasta. Scrape the pasta mixture into the prepared baking dish and pour the topping evenly on top.

Bake for 20 minutes, or until the topping is golden brown. Let rest for 15 minutes before serving.

YIELD: 4 to 6 servings

CHORIZO AND POTATO LASAGNA BAKE

There is no need to add salt to this flavor-rich dish: The capers and olives take care of that. If you are concerned about your sodium intake, consider rinsing both the capers and the olives before adding them (drain them well) or cut back on the amount a little.

INGREDIENTS:

2 pounds (908 g) thinly sliced russet potatoes, peeling optional

FOR THE TOPPING:

1 cup (235 ml) unsweetened soymilk

¼ cup (60 ml) extra-virgin olive oil

1 tablespoon (8 g) cornstarch

1 tablespoon (15 ml) mild vinegar

1 clove garlic, halved

1 teaspoon granulated onion

½ teaspoon sea salt

Freshly ground pepper, to taste

FOR THE SAUCE:

2 teaspoons (10 ml) extra-virgin olive oil

3 tablespoons (30 g) minced shallot

2 cloves garlic, minced

1.2 pounds (544 g) Roma tomatoes, finely diced

½ cup (80 g) green olives with pimientos, chopped

¼ cup (60 g) capers, drained

1 tablespoon (17 g) tomato paste

2 teaspoons (2 g) dried oregano

2 teaspoons (5 g) paprika

Freshly ground pepper, to taste

12 ounces (340 g) TVP Chorizo (page 216) or store-bought soy chorizo

¼ cup (60 ml) red wine

DIRECTIONS:

Cover the potatoes with water in a large pot. Bring to a boil. Lower the heat to medium-high and cook until tender, about 15 minutes; drain and set aside.

To make the topping: Add all the ingredients to a microwave-safe bowl and stir to combine. Heat in the microwave for 2 minutes, making sure the mixture doesn't boil over. Set aside to cool and thicken. Stir with a fork before using.

To make the sauce: Heat the oil in saucepan. Add the shallot, garlic, and tomatoes. Cook for 2 minutes.

Add the olives, capers, tomato paste, oregano, paprika, pepper, and chorizo. Cook for 4 minutes.

Add the wine and simmer for 10 minutes, uncovered. Use a potato masher and press down on the mixture and crush it just slightly.

Preheat the oven to 375°F (190°C, or gas mark 5).

In a 9-inch (23-cm) square, deep baking dish, ladle in enough sauce to thinly cover the bottom. Top with a single layer of potatoes. Apply more sauce, then potatoes, and repeat until you run out of ingredients. Evenly sprinkle on the topping.

Bake for 20 to 25 minutes, or until golden brown on top. Let stand for 20 minutes before serving.

YIELD: 4 to 6 servings

CHEESY CHILI BAKE

The first time we combined chili, pasta, and cheesy sauce, we were officially hooked. This dish is part of what makes simple comfort food simply irresistible!

FOR THE TOPPING:

1 cup (235 ml) unsweetened nondairy milk

½ cup (66 g) macadamia nuts

½ cup (60 g) sliced almonds

½ teaspoon fine sea salt

¼ teaspoon ground pepper

2 teaspoons (10 ml) freshly squeezed lemon juice

2 cloves garlic

1 teaspoon granulated onion

1 tablespoon (8 g) nutritional yeast

1 tablespoon (15 g) maca powder or (8 g) extra nutritional yeast

FOR THE CHEESY SAUCE:

1¼ cups (295 ml) unsweetened soymilk

¾ cup (90 g) nutritional yeast

1 tablespoon (18 g) miso

2 tablespoons (32 g) tahini

2 tablespoons (28 g) nondairy butter

2 teaspoons (31 g) Dijon mustard

2 cloves garlic

1 tablespoon (8 g) cornstarch

12 ounces (340 g) uncooked elbow macaroni

4 cups (995 g) Chocolate Stout Chili (page 81) or any chili

DIRECTIONS:

Preheat the oven to 375°F (190°C, or gas mark 5).

To make the topping: Combine all the ingredients in a blender and process until perfectly smooth. Set aside.

To make the cheesy sauce: Combine all the ingredients in a blender and process until perfectly smooth. Microwave for 2 minutes. Stir with a fork, and set aside.

Cook the pasta according to package directions until just slightly undercooked, because it will continue cooking in the oven. Drain well.

Add the chili and cheesy sauce and stir to combine. Pour into a deep 10-inch (25-cm) baking dish. Cover evenly with the topping.

Bake for 25 minutes, or until golden brown on top. Serve.

YIELD: 4 to 6 servings

CREAMY ALL-IN-ONE BOWL

Supper time is just around the corner of a long, draining day but you barely have enough energy to walk from door to couch. If you happen to have cooked rice and steamed broccoli left over from previous meals, this peanutty rice bowl can be ready just in time to rejuvenate you and fill you up nicely in order to enjoy some well-deserved time with family and friends.

FOR THE TOFU:

2 tablespoons (30 ml) peanut oil

1 tablespoon (5 g) ground ginger

Pinch of fine sea salt

1 pound (454 g) super-firm tofu, cut into tiny cubes

FOR THE DRESSING:

½ cup (128 g) natural crunchy cashew, almond, or peanut butter

¼ cup (60 ml) seasoned rice vinegar (if you are sensitive to vinegar, replace some of it with vegetable broth)

2 tablespoons (30 ml) reduced-sodium soy sauce

1 tablespoon (18 g) miso

2 cloves garlic, grated

1 teaspoon Sriracha, or to taste

2 tablespoons (30 ml) freshly squeezed lemon juice

2 cups (312 g) steamed chopped broccoli florets

1 cup (165 g) chopped fresh pineapple

2½ cups (488 g) cooked brown jasmine rice

¼ cup (5 g) chopped fresh cilantro

¼ cup (35 g) chopped dry-roasted cashews, almonds, or peanuts

DIRECTIONS:

To make the tofu: Combine the oil, ginger, and salt in a skillet and heat over medium-high heat. Add the tofu cubes and fry for 10 minutes, stirring often, until brown and crispy.

To make the dressing: Combine all the ingredients and stir until emulsified.

Add the broccoli, pineapple, and rice to the tofu skillet, and cook for a few minutes until heated through. Stir in the dressing, sprinkle with the cilantro and nuts, and serve immediately.

YIELD: 4 servings

SAUERKRAUT AND DUMPLINS

Joni here to tell you that throughout my entire life I thought my family was the only one who ate this ridiculous dish every year on New Year's Day. Come to find out, when I went to my mommy to get the beloved family recipe, she told me, "Hold on a second, let me get out my box of Bisquick, the recipe is on the side of the box." Ha! Well, when she and my Gramma Jo made it, they would make the "dough balls" floating in a broth of sauerkraut and pork. It is with my pleasure that I share with you this very top-secret recipe, without the pork, of course.

FOR THE SAUERKRAUT:

6 cups (1.410 l) vegetable broth

1 large jar (32 ounces, or 896 g) prepared sauerkraut, with liquid

8 ounces (227 g) large-chunk TVP or Soy Curls

FOR THE DUMPLINS:

3½ cups (438 g) all-purpose flour

1 teaspoon baking powder

1 teaspoon baking soda

½ teaspoon salt

2 cups (470 ml) soymilk

2 tablespoons (30 ml) freshly squeezed lemon juice

¼ cup (56 g) nondairy butter, melted

DIRECTIONS:

To make the sauerkraut: In a large pot with a tight-fitting lid, combine the vegetable broth and sauerkraut with liquid and bring to a boil. Reduce to a simmer and add the TVP.

To make the dumplins: In a large mixing bowl, combine the flour, baking powder, baking soda, and salt.

In a separate small bowl, combine the soymilk and lemon juice. It will curdle and become like buttermilk. Add the melted butter to the buttermilk mixture and stir to combine.

Add the wet ingredients to the dry and stir to combine. Some lumps are okay. The batter will be wet, like a very thick pancake batter.

Using an ice-cream scoop, carefully drop the dumplin's into the simmering sauerkraut. Repeat until all of the batter is used and the dough balls almost create a solid layer on top of the sauerkraut.

Cover and cook for about 30 minutes, or until the dough balls are fully cooked. They will still look moist on the outside, but the insides should be fluffy.

Divide the dough balls among 8 bowls and ladle the sauerkraut broth on top. Serve hot.

YIELD: 8 servings

RECIPE NOTE

You can use any of your favorite proteins here—Gardein strips, seitan, tempeh, even Tofurky sandwich slices.

PATATAS BRAVAS FRITTATA

We're breaking all the rules by serving traditionally flavored potatoes alongside a non-tofu-based frittata flavored with the spices commonly used in patatas bravas (a popular Catalan appetizer translating to "fierce potatoes"), which makes for a spicy and satisfying dish best left to chill overnight, so that it holds its shape when sliced.

INGREDIENTS:

1 can (15 ounces, or 425 g) fire-roasted or regular diced tomatoes, with juice

1 can (28 ounces, or 793 g) whole roasted red peppers, drained and chopped

8 cloves garlic

2 dried guarillo peppers, seeds and tails removed, rinsed, or 1 tablespoon (7 g) mild to medium chili powder

½ teaspoon fine sea salt

¼ teaspoon ground black pepper

2 tablespoons (14 g) granulated onion

2 tablespoons (14 g) mild paprika

2 tablespoons (30 g) ketchup

2 cans (each 15 ounces, or 425 g) chickpeas, drained and rinsed

1 cup (144 g) vital wheat gluten flour

¼ cup (30 g) nutritional yeast

1 can (15 ounces, or 425 g) black beans, drained and rinsed

1 tablespoon (15 ml) extra-virgin olive oil

½ cup (56 g) shredded nondairy cheese, such as Daiya (optional)

1 recipe Home Fries (page 151), seasoned with ½ teaspoon fine sea salt and ¼ teaspoon ground pepper instead of the chipotle seasoning

¼ cup (11 g) chopped fresh basil or (15 g) parsley

DIRECTIONS:

Combine the tomatoes, roasted peppers, garlic, guarillo peppers, salt, pepper, onion, paprika, and ketchup in a large saucepan. Bring to a boil, lower the heat to medium-low, and simmer for 15 minutes.

Using a food processor, process the chickpeas until broken into small pieces. Alternatively, for a smoother texture and more firmness for the frittata as a whole, process the chickpeas at the same time you do the tomato mixture, until smooth. Transfer to a large bowl.

Carefully transfer the tomato mixture to the food processor and blend until smooth.

Transfer the tomato mixture back to the large saucepan, along with the processed chickpeas, wheat gluten, and nutritional yeast. Stir for 1 minute, until very well combined. Stir in the black beans.

Preheat the oven to 400°F (200°C, or gas mark 6). Coat a 10-inch (25-cm) cast-iron skillet or deep baking dish with the olive oil.

Press the tomato mixture evenly into the prepared dish. Sprinkle with the cheese. Place on top of a baking sheet in case of overflow. Bake for 30 minutes, or until golden brown and set.

Sprinkle with the optional cheese and serve alongside the potatoes.

YIELD: 6 servings

FIVE-CHEESE BAKED MACARONI AND CHEESE

This baked version of macaroni and cheese gets its cheesiness from 1) a noochy sauce 2) a tofu ricotta-like mixture 3) nondairy cream cheese 4) Daiya or other shredded vegan cheese, and 5) Walnut Parmesan Sprinkles. Yep, that's five cheeses!

FOR THE SAUCE:

½ cup (112 g) nondairy butter

1 cup (235 ml) plain nondairy creamer or nondairy milk

¼ cup (30 g) nutritional yeast

1 tablespoon (8 g) garlic powder

1 tablespoon (8 g) onion powder

1 teaspoon smoked paprika

2 tablespoons (16 g) all-purpose flour

FOR THE TOFU:

10 ounces (280 g) extra-firm tofu, drained, pressed, and crumbled

2 tablespoons (36 g) miso

2 tablespoons (30 g) yellow mustard

2 tablespoons (30 ml) olive oil

1 pound (454 g) elbow macaroni, prepared according to package directions

8 ounces (227 g) nondairy cream cheese

1 cup (4 ounces, 112 g) shredded nondairy cheese, such as Daiya

Salt and pepper, to taste

½ cup (43 g) Walnut Parmesan Sprinkles (page 212)

DIRECTIONS:

Preheat the oven to 350°F (180°C, or gas mark 4).

To make the sauce: Melt the butter in a small pot over medium-high heat. Stir in the creamer, nutritional yeast, garlic powder, onion powder, and paprika. Bring to a boil. Reduce the heat to medium and stir in the flour. Whisk vigorously until thickened and there are no lump. Remove from the heat and set aside.

To make the tofu: In a large mixing bowl, combine the tofu, miso, mustard, and olive oil and mash with your hands until well incorporated.

Drain the pasta and return to the pot. Add the sauce, tofu mixture, cream cheese, and shredded cheese. Season with salt and pepper to taste. Stir to combine.

Transfer the mixture to a 9 × 13-inch (23 × 33-cm) baking dish. Sprinkle an even layer of Walnut Parmesan Sprinkles over the top. Bake, uncovered, for 30 minutes, or until slightly browned.

Remove from the oven and allow to sit for about 10 minutes before serving.

YIELD: 6 servings

EAT YOUR VEGGIES!

Both this recipe and the Beefy-Cheesy Mac on the opposite page taste great with the addition of green peas, broccoli florets, or green beans tossed into the mix!

BEEFY-CHEESY MAC

Joni's mom used to make her and her sister Hamburger Helper at least once a week for dinner (Tuna Helper on at least one other night). Cheeseburger Macaroni was their favorite flavor. After a while, she started adding peas or broccoli to the mix—you know, to make it healthier—so you can do that if you choose, but as a Hamburger Helper purist, Joni likes it without any add-ins.

Using a big old frying pan (with a lid) is key here, and no, you won't have to fry the pasta, but it will almost taste that way! If you don't have a huge frying pan, use a big soup pot, the wider the better.

INGREDIENTS:

¼ cup (56 g) nondairy butter

1 cup (160 g) finely diced onion

4 cups (940 ml) vegetable broth, divided

1 cup (96 g) TVP granules

1 cup (235 ml) soymilk

¼ cup (60 ml) vegetable oil

1 tablespoon (15 ml) sesame oil

1 tablespoon (8 g) garlic powder

2 teaspoons (4.4 g) turmeric

2 tablespoons (36 g) miso

1 tablespoon (7 g) paprika

1 tablespoon (15 g) yellow mustard

¼ cup (30 g) nutritional yeast

12 ounces (340 g) uncooked elbow macaroni

½ cup (120 g) nondairy sour cream, store-bought or homemade (page 211)

½ cup (120 g) ketchup

Salt and pepper, to taste

DIRECTIONS:

In a large frying pan, melt the butter over medium-high heat. Add the onion and sauté until just beginning to brown. Add 1 cup (235 ml) of the vegetable broth. Bring to a boil. Reduce the heat to low, and stir in the TVP. Continue to cook until the TVP has absorbed most of the liquid, 5 to 7 minutes.

Meanwhile, combine the remaining 3 cups (705 ml) vegetable broth, soymilk, vegetable oil, sesame oil, garlic powder, turmeric, miso, paprika, mustard, and nutritional yeast.

Add the mixture to the pan, stir, and bring to a boil. Add the macaroni, reduce to a simmer, cover, and simmer until the pasta is tender, 12 to 15 minutes, stirring often to prevent scorching.

Uncover and stir in the sour cream, ketchup, salt, and pepper to taste.

Remove from the heat and let stand for 10 minutes to thicken up before serving.

YIELD: 4 to 6 servings

PASTA ALFREDO

Fettucine is the traditional pasta of choice here, but any pasta will do. Sometimes we use this sauce over macaroni, as a change from the usual mac and cheese.

INGREDIENTS:

¼ cup (56 g) nondairy butter

1 cup (240 g) nondairy sour cream, store-bought or homemade (page 211)

½ cup (120 g) nondairy cream cheese

¼ cup (60 ml) soymilk

¼ cup (30 g) nutritional yeast

1 tablespoon (8 g) garlic powder

½ cup (60 g) finely ground cashews

Salt and pepper, to taste

1 pound (454 g) pasta of choice, prepared according to package directions

DIRECTIONS:

Add the butter, sour cream, cream cheese, and soymilk to a pot. Heat over medium heat until melted and creamy, 5 to 7 minutes.

Stir in the nutritional yeast, garlic powder, and cashews. Cook for about 3 minutes, until thickened. Season with salt and pepper to taste.

Serve immediately over the pasta.

YIELD: 4 servings

PESTO, FARRO, AND FAGIOLI

Farro is a super-chewy and delicious grain that pairs nicely here with the texture of the beans and the freshness of the pesto. It's another dish that takes no time to prepare and won't make a huge dent in your pocketbook while filling you up just right.

INGREDIENTS:

1 cup (180 g) uncooked semi-pearled farro

1¾ cups (415 ml) reduced-sodium vegetable broth

½ teaspoon fine sea salt

¼ teaspoon ground white pepper

1 recipe Spinach Pesto (page 210)

1 can (15 ounces, or 425 g) cannellini beans, drained and rinsed

2 tablespoons (30 ml) balsamic vinegar

¼ teaspoon red pepper flakes

2 tablespoons (30 ml) capers, with brine

2 tablespoons (30 ml) freshly squeezed lemon juice

DIRECTIONS:

Toast the farro in a dry skillet over medium heat until fragrant, about 2 minutes, stirring constantly. Add the broth, salt, and pepper. Bring to a boil, cover, reduce the heat, and simmer for 15 minutes, until the grain is cooked but still chewy and the water has evaporated.

Stir in the pesto, beans, vinegar, red pepper flakes, and capers. Cook, uncovered, for 2 minutes longer.

Divide among 4 bowls and top each portion with ½ tablespoon (8 ml) lemon juice. Enjoy hot or cold.

YIELD: 4 servings

PASTA ALLA FORMIANA

Baking the uncooked pasta directly in tomato sauce imparts the whole dish with deep and rich Italian-style flavors you'll have to try to believe.

FOR THE PARMESAN:

1 cup (100 g) walnut halves

¾ cup (90 g) nutritional yeast

1 tablespoon (15 g) maca powder

¼ cup (20 g) panko bread crumbs

½ teaspoon fine sea salt

½ teaspoon garlic powder

½ teaspoon granulated onion

1 tablespoon (18 g) miso

FOR THE PASTA:

¼ cup (60 ml) extra-virgin olive oil, divided

4 small beefsteak tomatoes, cut into ¼-inch (6-mm) thick slices, divided

2½ cups (590 ml) tomato juice

1¼ cups (170 g) whole pitted black olives

1 teaspoon dried basil

½ teaspoon red pepper flakes

4 cloves garlic

2 teaspoons (4.8 g) granulated onion

8 ounces (227 g) uncooked whole wheat elbow macaroni

DIRECTIONS:

To make the parmesan: Combine the walnuts, nutritional yeast, maca powder, bread crumbs, salt, garlic, and onion in a food processor. Blend until finely ground. Add the miso and pulse until combined. Store in an airtight container in the refrigerator for up to 2 weeks.

To make the pasta: Preheat the oven to 400°F (200°C, or gas mark 6). Coat an 8-inch (20-cm) square baking dish with 1 tablespoon (15 ml) of the oil.

Cover the bottom of the dish with the slices of 2 tomatoes.

Using a blender, combine the juice, olives, basil, red pepper flakes, 2 tablespoons (30 ml) of the oil, garlic, and onion. Add to the uncooked macaroni in a large bowl and stir to combine.

Transfer to the dish, on top of the tomato slices. Cover with the slices of the remaining 2 tomatoes. Drizzle the tomatoes with the remaining 1 tablespoon (15 ml) oil. Place on a baking sheet in case it overflows.

Bake, uncovered, for 1 hour, or until the tomatoes are brown on top. Sprinkle each serving with the parmesan.

YIELD: 4 servings, 2¼ cups (225 g) parmesan

SAUTÉED CHEESE TORTELLINI

If you have a pasta roller, this is a breeze. If you don't, just use a well-floured surface
and a rolling pin. These are great sautéed in a frying pan with salt and pepper,
because the filling is so rich. A simple marinara would also be a nice accompaniment.

FOR THE FILLING:

8 ounces (227 g) nondairy cream cheese

1 tablespoon (18 g) white or yellow miso

¼ cup (30 g) nutritional yeast

1 tablespoon (8 g) garlic powder

1 teaspoon dried basil

FOR THE DOUGH:

2½ cups (313 g) all-purpose flour

1 teaspoon salt

¼ cup (60 ml) olive oil

¾ cup (180 ml) water

3 tablespoons (45 ml) olive oil, for sautéing

Salt and pepper, to taste

DIRECTIONS:

To make the filling: Mash together all the ingredients. Refrigerate until ready to use.

To make the dough: In a medium-size mixing bowl, combine the flour and salt. Make a well in the center of the flour and add the oil and water. Knead in the bowl until the dough begins to come together.

Turn out onto a well-floured surface and knead into a stiff but elastic dough, about 5 minutes. If needed, add more water, 1 tablespoon (15 ml) at a time. To make it easier to work with, divide into 4 equal pieces.

Roll each piece as thin as possible, about ¹⁄₁₆ inch (1.5 mm). Using a 3-inch (7.5-cm) round cookie cutter, or the top of a pint glass, cut out 40 pieces.

Add about 1 teaspoon of filling to the edge of each of a round. Roll it up like a little burrito, then twist the edges tightly (the dough should be plenty elastic and not give you trouble here). Bring the ends together and pinch to form a ring; it will look almost like a little crab. Repeat with all 40 rounds.

Spread in a single layer on the counter and allow to dry for about 1 hour. You can also freeze them at this point for later use. They will keep for at least a month if stored in an airtight container in the freezer.

Bring a large pot of lightly salted water to a rolling boil. Gently place the tortellini in the boiling water. Boil for about 6 minutes, or until they float to the top of the water.

Pour some of the oil into a frying pan, and heat over medium-high heat. Using a slotted spoon, lift the tortellini out of the water, drain the excess water, and transfer some to the hot oil, being careful of splatters. Do not overcrowd the pan. Sauté for 3 to 4 minutes per side, adding salt and pepper to taste. Repeat in batches to fry all of the tortellini.

Let sit for about 10 minutes before serving to allow the filling to cool.

YIELD: 4 to 6 servings

TRADITIONAL RED LASAGNA

This rich and filling lasagna is so much like the real thing that any skeptics in your household will be hard-pressed to notice a difference!

FOR THE RICOTTA:

14 ounces (397 g) extra-firm tofu, drained and pressed

¼ cup (35 g) finely ground raw cashews

¼ cup (30 g) nutritional yeast

3 tablespoons (45 ml) extra-virgin olive oil

2 tablespoons (6 g) finely chopped fresh basil or 1 tablespoon (2 g) dried

Salt and pepper, to taste

FOR THE SAUCE:

28 ounces (784 g) canned diced tomatoes with juice, no salt added

8 ounces (227 g) tomato sauce

6 ounces (170 g) tomato paste

1 tablespoon (2 g) dried basil or 3 tablespoons (9 g) fresh, chopped

1 tablespoon (12 g) evaporated cane juice or granulated sugar

1 tablespoon (22 g) molasses

2 tablespoons (30 ml) extra-virgin olive oil

6 cloves garlic, minced

1 cup (160 g) finely diced white or yellow onion

1¼ cups (120 g) TVP granules

12 uncooked no-boil lasagna noodles

2 tablespoons (15 g) nutritional yeast

2 tablespoons (14 g) ground cashews or walnuts

DIRECTIONS:

To make the ricotta: Crumble the tofu into a bowl until it resembles ricotta. Add all the remaining ingredients and mix together with your hands. Set aside.

To make the sauce: Place the tomatoes, sauce, tomato paste, basil, sugar, and molasses in a large stockpot. Bring to a simmer over medium-low heat.

Meanwhile, in a skillet, heat the olive oil and sauté the garlic and onion until fragrant and translucent, about 10 minutes. Add the garlic and onion to the pot. Cover and continue to simmer for 20 minutes longer. Uncover and simmer for 10 minutes longer. Stir in the TVP, cover, and let sit for 10 minutes.

Preheat the oven to 375°F (190°C, or gas mark 5).

To assemble the lasagna, be sure to reserve some sauce and ricotta for the very top of the lasagna. You will have 4 layers of pasta in all, so divide each ingredient accordingly.

In a square 8- or 9-inch (20- or 23-cm) baking dish, spread a thin layer of sauce, add 3 noodles in a single layer, add another layer of sauce, and then a layer of ricotta. Repeat until there are 4 layers of noodles. Top with a final light layer of sauce and ricotta, and then sprinkle with the nutritional yeast and cashews.

Bake, uncovered, for 30 to 40 minutes, or until the top is beginning to brown and the noodles are nice and tender.

Let stand for at least 15 minutes before serving, so that the portions don't fall apart when cut.

YIELD: 6 servings

◄ PASTA ALLA CARB-ONARA

We think the taste of this creamy, animal-friendly version comes
really close to its original cholesterol-unfriendly incarnation.

INGREDIENTS:

2 tablespoons (30 ml) extra-virgin olive oil

½ cup (51 g) Hemp Almond Parmesan (page 213)

14 ounces (414 ml) light coconut milk or
nondairy creamer

1 tablespoon (8 g) cornstarch

4 cloves garlic, minced

½ teaspoon ground black pepper, or to taste

1 tablespoon (8 g) granulated onion

10 ounces (283 g) uncooked spaghetti

½ cup (40 g) imitation bacon bits

2 cups (320 g) frozen green peas, thawed

⅓ cup (20 g) chopped fresh parsley

Freshly squeezed lemon juice or zest, to taste

DIRECTIONS:

In a blender, combine the oil, parmesan, coconut milk,
cornstarch, garlic, pepper, and onion and process
until smooth.

Bring water in a large pot to a boil. Cook the pasta just
short of al dente; it will cook some more when combined
with the sauce. Drain well. Return the pasta to the pot.

Pour the sauce onto the pasta and add the bacon bits
and peas. Cook over low heat for a few minutes, just until
heated through and thickened.

Sprinkle with the parsley, add a touch of lemon juice or
zest to brighten up the flavors, and serve.

YIELD: 6 servings

TWICE-BAKED SPAGHETTI

Growing up at Joni's house, she would have spaghetti one night, and twice "baked"
spaghetti the next night, presumably with the leftovers from the night before.

INGREDIENTS:

1 pound (454 g) prepared spaghetti

1 can (14 ounces, or 392 g) diced tomatoes, drained

1 cup (244 g) marinara sauce

½ cup (112 g) vegan mayonnaise,
store-bought or homemade (page 211)

8 ounces (227 g) nondairy cream cheese

¼ cup (30 g) nutritional yeast

½ cup (40 g) panko bread crumbs or
Walnut Parmesan Sprinkles (page 212)

Salt and pepper, to taste

DIRECTIONS:

Preheat the oven to 350°F (180°C, or gas mark 4).

Add the tomatoes, marinara, mayonnaise, cream cheese,
and nutritional yeast to the prepared spaghetti. Stir to
combine. Transfer to a 9-inch (23-cm) square baking dish.
Smooth out the top.

Sprinkle the top evenly with the panko. Season with salt
and pepper to taste.

Bake for 1 hour, or until the topping is just beginning
to brown. Let rest for about 10 minutes before slicing
and serving.

YIELD: 9 servings

EGGPLANT PARMIGIANA

"Hearty, fruity, filling, and just wonderful" is the way this one-stop meal was described by one of our testers, Constanze, of the popular German site Seitan Is My Motor. We think that says it all and hope you'll feel the same way Constanze does.

FOR THE EGGPLANT:

2 large eggplants, sliced into ⅛-inch (3-mm) thick rounds

3 tablespoons (45 ml) olive oil

½ teaspoon fine sea salt

FOR THE MARINARA:

1 tablespoon (15 ml) olive oil

4 sun-dried tomatoes, packed in oil, chopped

4 cloves garlic, minced

2 teaspoons (4.8 g) granulated onion

2 teaspoons (3.6 g) dried oregano

2 teaspoons (2.8 g) dried basil

2 teaspoons capers, with brine

¼ teaspoon red pepper flakes

4 ounces (113 g) tomato paste

1 can (15 ounces, or 425 g) fire-roasted or regular diced tomatoes, with juice

1 cup (235 ml) tomato sauce

½ cup (50 g) Hemp Almond Parmesan (page 213)

1 recipe mozzarella (page 214)

DIRECTIONS:

To make the eggplant: Preheat the oven to 400°F (200°C, or gas mark 6). Divide the eggplant slices between 2 large, rimmed baking sheets. Lightly brush each side with oil and sprinkle with salt.

Roast for 20 minutes, or until tender. Remove from the oven and set aside until cool enough to handle.

To make the marinara: Combine the oil, sun-dried tomatoes, garlic, onion, oregano, basil, capers, and red pepper flakes in a saucepan. Cook over medium-high heat for 2 minutes, to let the flavors develop. Add the tomato paste, diced tomatoes, and tomato sauce. Bring to a low boil, lower the heat, and simmer, uncovered, for 15 minutes.

Have ready a 9 × 13-inch (23 × 33-cm) baking dish. There will be 3 layers of marinara, 2 of eggplants and 2 of parmesan. Cover the bottom of the dish with 1 cup (235 ml) of the marinara. Evenly top with half of the eggplant slices (it's okay if you layer them a bit). Top with ¼ cup (25 g) of the parmesan. Repeat with 1 cup (235 ml) marinara, the remaining eggplant slices, and the remaining ¼ cup (25 g) parmesan. Cover with the remaining marinara and dollop circles of the mozzarella over the top.

Bake for 20 minutes, or until the mozzarella is golden brown. Let stand for 15 minutes before slicing and serving.

YIELD: 6 servings

ROASTED BROCCOLI AND GARLIC PIZZA

Roasting broccoli brings out a nutty taste that makes even the biggest vegetable hater unable to resist it. Pair it with a thin, crispy crust and the inimitable flavor of garlic, and you can safely say you've got a winner here. You can also make 2 smaller pizzas, adjusting the baking time accordingly.

FOR THE ROASTED BROCCOLI:

3½ cups (250 g) broccoli florets, cut into even smaller florets

2 teaspoons (10 ml) red balsamic vinegar

2 tablespoons (30 ml) olive oil

4 cloves garlic, minced

½ teaspoon red pepper flakes

½ teaspoon fine sea salt

FOR THE WHITE MARINARA:

1 cup (180 ml) unsweetened nondairy creamer or milk

1 cup (100 g) Hemp Almond Parmesan (page 213)

2 tablespoons (30 ml) olive oil

2 teaspoons (4.8 g) granulated onion

¼ teaspoon fine sea salt

¼ teaspoon ground pepper, or to taste

1 recipe Garlic Knots dough (page 202), prepared following the recipe note (but not baked)

Extra-virgin olive oil, for drizzling

DIRECTIONS:

To roast the broccoli: Preheat the oven to 400°F (200°C, or gas mark 6). Combine all the ingredients in a large bowl, using your hands to massage the oil into the broccoli florets. Roast for 20 minutes, or until the broccoli just starts to become tender, because it will roast some more when the pizza bakes. Alternatively, you can choose to simply steam the broccoli until just tender, about 4 minutes, and then combine it with the other ingredients.

To make the marinara: Combine all the ingredients in a blender and process until smooth. Transfer to a small saucepan and cook over medium heat until slightly thickened, about 3 minutes, stirring constantly. Set aside.

Gently deflate the dough, roll into a large, thin rectangle about 14 × 12 inches (36 × 30 cm), and place on a lightly floured baking sheet. Evenly spread the marinara almost to the edges of the pizza, top with the roasted broccoli, and let rest for 15 minutes.

Preheat the oven to 400°F (200°C, or gas mark 6).

Bake the pizza for 20 minutes, or until the edges are golden brown. Transfer to a wire rack if not eating immediately. Drizzle a small amount of extra-virgin olive oil over the pizza upon serving.

YIELD: 8 servings

DEEP-DISH PIZZA PIE

Make no mistake, this is a PIE. A knife-and-fork pizza. We have listed some fillings
in the recipe, but you can add whatever you want here. Go simple, or go all out.
A 10- to 12-inch (25- to 30-cm) cast-iron skillet is perfect for this recipe.

INGREDIENTS:

2 recipes Garlic Knots dough (page 202),
prepared following the recipe note (but not baked)

1 cup (257 g) marinara or pizza sauce

1 cup (160 g) diced onion

1 cup (149 g) diced bell pepper

1 cup (70 g) sliced mushrooms

½ cup (68 g) sliced black olives

1 recipe TVP Pepperoni (page 214)

1 recipe mozzarella (page 214)

½ teaspoon garlic powder

Salt and pepper, to taste

DIRECTIONS:

Gently punch down the dough. Divide into 2 equal pieces.
Stretch 1 piece into the bottom of the cast-iron pan so
that it also goes up the sides, leaving about ½ inch
(1.3 cm) overhang around the edge. Set the other piece
aside while you fill the pie.

Preheat the oven to 400°F (200°C, or gas mark 6).

Fill the pie the same way that you fill a lasagna—in layers.
Three layers is a good number to shoot for, so divide your
ingredients accordingly. Layer the marinara, then the
veggies, then the pepperoni, then the mozzarella. Repeat,
finishing with a final thin layer of marinara.

Divide the remaining piece of dough into 10 equal pieces.
Roll each piece into a rope the length of the diameter
of the pie. Weave the ropes (5 going each way) to form
the top crust. Roll the edge of the bottom crust over the
edge of the top crust and crimp with the tines of a fork.
Sprinkle the top with garlic powder, salt, and pepper.

Bake for 30 minutes, or until the top is golden brown.
Allow to rest for at least 10 minutes before cutting
and serving.

YIELD: 8 servings

RECIPE NOTE

Did you know that, contrary to popular belief, pizza was
first invented by the Greeks, who baked large round flat-
breads and topped them with olive oil, spices, potatoes
and other vegetables? Cheese and tomatoes weren't
even introduced as toppings until much later—in the late
1800s—by Italians in Naples.

PESTO CON GUSTO PIZZA

It's so easy being green! This big pizza is loaded with the inimitable flavors of garlic, basil, and olive oil. Kind of like a vacation in Italy, without the cost. Or jet lag. Bear in mind that the mozzarella will have a creamy consistency, but it will not be solid like its dairy version.

FOR THE MOZZARELLA:

1 cup (235 ml) unsweetened soymilk

¼ cup (60 ml) extra-virgin olive oil

1 tablespoon (15 ml) white balsamic vinegar

2 cloves garlic, minced

1 teaspoon granulated onion

½ teaspoon fine sea salt

Freshly ground pepper, to taste

2 tablespoons (16 g) cornstarch

FOR THE PESTO:

¾ cup (90 g) walnuts

1 tablespoon (18 g) miso

Juice of ½ lemon

2 cloves garlic, minced

Freshly ground pepper, to taste

1½ cups (36 g) packed fresh basil

½ cup (120 ml) extra-virgin olive oil

FOR THE CRUST:

1 recipe Garlic Knots dough (page 202), prepared following the recipe note (but not baked)

DIRECTIONS:

To make the mozzarella: Combine all the ingredients in a blender and process until smooth. Transfer to a 4-cup (940-ml) glass measuring cup and microwave on High for 2 minutes, keeping a close eye so that it doesn't bubble over, because it needs to boil to thicken. Let stand for 15 minutes, then stir with a fork. Chill for 2 hours. Stir with a fork before using.

To make the pesto: In a food processor, grind the walnuts and miso until a smooth paste forms. Add the lemon juice, garlic, and pepper; pulse several times. Add the basil, pulse several times. Drizzle in the oil while the machine is running until the desired consistency is reached.

Preheat the oven to 400°F (200°C, or gas mark 6).

Gently deflate the dough and roll into a large, thin rectangle 14 × 12 inches (36 × 30 cm), and place on a lightly floured baking sheet. Spread the pesto evenly on top of the crust. Dollop circles of the mozzarella over the pesto.

Bake for 24 minutes, or until golden brown. Let cool on a wire rack before slicing and serving.

YIELD: 8 servings

CHAPTER 4

Over-the-Top, Totally Tantalizing Sides

Nutritious and nourishing ways to fill your plate and build a completely satisfying meal.

Let these lip-smacking, scrumptious side dishes be the Robin to your Batman! These sides, snacks, and starters are so tasty and filling, you might just end up eating them as a meal all by themselves. (No offense to Batman.)

With so many irresistible recipes to choose from—wings, fries, deli salads, mashed potatoes, and so much more—you'll have a mighty hard time choosing a family "favorite." Recipe throw down, anyone?

MUCHO MACHO NACHOS

A plateful of these nachos, your favorite show on TV, a cuddly companion of the furry or non-furry persuasion at hand and you're all set for the best couch potato session ever.

INGREDIENTS:

1 recipe Spelt Flour Tortillas (page 199), made into chips following instructions below

1 recipe Pico de Gallo (page 206)

1 recipe Creamy Cheesy Sauce (page 212), made with cheddar-style vegan cheese

DIRECTIONS:

Prepare tortillas, and cut them into eighths. You can then either bake or fry them to make your tortilla chips.

To bake: Preheat the oven to 375°F (190°C, or gas mark 5). Lightly brush the tortilla pieces with 2 tablespoons (30 ml) peanut oil or coat with nonstick cooking spray. Sprinkle with sea salt. Place evenly in single layers on several large baking sheets. Bake for 8 minutes, or until lightly golden and crisp. Keep a close eye so they don't burn. Let cool on wire rack.

To fry: Use a deep fryer, or fill a heavy, deep saucepan with 3 inches (7.5 cm) oil. Heat to 350°F (180°C). Do not overcrowd! Fry the chips in batches until golden brown, flipping them once, for 1 to 2 minutes. Remove from the oil with a heat-proof slotted spoon. Drain on paper towels. Immediately sprinkle with sea salt. Repeat with the remaining tortillas. Let cool on a wire rack.

To assemble the nachos: Place a generous handful of chips on a plate. Top with lots of pico de gallo so that you get some healthy veggies in your belly. Cover with as much cheesy sauce as wanted. Serve immediately.

YIELD: 4 to 6 servings

IRISH NACHOS

Traditionally made with waffle fries, this version is made home-kitchen friendly by using tater tots. They also taste great with sweet potato fries.

FOR THE SAUCE:

1 cup (235 ml) plain nondairy soy creamer

1 tablespoon (15 ml) soy sauce

1 tablespoon (14 g) nondairy butter

1 tablespoon (18 g) white or yellow miso

¼ cup (30 g) nutritional yeast

½ teaspoon yellow mustard

½ teaspoon garlic powder

½ teaspoon onion powder

½ teaspoon paprika

2 tablespoons (16 g) cornstarch mixed with ¼ cup (60 ml) water to make a slurry

½ teaspoon liquid smoke (optional)

Salt and pepper, to taste

FOR THE NACHOS:

1 pound (454 g) tater tots, prepared according to package directions

½ cup (120 g) nondairy sour cream, store-bought or homemade (page 211)

¼ cup (24 g) diced scallion or chives

1 tomato, seeded and diced

½ cup (48 g) imitation bacon bits, store-bought or homemade (page 216), or 5 slices Hickory-Smoked Breakfast Strips (page 38), broken into bits

A few slices jarred jalapeños, or to taste

DIRECTIONS:

To make the sauce: In a sauce pot, add the creamer, soy sauce, butter, miso, nutritional yeast, mustard, garlic powder, onion powder, and paprika. Bring to a boil, stirring often. Decrease the heat to low, and stir in the cornstarch slurry to thicken. Stir in the liquid smoke, salt, and pepper.

To assemble the nachos: On a plate, layer first the tater tots, then the sauce, then the sour cream, then the scallion, then the tomato, then the bacon bits, and finally the jalapeños.

YIELD: 2 to 4 servings

RECIPE NOTE

Take this dish from snack to main course by adding a heaping pile of Chocolate Stout Chili (page 81) or another favorite chili recipe.

BACON-WRAPPED WATER CHESTNUTS

These little guys are a perfect appetizer or snack. Serve with maple syrup for dipping.

INGREDIENTS:

½ recipe Hickory-Smoked Breakfast Strips dough (page 38)

24 canned whole water chestnuts, drained

1 cup (235 ml) water

¼ cup (60 ml) soy sauce

1 tablespoon (15 ml) hickory-flavored liquid smoke

DIRECTIONS:

Preheat the oven to 400°F (200°C, or gas mark 6). Have ready a 9-inch (23-cm) square baking dish.

On a lightly floured surface, roll out the dough to about ⅛ inch (3 mm) thick. Cut into 24 strips, 1 inch (2.5 cm) wide by 4 inches (10 cm) long.

Roll 1 water chestnut up in 1 strip of dough and secure with a toothpick. Place in the baking dish. Repeat until all 24 water chestnuts are wrapped.

In a small bowl, combine the water, soy sauce, and liquid smoke. Pour over the wrapped water chestnuts.

Bake for 30 minutes. Remove from the oven and carefully drain the liquid. Return to the oven and bake for 20 minutes longer. Serve warm.

YIELD: 24 pieces

PESTO PEA-DAMAME SOUP

QUICK AND EASY

This nutritious green soup is packed with flavor and involves very little work.

FOR THE PESTO:

½ cup (80 g) dry-roasted whole almonds

1 tablespoon (18 g) miso

2 cloves garlic, minced

1 cup (24 g) packed fresh basil

⅓ to ½ cup (80 to 120 ml) extra-virgin olive oil

FOR THE SOUP:

1 pound (454 g) frozen green peas

1⅔ cups (255 g) ready-to-eat shelled edamame

4 cups (940 ml) vegetable broth

Salt and pepper, to taste

DIRECTIONS:

To make the pesto: In a food processor, blend the almonds, miso, and garlic until finely ground. Add the basil, and pulse several times until no whole leaves are left. Drizzle in the oil while the machine is running until the desired consistency is reached. Set aside.

To make the soup: Combine the peas, edamame, and broth in a large saucepan. Bring to a boil, decrease the heat, and simmer, uncovered, for 15 minutes. Add the pesto and stir until combined. Using a blender, partially blend some of the soup to leave some character and texture to it. Season with salt and pepper upon serving.

YIELD: 4 to 6 servings

HOME FRIES WITH CHIPOTLE BBQ SEASONING

Serve these potatoes that aren't afraid to show their true colors alongside even more spicy goodness, such as Orange Chipotle Wings (page 154) or Taco Salad (page 118). If you prefer cooling things down a bit, try them with the filling for Waldorf Salad Wraps (page 89) served as a salad.

FOR THE SEASONING:

2 tablespoons (15 g) medium chili powder

1 tablespoon (8 g) chipotle chile powder

2 teaspoons (4.2 g) ground cumin

2 teaspoons (4.8 g) granulated onion

2 teaspoons imitation bacon bits, store-bought or homemade (page 216), or 1 teaspoon smoked salt

1 teaspoon dried basil

1 teaspoon Mexican oregano

1 teaspoon dried cilantro

½ teaspoon garlic powder

½ teaspoon Worcestershire-flavored or regular ground pepper

FOR THE POTATOES:

2 tablespoons (30 ml) peanut oil

2 tablespoons (28 g) nondairy butter, divided

1¾ pounds (800 g) mix of red and Yukon gold potatoes, brushed clean, peeling optional, cut into ½-inch (1.3-cm) cubes

Salt, to taste

DIRECTIONS:

To make the seasoning: Combine all the ingredients using a coffee grinder or small food processor. Store in an airtight container for a limitless amount of time.

To make the potatoes: Heat the oil and 1 tablespoon (14 g) of the butter in a large skillet over medium-high heat. Once the butter melts, add the potatoes. Cook over medium heat, stirring often, until the potatoes are golden brown and tender, about 20 minutes. If you see the potatoes need a little more moisture, add the remaining 1 tablespoon (14 g) butter.

Add 2 tablespoons (10 g) of the seasoning and stir to combine. Cook for 2 minutes longer. Season with salt and serve immediately.

YIELD: 4 servings, ½ cup (40 g) seasoning

RECIPE NOTES

- For the crispiest potatoes, get rid of the starch. Put the potato cubes in a bowl of cold water; let stand for 1 hour in the refrigerator. Dry thoroughly by patting with a clean, dry kitchen towel.

- Use the leftover seasoning as a rub for tofu or tempeh, or to flavor TVP.

GARLIC TRUFFLE FRIES

GLUTEN FREE   SOY FREE

Taking french fries from yum to whoa! A deep fryer works best here, but if you don't have one a pot filled with about 4 inches (10 cm) of oil will work just fine.

INGREDIENTS:

1 pound (454 g) russet potatoes, peeled

2 tablespoons (30 ml) black truffle oil

½ teaspoon sea salt

2 cloves garlic, pressed

Vegetable oil, for frying

1 tablespoon (2 g) dried parsley

DIRECTIONS:

Cut the potatoes into thin fries. You can make them thicker, but thinner means crispier, and more surface area to absorb the flavors! If you have a mandolin, this would be an excellent time to use it. If not, just use your awesome knife skills to cut them into a thin julienne.

Rinse the fries in ice cold water to get rid of the extra starch and prevent discoloration. Pat dry with a kitchen towel, being sure to get rid of excess moisture; wet potatoes can be dangerous when they come into contact with hot oil.

In a large, heat-resistant bowl, whisk together the truffle oil, salt, and garlic.

Preheat the oil to 350°F (180°C). Have ready a wire cooling rack with a kitchen towel or paper towels under it to catch the excess oil.

Add the fries in small batches to the oil and fry for about 1½ minutes. Transfer to the wire rack to drain and cool. Repeat until all the fries have been cooked.

Now repeat the process, this time leaving the fries in a little longer to get golden and crispy. Transfer to the wire rack to drain for a few moments.

Transfer to the bowl and toss to coat with the truffle mixture while they are still hot. Sprinkle with parsley and give a final toss to coat before serving.

YIELD: 1 pound (454 g) of fries . . . how many servings that is, well, that is subjective!

TWICE-BAKED POTATOES

Nothing says comfort food quite the way potatoes do! Throw a deliciously creamy sauce into the mix, and have a joyous trip into perfect bliss.

FOR THE POTATOES:

3 large russet potatoes, scrubbed clean

1 tablespoon (15 ml) peanut oil

Salt and pepper, to taste

FOR THE SAUCE:

1 cup (235 ml) unsweetened soymilk

¼ cup (60 ml) extra-virgin olive oil, melted coconut oil, or melted nondairy butter

1 tablespoon (15 ml) white balsamic vinegar

2 cloves garlic, minced

2 teaspoons (4.8 g) granulated onion

½ teaspoon fine sea salt

¼ teaspoon ground nutmeg or 1½ teaspoons herbes de Provence

Freshly ground pepper, to taste

1 tablespoon (8 g) arrowroot powder

DIRECTIONS:

To make the potatoes: Preheat the oven to 400°F (200°C, or gas mark 6). Pierce the ends of all the potatoes with a knife. Rub with the oil and sprinkle with the salt and pepper. Place the potatoes directly on the oven rack, with a baking pan at the lower level to catch drippings. Bake for 1 hour, or until the skin is crispy and the flesh tender.

To make the sauce: Combine all the ingredients in a blender and process until smooth. Transfer to a microwave-safe container and microwave on High for 2 minutes, keeping a close eye so that it doesn't bubble over. Let stand for 15 minutes, then stir with a fork. Let stand or 20 minutes longer. Stir with a fork before using.

Lower the oven temperature to 375°F (190°C, or gas mark 5). Wearing an oven mitt, cut the potatoes in half and carefully scoop out most of the flesh. Place the potato skins on a baking sheet.

Mash the scooped-out flesh with the sauce. Scoop into the potato skins, smoothing the top. Bake for 20 minutes, or until the top is golden brown.

YIELD: 6 potato halves

RECIPE NOTE

Serve these topped with nondairy shredded cheese or sour cream, imitation bacon bits, and chopped chives. Or serve alongside Root Beer Beans (page 167) or Lentil and Bacon Pot O' Stew (page 75).

ORANGE CHIPOTLE WINGS

Not that you need any special occasion to prepare this easy and delicious finger food, but these wings will be especially welcome during football season.

INGREDIENTS:

1 teaspoon orange zest

½ cup (120 ml) freshly squeezed orange juice

1 tablespoon (15 ml) blended chipotle and adobo sauce

2 teaspoons (4.8 g) granulated onion

1 clove garlic, minced

¼ teaspoon sea salt, or to taste

8 ounces (227 g) tempeh, cut lengthwise into 8 pieces

Scant ½ cup (55 g) arrowroot powder or cornstarch

½ cup (40 g) panko or other bread crumbs, plus more as needed

2 tablespoons (28 g) nondairy butter, melted

2 teaspoons (1.2 g) dried cilantro

1 tablespoon (14 g) packed light brown sugar

DIRECTIONS:

In a shallow dish, combine the orange zest, juice, chipotle sauce, onion, garlic, and salt. Place the tempeh pieces in the dish and marinate for 10 minutes, flipping them over occasionally.

In the meantime, place the arrowroot powder in another shallow dish. Place the bread crumbs in yet another shallow dish.

Preheat the oven to 400°F (200°C, or gas mark 6). Line a baking sheet with parchment paper or a silicone baking mat.

Dredge a piece of tempeh in the arrowroot powder, making sure every side is covered and shaking off the excess powder. Dip back into the marinade on each side. Dredge in the bread crumbs, making sure every side is covered. Place on the prepared baking sheet. Repeat with the remaining 7 tempeh slices. There will be leftover marinade; don't worry if some of the arrowroot powder or bread crumbs are left in there.

Coat each tempeh piece with cooking spray. Bake for 15 minutes, flip over, and bake for 15 minutes longer.

As the tempeh bakes, whisk together the remaining marinade, melted butter, cilantro, and sugar.

Remove the wings from the oven and cover them with the sauce. Serve immediately.

YIELD: 8 wings

RECIPE NOTE

If you usually find tempeh to have a slightly bitter taste to it, simmer it in 2 cups (470 ml) vegetable broth, along with a dried bay leaf, for 20 minutes. Drain well and use in any recipe.

EAT YOUR VEGGIES!

Serve with broccoli and garlic sautéed in olive oil, or if you have a little leftover orange sauce from the wings, pour it on top of the broccoli, too.

HAM-ISH SAUCISSES

A quick and easy protein-rich treat sure to please everyone in the family. Make it a healthy snack by simply dunking the saucisses into mustard or ketchup and munching away.

INGREDIENTS:

1 cup (144 g) vital wheat gluten flour

¼ cup (30 g) garbanzo fava bean flour

¼ cup (30 g) nutritional yeast

2 teaspoons (4.8 g) granulated onion

1 teaspoon garlic powder

½ teaspoon ground pepper

½ teaspoon dried oregano

½ teaspoon dried sage

2 tablespoons (30 ml) soy sauce

1 tablespoon (15 ml) pure maple syrup

1 tablespoon (15 ml) peanut oil

1 tablespoon (15 ml) apple cider vinegar

1 teaspoon liquid smoke

1 teaspoon mustard

½ cup (120 ml) water

DIRECTIONS:

Preheat the oven to 375°F (190°C, or gas mark 5). Have 2 baking sheets ready. Cut a large piece of parchment paper or foil into eight 8 × 4-inch (20 × 10-cm) pieces.

In a medium-size bowl, combine the wheat gluten, flour, nutritional yeast, onion, garlic powder, pepper, oregano, and sage. Add the soy sauce, syrup, oil, vinegar, liquid smoke, mustard, and water and use your hands to knead and incorporate, about 2 minutes. Let rest for 15 minutes to let the gluten develop.

Divide the dough into 8 equal portions, a little over 2 tablespoons (50 g) each. Shape the dough into mini sausages. Tightly wrap in the parchment paper or foil pieces. Place on a baking sheet and top with the other baking sheet to weight down the sausages so they don't expand too much.

Bake for 30 minutes. Remove the top baking sheet. Unwrap the sausages: they should be golden and firm, but if they aren't, bake them unwrapped until they are done.

Let cool on a wire rack. These freeze beautifully.

YIELD: 8 mini sausages

RECIPE NOTE

These saucisses are great as a snack or used in Haute Pockets (page 98). They can also be wrapped and baked in cut-out puff pastry until golden brown for easy peasy pigs in a blanket, and they will make your kids (and grown-ups) go bananas when served with Ants on a Log in a Bowl (page 163).

SLOW COOKER COCKTAIL WEENIES

A little prep work ahead of time, turn the slow cooker on, set out a pack of toothpicks, and let the guests snack on these little guys all night!

INGREDIENTS:

1 bottle (28 ounces, or 784 g) barbecue sauce

1 jar (10 ounces, or 280 g) grape jelly

1 cup (96 g) TVP granules

1 cup (235 ml) water

1 tablespoon (15 ml) liquid smoke

2 tablespoons (15 g) nutritional yeast

¾ cup (108 g) vital wheat gluten flour

¼ cup (32 g) cornstarch

2 teaspoons (5 g) paprika

1 tablespoon (8 g) garlic powder

1 tablespoon (8 g) onion powder

3 tablespoons (45 ml) vegetable oil

2 tablespoons (32 g) creamy no-stir peanut butter

¼ cup (60 g) plain soy yogurt

DIRECTIONS:

Add the barbecue sauce and grape jelly to the bottom of your slow cooker. Stir to combine. Cover and turn on the slow cooker to the High setting.

To reconstitute the TVP, stir together the granules, water, liquid smoke, and nutritional yeast in a microwave-safe dish, cover tightly with plastic wrap, and microwave on High for 5 to 6 minutes. Alternatively, bring the water to a boil and pour over the granules mixed with the liquid smoke and nutritional yeast, cover, and let sit for 10 minutes.

Add the reconstituted TVP mixture to the bowl of a food processor. Add the wheat gluten, cornstarch, paprika, garlic powder, onion powder, oil, peanut butter, and yogurt and pulse until well combined and resembles loose ground beef.

Using about 1 teaspoon of the mixture at a time, form into a small cocktail weenie shape and place in the now hot barbecue sauce mixture. Repeat until all of the mixture is used, about 40 weenies, trying to add them to the slow cooker in a single layer.

Cook on High for 2 hours. Change to the Keep Warm setting and serve as an appetizer right out of the cooker!

YIELD: 40 weenies

CRISPY MAC AND CHEESE BALLS

Oh, yes. We did. We find it easiest to make these over a 2-day period. Make the mac and cheese and form it into balls one night. Place them in the freezer overnight, and then do the battering and frying the next day. You will only make yourself miserable if you try to batter an unfrozen ball. It won't work. They will fall apart and leave you cursing and throwing them all about the kitchen. Trust us on this one.

So here you have it—pasta mixed with bread, dipped in batter, and deep-fried! Oh my!

FOR THE MAC AND CHEESE BALLS:

8 ounces (227 g) uncooked elbow macaroni

½ cup (112 g) nondairy cream cheese

1 tablespoon (18 g) miso paste

2 tablespoons (28 g) nondairy butter

½ teaspoon paprika

1½ teaspoons (4.5 g) garlic powder

1½ teaspoons (3.6 g) onion powder

½ cup (40 g) panko bread crumbs

2 tablespoons (15 g) nutritional yeast

1½ teaspoons yellow mustard

Vegetable oil or shortening, for frying

FOR THE BATTER:

2 cups (250 g) all-purpose flour

¼ cup (30 g) nutritional yeast

½ teaspoon paprika

1 teaspoon dried parsley

Salt and black pepper, to taste

2 cups (470 ml) nondairy creamer or milk

Marinara or ranch dressing, for dipping sauce (optional)

DIRECTIONS:

To make the mac and cheese balls: Prepare the pasta according to package directions. Drain and return to the pot. Add the cream cheese, miso, butter, paprika, garlic powder, onion powder, bread crumbs, nutritional yeast, and mustard and stir until well combined.

Line a baking sheet with parchment or waxed paper. Take about 2 tablespoons (28 g) of the mac and cheese and form it into a small ball, about the size of a golf ball. Place on the baking sheet, and repeat until all of the mixture is used.

Place the baking sheet in the freezer for several hours, or overnight, for the balls to get hard and stiff.

Preheat a deep fryer filled with oil. If you don't have a deep fryer, use a pot filled with 4 inches (10 cm) of oil, heated to 350°F (180°C). Line a platter or plate with paper towels to absorb the excess oil.

To make the batter: In a medium-size bowl, mix together all of the batter ingredients.

Dip 1 frozen ball into the batter, and then place in the hot oil. Repeat with 2 or 3 more balls, but avoid overcrowding. Fry for about 4 minutes, or until golden and crispy. Transfer to the plate to drain. Repeat with the remaining balls, frying in batches of 3 or 4 balls at a time.

Serve warm. Enjoy on their own or serve with marinara or ranch dressing for a dipping sauce.

YIELD: 25 balls

HUSH PUPPIES

This version of a Southern classic is beefed up a bit with chopped onions, peppers, and whole kernels of corn. They taste great on their own, but even better dipped in Creamy Cheesy Sauce (page 212) or the Mexican-Style Dipping Sauce for Corn (page 207). A deep fryer works best here, but if you don't have one, a pot filled with about 4 inches (10 cm) of oil will do just fine.

INGREDIENTS:

Vegetable oil, for frying

1 cup (235 ml) plain soymilk

2 tablespoons (30 ml) freshly squeezed lemon juice

1 cup (140 g) cornmeal

1 cup (125 g) all-purpose flour

1 teaspoon sugar

1 teaspoon baking powder

1 teaspoon baking soda

¼ teaspoon salt

¼ teaspoon cayenne pepper

1 cup (136 g) yellow corn kernels

¼ cup (40 g) finely diced onion

¼ cup (40 g) finely diced red or green bell pepper

1 tablespoon (15 g) minced garlic

1 recipe Creamy Cheesy Sauce (page 212) or Mexican-Style Dipping Sauce for Corn (page 207) (optional)

DIRECTIONS:

Combine the lemon juice and soymilk in a measuring cup: It will curdle and become like buttermilk.

In a mixing bowl, combine the cornmeal, flour, sugar, baking powder, baking soda, salt, and cayenne pepper. Add the buttermilk mixture to the flour mixture and stir to combine. Fold in the corn, onion, bell pepper, and garlic. Let rest for about 10 minutes.

Heat the oil in a deep or pot to 350°F (180°C).

Carefully drop a heaping rounded tablespoon (30 g) of batter into the hot oil. (You can add about 4 at a time, just be sure not to overcrowd them.) Fry for 3 to 4 minutes, turning often, until deep golden brown. Transfer to a paper towel-lined plate to absorb the excess oil. Repeat until all the batter is used.

Serve warm with the dipping sauce.

YIELD: About 20 hush puppies

EAT YOUR VEGGIES!

Serve these *puppies* as a starchy side, but make sure to include a nice vegetable side like the Collard Greens (page 173) to round out your meal.

TOFU JERKY

LOW FAT

Chewy, salty, protein-rich and readily enjoyable at any time of the day,
this jerky is healthier than chips and possibly even more addictive.

INGREDIENTS:

1 pound (454 g) super-firm tofu or frozen, thawed,
and pressed extra-firm tofu, sliced between ⅛ and
¼ inch (3 and 6 mm) thick (about 10 slices)

2 tablespoons (30 ml) reduced-sodium soy sauce
(if you cannot find reduced-sodium, use 1 tablespoon
[15 ml] water and 1 tablespoon [15 ml] soy sauce)

2 tablespoons (30 ml) liquid smoke

¼ cup (68 g) ketchup

¼ cup (68 g) brown sauce, such as HP

½ teaspoon hot sauce, or to taste

¼ cup (60 ml) water

2 tablespoons (30 ml) pure maple syrup

2 cloves garlic, minced

DIRECTIONS:

Preheat the oven to 400°F (200°C, or gas mark 6).

Place the tofu slices in a shallow baking dish. Combine
the remaining ingredients in a small bowl. Pour the marinade over the tofu, making sure every side gets coated.

Bake for 20 minutes. Lower the temperature to 250°F
(120°C, or gas mark ½). Flip the tofu slices and bake for
20 minutes longer. Flip again, brushing the tofu slices
with the marinade that is on the sides of the baking dish.
Bake for 20 minutes longer. Repeat flipping and brushing 3 more times in 20-minute intervals, baking for 60
minutes longer, or until the marinade is gone and the tofu
looks suitably dry without being shriveled or burnt.

Enjoy hot, at room temperature, or cold. Delicious as is
or in sandwiches.

YIELD: About 10 slices

RECIPE NOTE

For a quick and delicious snack or meal, spread a
generous amount of Spinach Pesto (page 210) in a
cut-up fresh and crusty artisan bread roll. Top with
as many tofu jerky slices as you want, along with
fresh baby spinach leaves or any other tender
greens, and have a big bite.

CRISPY PEPPERONI BITES

These are like mini crispy pizzas, perfect for a filling snack or as a side dish to a big whopping mixed and crunchy vegetable salad. Use your favorite marinara instead if you prefer. The one offered here is super simple but does the job perfectly!

FOR THE SIMPLE MARINARA:

½ cup plus 2 tablespoons (142 g) diced fire-roasted or regular tomatoes

2 teaspoons (5.5 g) tomato paste

1 clove garlic, minced

1 teaspoon granulated onion

1 teaspoon dried basil

1 teaspoon capers, with brine (optional)

½ teaspoon dried oregano

Pinch of salt

Pinch of ground pepper

Pinch of red pepper flakes

FOR THE CRUST:

1½ cups (180 g) all-purpose flour

1 teaspoon baking powder

⅓ cup (75 g) cold nondairy butter

½ teaspoon fine sea salt

¼ teaspoon freshly ground pepper

¼ cup (60 ml) any nondairy milk, as needed

½ recipe TVP Pepperoni (page 214)

⅓ cup (37 g) shredded nondairy cheese (optional)

DIRECTIONS:

To make the marinara: Combine all the ingredients in a blender and process until smooth. Set aside.

Preheat the oven to 375ºF (190ºC, or gas mark 5). Coat 6 jumbo muffin cups with cooking spray.

To make the crust: Combine the flour, baking powder, butter, salt, and pepper in a food processor. Pulse a few times until the butter is cut throughout the flour. Slowly add the milk, pulsing while drizzling it in, until a dough forms. Divide the dough into 6 equal portions. Shape each into a disk. Press down into the bottom of each muffin cup, bringing the edges halfway up the cup.

Place 1 tablespoon (15 g) pepperoni on top of each crust. Top with 1 tablespoon (15 ml) marinara. Top with another 1 tablespoon (15 g) pepperoni. Top with 1 scant tablespoon (6 g) optional cheese.

Bake for 25 minutes, or until the edges of the crust are light golden brown. Carefully remove from the muffin pan and enjoy.

YIELD: 6 pepperoni bites

EAT YOUR VEGGIES!

Serve with Salade Russe (page 170); mixed greens, shredded carrots, or sliced roasted beets dressed with Mamou's Magical Vinaigrette (page 209); or any thick vegetable soup.

ANTS ON A LOG IN A BOWL

GLUTEN FREE **SOY FREE**

Enjoy this with Piggies in a Blanket (page 112).

INGREDIENTS:

1 pound (454 g) hearts of celery, trimmed and thinly chopped

5 tablespoons (80 g) natural crunchy peanut butter

¼ cup (60 ml) rice vinegar (replace 1 to 2 tablespoons [15 to 30 ml] with either broth or lemon juice if you are sensitive to vinegar)

2 cloves garlic, minced

½ teaspoon Sriracha, or to taste

¼ cup (40 g) raisins

1 tablespoon (15 ml) toasted sesame oil

DIRECTIONS:

Place the celery in a colander and rinse well. Let drain while you prepare the sauce.

Combine all the remaining ingredients in a salad bowl. Add the celery. Stir well. Chill for 1 hour to let the flavors meld.

YIELD: 4 servings

SPICY CHICKPEAS

QUICK AND EASY

Spice is nice, and filling, too!

INGREDIENTS:

2 tablespoons (30 ml) peanut oil

1 large red bell pepper, stemmed, seeded, and diced

¼ cup (40 g) chopped red onion

2 tablespoons (20 g) minced shallot

4 cloves garlic, minced

2 cans (each 15 ounces, or 425 g) chickpeas, drained and rinsed

1 teaspoon ground ginger

1 tablespoon (6 g) garam masala

2 teaspoons sambal oelek, or to taste

½ cup (120 ml) light coconut milk

1 tablespoon (15 ml) rice vinegar

1½ teaspoons reduced-sodium soy sauce

1 tablespoon (2 g) dried cilantro

DIRECTIONS:

Heat the oil in a large skillet over medium heat. Add the bell pepper, onion, shallot, and garlic and cook for 2 minutes.

Add the chickpeas, ginger, garam masala, and sambal oelek and cook for 2 minutes longer, or until fragrant.

Stir in the coconut milk, vinegar, and soy sauce. Add dried cilantro (If you'd rather use fresh cilantro, sprinkle it on top upon serving, instead) Cook for 8 minutes, uncovered, until heated through.

Pair this with quinoa, jasmine rice, black lentils, or steamed cubed potatoes and you've got yourself a beautifully complete meal.

YIELD: 4 servings

CHORIZO FLAUTAS

If you use corn tortillas, the name for these crunchy, delicate, and irresistibly filled-then-fried tortillas magically switches from *flautas* to *taquitos*—fancy that! If you want to avoid the fryer, though, these don't disappoint when baked, either.

INGREDIENTS:

12 ounces (340 g) TVP Chorizo (page 216) or store-bought soy chorizo

¼ cup (60 ml) salsa verde, store-bought or homemade (page 206), plus more for serving

2 teaspoons (4.6 g) granulated onion

1 clove garlic, minced

1 tablespoon (2 g) dried cilantro

Six 7-inch (18-cm) flour tortillas

Vegetable oil for frying or nonstick cooking spray for baking

DIRECTIONS:

Combine the chorizo, ¼ cup (60 ml) salsa, onion, garlic, and cilantro in a medium-size skillet. Brown for 5 minutes over medium-high heat.

Place about ¼ cup (60 g) of the filling along one edge of each tortilla. Roll the tortillas closed and secure with toothpicks.

To fry: Use a deep fryer, or fill a heavy, deep saucepan with 3 inches (7.5 cm) of vegetable oil. Heat to 350°F (175 °C). Fry 1 flauta at a time, flipping over once, until golden brown on both sides, 2 to 4 minutes. Remove from the oil with a heat-proof slotted spoon. Transfer to a paper towel-lined plate to absorb the excess oil. Repeat with the remaining flautas. Serve hot with extra salsa.

To bake: Preheat the oven to 400°F (200°C, or gas mark 6). Place the flautas on a nonstick baking sheet. Coat with cooking spray on both sides. Bake for 10 minutes, flip over, and bake for 10 minutes longer, or until golden brown and crispy. Serve hot with extra salsa.

YIELD: 6 flautas

EAT YOUR VEGGIES!

Add some extra crunch, fiber, vitamins, and overall good conscience to this meal by serving it alongside our Roasted Cauli-mole Salad (page 169).

BAKED ASPARAGUS
WITH MUSHROOM SAUCE

A classy and traditional side dish sure to please the most discerning palates. Serve this alongside a nice savory protein, or serve family style at your next holiday get-together. The sauce is rich and flavorful. We won't tell anybody if you sop the extra up with a piece of bread.

INGREDIENTS:

1 bunch asparagus, snapped at their natural weak point, ends discarded

¼ cup (56 g) nondairy butter

1 medium-size yellow or white onion, roughly chopped

8 ounces (227 g) sliced button mushrooms

4 cloves garlic, thinly sliced

1 cup (235 ml) vegetable broth

2 tablespoons (15 g) nutritional yeast

2 tablespoons (16 g) all-purpose flour mixed with ¼ cup (60 ml) water to make a slurry

½ cup (120 g) nondairy sour cream, store-bought or homemade (page 211)

Salt and pepper, to taste

DIRECTIONS:

Preheat the oven to 400°F (200°C, or gas mark 6).

Place the asparagus in an 8-inch (20-cm) square baking dish.

In a frying pan or skillet, melt the butter over medium-high heat. Add the onion, mushrooms, and garlic. Sauté until translucent and fragrant, 5 to 7 minutes.

Add the broth and bring to a boil. Stir in the nutritional yeast. Stir in the slurry to thicken, and remove from the heat. Stir in the sour cream. Season with salt and pepper. Pour the mixture over the asparagus.

Bake, uncovered, for 20 minutes, or until the desired tenderness.

YIELD: 4 servings

ROOT BEER BEANS

Serve this bean-y goodness alongside Twice-Baked Potatoes (page 153), and stir some Creamy Cheesy Sauce (page 212) directly into your bowl. You may find yourself diving headfirst to lick any remnants from the bowl. Are we speaking from experience? Maaaaybe . . .

INGREDIENTS:

3 cans (each 15 ounces, or 425 g) beans of choice (black beans, kidney beans, pinto beans), drained and rinsed

12 ounces (355 ml) natural root beer (avoid brands that contain high-fructose corn syrup)

2 tablespoons (44 g) regular molasses

1 tablespoon (15 g) stone-ground mustard

2 tablespoons (34 g) ketchup or tomato paste

1 teaspoon liquid smoke

1 teaspoon hot sauce, or to taste

3 cloves garlic, grated

2 tablespoons (10 g) imitation bacon bits, store-bought or homemade (page 216, optional)

2 tablespoons (14 g) granulated onion or ⅓ cup (80 g) caramelized chopped onion (see page 122)

DIRECTIONS:

Combine all the ingredients in a medium-size saucepan. Bring to a boil. Lower the heat to medium and simmer, uncovered, for 20 minutes, stirring occasionally. Using a potato masher, only partially crush some of the beans to thicken the sauce.

YIELD: 6 servings

CHEESY GARLIC MASHED POTATOES

GLUTEN FREE   QUICK AND EASY

Mashed potatoes are good, but cheesy garlic mashed potatoes are simply fantastic!

INGREDIENTS:

2 pounds (908 g) red potatoes, with skins

½ cup (120 g) nondairy sour cream, store-bought or homemade (page 211)

¼ cup (56 g) nondairy butter

¼ cup (30 g) nutritional yeast

1 tablespoon (8 g) garlic powder

1 tablespoon (18 g) white or yellow miso

1½ teaspoons maca powder (optional)

Salt and pepper, to taste

DIRECTIONS:

Bring a large pot of lightly salted water to a boil.

Cut the potatoes into chunks and add to the boiling water. Boil until fork-tender, 12 to 15 minutes. Drain, and return the potatoes to the pot.

Add all the remaining ingredients and mash with a potato masher. Don't worry about lumps—they're almost a requirement here!

YIELD: 6 servings

GERMAN POTATO SALAD

This one tastes great warm or cold. Remember that it's very important to caramelize those onions, because raw onions won't give you the right flavor.

INGREDIENTS:

3 pounds (1362 g) red potatoes, cut into bite-size chunks

3 tablespoons (45 ml) canola or other mild-flavored vegetable oil

2 cups (320 g) diced white or yellow onion

1 tablespoon (15 g) minced garlic

¼ cup (60 ml) rice vinegar

¼ cup (60 ml) water

¼ cup (40 g) diced scallion

2 tablespoons (25 g) evaporated cane juice or granulated sugar

1 tablespoon (15 ml) liquid smoke

½ cup (40 g) imitation bacon bits, store-bought or homemade (page 216)

Salt and pepper, to taste

DIRECTIONS:

Bring a large pot of lightly salted water to a boil. Add the potatoes and boil until fork-tender, but still firm, about 12 minutes.

While the potatoes are boiling, in a frying pan, heat the oil over medium-low heat. Add the onion and cook until very soft and caramelized, 5 to 7 minutes. Add the garlic and cook for 3 minutes longer.

In a small bowl, whisk together the rice vinegar, water, scallion, sugar, and liquid smoke. Add to the onions. Cook, stirring constantly, until the sugar is dissolved, about 2 minutes.

Drain potatoes and return to the pot. Pour the onion mixture over the potatoes and toss to coat. Add the bacon bits and toss to combine. Season with salt and pepper. Serve warm or cold.

YIELD: 8 servings

GREEN POTATOES

GLUTEN FREE   **QUICK AND EASY**

We have been known to make just the dressing and use it over green salad
or pasta, or mix it with rice. Sometimes we double the dressing recipe, and use half
on the potatoes and reserve the rest for those other uses. For this one we leave
the skin on the potatoes, but feel free to peel yours if that's how you roll.

INGREDIENTS:

3 pounds (1362 g) red potatoes, cut into bite-size chunks

1 ounce (28 g) baby spinach

1½ ounces (42 g) cilantro, stems removed

1 shallot, chopped

2 cloves garlic, chopped

6 ounces (170 g) soft silken tofu, drained

¼ cup (60 ml) olive oil

1 tablespoon (15 ml) freshly squeezed lemon juice

Salt and pepper, to taste

DIRECTIONS:

Bring a large pot of lightly salted water to a boil. Add the potatoes and boil for 12 to 15 minutes, or until fork-tender. Drain and return to the pot.

In a blender or food processor, blend the remaining ingredients together until smooth. Pour over the potatoes and gently toss. Serve hot or cold.

YIELD: 6 to 8 servings

ROASTED CAULI-MOLE SALAD

GLUTEN FREE   **SOY FREE**

Enjoy this refreshing and rich salad with Haute Pockets (page 98), Scalloped
Potato Pie (page 122), or Chorizo Flautas (page 164). Not all at the same time, though.

INGREDIENTS:

1 medium-size head cauliflower

4 cloves garlic, minced

3 tablespoons (45 ml) freshly squeezed lemon juice

3 tablespoons (45 ml) extra-virgin olive oil

½ teaspoon fine sea salt

¼ teaspoon ground black pepper

8 ounces (227 g) store-bought pico de gallo–flavored guacamole

¼ cup (25 g) chopped scallion or (40 g) red onion

DIRECTIONS:

Preheat the oven to 425°F (220°C, or gas mark 7).

Trim, clean, and cut the cauliflower into ½-inch (1.3-cm) thick slices, then cut widthwise. Place the cauliflower, garlic, lemon juice, oil, salt, and pepper in a 9-inch (13-cm) baking dish.

Bake for 30 minutes, turning once halfway through, or until the cauliflower is al dente. Remove from the oven and let cool.

Place the cauliflower and all its juices in a large bowl; add the guacamole and scallion and stir to combine. Serve immediately.

YIELD: 4 servings

SALADE RUSSE

Creamy and tasty, this is the perfect accompaniment to Haute Pockets
(page 98), Crispy Pepperoni Bites (page 162), or any sandwich.

INGREDIENTS:

6 cups (1.4 l) water

2½ cups (375 g) diced red potatoes

1½ cups (200 g) diced carrots

1½ cups (200 g) frozen green peas

3 tablespoons (30 g) chopped red onion

1 teaspoon drained and minced capers

½ cup (112 g) vegan mayonnaise,
store-bought or homemade (page 211)

1 teaspoon Dijon mustard

1 tablespoon (15 ml) apple cider vinegar

Salt and pepper, to taste

Dried or fresh dill, to taste (optional)

DIRECTIONS:

Bring the water to a boil in a medium-size pot. Add the
potatoes and carrots. Boil for 8 minutes, or until the
vegetables are fork-tender without being mushy. Add the
peas and boil for 1 minute. Drain well, and let cool.

In the meantime, combine the onion, capers, mayonnaise,
mustard, vinegar, salt, and pepper in a large bowl. Add
the cooled veggies and toss to coat.

Divide among 6 bowls and sprinkle each serving with
a little dill for extra color and flavor.

YIELD: 6 servings

DELI-STYLE MACARONI SALAD

So traditional, no one will ever know it's vegan.

INGREDIENTS:

1 cup (224 g) vegan mayonnaise

¼ cup (60 ml) apple cider vinegar

2 tablespoons (30 g) Dijon mustard

1 teaspoon dried dill or 1 tablespoon (3 g) fresh

Salt and pepper, to taste

1 pound (454 g) elbow macaroni, prepared

1 bell pepper, cored, seeded, and diced

1 cup (160 g) diced red onion

1 cup (48 g) diced scallion or chives

1 cup (100 g) chopped celery

1 cup (110 g) shredded carrot

¼ cup (60 g) sweet pickle relish

DIRECTIONS:

Whisk together mayonnaise, vinegar, mustard, and dill.
Season with salt and pepper.

Add the chopped veggies, relish, and dressing to the
cooled pasta and toss to combine.

Keep refrigerated until ready to serve.

YIELD: 16 servings

EAST COAST MEETS WEST COAST PASTA SALAD

This pasta salad has a fairly traditional vinaigrette dressing, typical of East Coast styles. But then a bit of that Mediterranean fusion sneaks in from the West Coast in the form of big chunky veggies.

FOR THE DRESSING:

½ cup (120 ml) extra-virgin olive oil

½ cup (120 ml) balsamic vinegar

1 tablespoon (15 g) minced garlic

2 tablespoons (30 g) Dijon mustard

2 tablespoons (42 g) agave nectar

Salt and pepper, to taste

FOR THE SALAD:

1 pound (454 g) spiral pasta, cooked according to package directions and cooled

6 ounces (170 g) extra-firm tofu, drained, pressed, and crumbled to resemble feta

1 medium-size red onion, julienned

1 can (14 ounces, or 397 g) artichoke hearts, drained and quartered

2 cups (142 g) broccoli florets, lightly steamed or raw

½ cup (67 g) sliced black olives

1 pint (454 g) cherry tomatoes, halved

½ cup (56 g) pepperochinis

DIRECTIONS:

To make the dressing: Whisk all the dressing ingredients together in a small bowl and set aside.

To make the salad: Toss all the salad ingredients together in a large salad bowl. Add the dressing and toss to coat. Refrigerate until ready to serve.

YIELD: 12 to 16 servings

RECIPE NOTE

This salad is a great way to use up extra veggies you may have lying around. Carrots, cucumbers, shredded yellow squash, zucchini, you name—if it can be chopped, then it probably tastes good in this salad!

SWEET PEPPERCORN COLESLAW

GLUTEN FREE **QUICK AND EASY**

This coleslaw takes the Sweet Potato Po' Boys (page 86) to a whole new level.

FOR THE SLAW:

½ head green cabbage, shredded

1½ cups (162 g) shredded carrots

½ cup (80 g) raisins or dried cranberries (optional)

FOR THE DRESSING:

½ cup (120 ml) plain soymilk

2 tablespoons (30 ml) freshly squeezed lemon juice

½ cup (112 g) vegan mayonnaise,
store-bought or homemade (page 211)

1 tablespoon (10 g) black peppercorns,
coarsely ground or cracked

1 tablespoon (2 g) chopped fresh fennel leaf

1 tablespoon (12 g) evaporated cane juice or
granulated sugar

Salt, to taste

DIRECTIONS:

To make the slaw: Toss together the slaw ingredients in a large mixing bowl.

To make the dressing: Add the soymilk to a small mixing bowl. Stir in the lemon juice and let sit for a few minutes. It will curdle and become like buttermilk. Whisk in the remaining ingredients.

Toss the slaw with the dressing and serve immediately.

You can make this ahead of time, but if you do, keep the dressing separate and toss together just before serving.

YIELD: 8 servings

KALE WITH A KICK

Serve as is for a glorious side dish or use as an ingredient in Kale Bagels (page 187).

INGREDIENTS:

1 bunch kale

2 tablespoons (30 g) orange marmalade

2 tablespoons (32 g) tahini

1 tablespoon (15 ml) seasoned rice vinegar

1 tablespoon (15 ml) tamari

1 tablespoon (15 ml) olive or peanut oil

1 large clove garlic, minced

2 tablespoons (20 g) finely chopped shallot or scallion

½ teaspoon toasted sesame oil

¼ teaspoon red pepper flakes

DIRECTIONS:

Remove stems and ribs from kale. Clean thoroughly and chop into tiny pieces. Spin the kale to remove excess water. Set aside.

Combine the remaining ingredients in a large bowl. Using your hands, massage the dressing onto the kale to coat thoroughly and tenderize. Let stand at room temperature for 1 hour, or until the kale is tender. Serve.

YIELD: 2 servings, about 2½ cups (280 g)

EAT YOUR COLLARD GREENS!

QUICK AND EASY

This preparation makes it easy to enjoy dark leafy greens.

INGREDIENTS:

½ cup (112 g) nondairy butter

1 medium-size yellow onion, finely minced

2 tablespoons (30 g) minced garlic

2 tablespoons (30 ml) balsamic vinegar

1 tablespoon (15 g) mild Dijon mustard

1 teaspoon red pepper flakes (optional)

1 teaspoon sesame oil

1 teaspoon agave nectar

3 bunches collard greens, torn from center vein into pieces

1 teaspoon toasted sesame seeds

Salt and pepper, to taste

DIRECTIONS:

In a large soup pot, melt the butter over medium-high heat. Add the onion and garlic, and sauté until translucent and fragrant, 3 to 5 minutes.

Stir in the vinegar, mustard, red pepper flake, sesame oil, and agave. Add the greens, and toss to coat. Cook until wilted to desired tenderness. For al dente greens it'll take 3 to 5 minutes.

Stir in the sesame seeds, season with salt and pepper, and serve.

YIELD: 4 servings

FRITTER FRIED OKRA

Sliced frozen okra is already the perfect size for frying. Talk about convenient!

INGREDIENTS:

1 pound (454 g) frozen okra

1 cup (235 ml) full-fat coconut milk

½ cup (70 g) cornmeal

½ cup (63 g) all-purpose flour

½ teaspoon paprika

½ teaspoon dried parsley

¼ teaspoon ground black pepper

¼ teaspoon salt

Vegetable oil, for frying

DIRECTIONS:

Place the frozen okra in a shallow dish. Pour the coconut milk over the okra, and let sit for about 10 minutes.

Meanwhile, prepare the flour mixture. Add the cornmeal, flour, paprika, parsley, pepper, and salt to a resealable plastic bag and shake to combine.

In a frying pan, pour the oil to a depth of 1 inch (2.5 cm) and heat over medium-high heat.

Drain the okra and place in the bag. Shake to coat.

Add the okra to the pan in a single layer and fry for 3 to 5 minutes, flipping halfway through, until golden and crispy. Transfer to a paper towel-lined plate to absorb the excess oil. Repeat until all the pieces are fried and erve immediately.

YIELD: 4 servings

BACON ONION PUFFS

These taste great as an appetizer, or instead of garlic bread. Try to find puff pastry that is not only vegan but also free of hydrogenated fats.

INGREDIENTS:

10 squares (6 × 6 inches, or 15 × 15 cm) vegan puff pastry

12 ounces (340 g) nondairy sour cream, store-bought or homemade (page 211)

¼ cup (40 g) finely diced white or yellow onion

3 tablespoons (18 g) imitation bacon bits, store-bought or homemade (page 216)

3 tablespoons (9 g) finely chopped fresh or freeze-dried chives

1 tablespoon (15 g) minced garlic

1 teaspoon dried dill or 1 tablespoon (3 g) chopped fresh

1 teaspoon liquid smoke

1 teaspoon red pepper flakes

¼ cup (56 g) nondairy butter, melted

Pinch of paprika

Pinch of garlic powder

Salt and pepper, to taste

DIRECTIONS:

Thaw the puff pastry according to the package directions.

Preheat the oven to 400°F (200°C, or gas mark 6). Line 2 baking sheets with parchment paper or silicone baking mats.

In a small mixing bowl, combine the sour cream, onion, bacon bits, chives, garlic, dill, liquid smoke, and red pepper flakes.

Add about ¼ cup (75 g) of filling to the center of 1 square of puff pastry. Using your fingertips, rub the edges of the square with water to moisten. Fold one corner over at a diagonal to the opposite corner to make a triangle. Using the tines of a fork, press the edges together to seal. Using a sharp knife, cut a few small slits in the top of the triangle. Brush the entire top with melted butter and sprinkle with paprika, garlic powder, salt, and pepper. Repeat with the remaining 9 squares.

Bake for 25 to 30 minutes, or until golden, puffy, and crispy. Let cool for a few minutes before serving.

YIELD: 10 puffs

POPCORN PEPPERS

QUICK AND EASY   **SOY FREE**

If jalapeños are too spicy, we won't tell anyone if you use your favorite pickles instead.

INGREDIENTS:

Vegetable oil, for frying

½ cup (70 g) cornmeal

½ cup (63 g) all-purpose flour

½ teaspoon salt

⅛ teaspoon ground black pepper

¼ teaspoon paprika

1 cup (235 ml) vegan light-colored beer (go to www.barnivore.com to check the vegan-ocity of your beer)

40 to 50 slices jarred jalapeños, drained and patted dry

DIRECTIONS:

Heat the oil to 350°F (180°C) in a deep fryer or pot. Have ready a plate lined with paper towels.

In a medium-size mixing bowl, whisk together the cornmeal, flour, salt, pepper, paprika, and beer until smooth. The batter should be like a thin pancake batter.

Dip each jalapeño ring into the batter and carefully drop into the hot oil. You can add quite a few to the pot at the same time, just make sure that they all have enough space to float around in the oil freely. Fry for about 3 minutes, or until golden brown and crispy. Using a slotted spoon, transfer to the paper towel–lined plate to absorb the excess oil. Repeat to dry all of the jalapeños.

Serve immediately.

YIELD: 40 to 50 pieces

CREAMED CORN WITH BACON

This rich, savory side dish pairs well with any meaty main course, especially I Would Do Anything for (Meat)loaf (page 101).

INGREDIENTS:

¼ cup (60 ml) vegetable oil

2 medium-size yellow onions, thinly sliced

¼ teaspoon salt

2 tablespoons (30 ml) balsamic vinegar

2 cups (470 ml) plain soy creamer

1 pound (454 g) yellow corn kernels

½ cup (120 g) nondairy sour cream, store-bought or homemade (page 211)

10 slices vegan bacon, store-bought or homemade (page 216), cut into chunks

DIRECTIONS:

Heat the vegetable oil in a stockpot over medium-low heat.

Add the onions and salt. Toss to coat. Cover and cook for about 20 minutes, or until soft, translucent, and golden brown, stirring occasionally.

Uncover, add the balsamic vinegar, toss to coat, raise the heat to high. Cook 5 minutes longer, stirring constantly.

Reduce the heat to medium and stir in the creamer. Add the corn. Bring to a simmer and simmer, uncovered, for 10 minutes. Remove from the heat.

Stir in the sour cream and bacon pieces. Let sit for about 10 minutes to thicken before serving.

YIELD: 8 servings

FRIED GREEN (OR YELLOW, OR RED) TOMATOES

The thing about green tomatoes is that, unless you have your own garden, it's nearly impossible to get 'em green! That's why we say to throw caution to the wind and fry up some yellow and red tomatoes. Why not? Just make sure they aren't too ripe, or the whole shebang will end up a big mushy mess.

INGREDIENTS:

½ cup (63 g) all-purpose flour

½ cup (120 ml) coconut milk

¾ cup (60 g) panko bread crumbs

½ teaspoon salt

¼ teaspoon pepper

¼ cup (60 ml) olive oil, divided

3 medium-size, firm green (or yellow, or red) tomatoes, sliced into rounds about ½ inch (1.3 cm) thick

DIRECTIONS:

Set up a breading station. In a shallow dish, place the flour; in another, the coconut milk; and in a third, the panko mixed with the salt and pepper.

Heat 2 tablespoons (30 ml) of the oil over high heat in a frying pan or cast-iron skillet.

Dip 1 slice of tomato into the flour to coat, then into the coconut milk, then into the panko, then place in the oil. Repeat until you have about half of the slices in a single layer in your pan.

Fry for 3 to 5 minutes, or until golden, then flip and cook for 3 to 5 minutes longer. Transfer to a paper towel-lined plate to absorb the excess oil. Repeat until all the slices are fried.

Serve immediately.

YIELD: About 15 slices

SOUTHERN FRIED CABBAGE

QUICK AND EASY   GLUTEN FREE

This Southern staple is traditionally prepared with bacon grease. We tend to think of our Earth Balance as better than bacon grease; besides, it's cholesterol free! This side dish tastes great alongside Breakfast Chicken-Fried Steak (page 32) and White Sausage Gravy (page 33).

INGREDIENTS:

½ cup (112 g) nondairy butter

1 tablespoon (15 ml) liquid smoke

1 head green cabbage, finely shredded

Salt and pepper, to taste

¼ cup (24 g) imitation bacon bits, store-bought or homemade (page 216, optional)

DIRECTIONS:

Melt the butter in a large pot over medium-high heat. Add the liquid smoke, cabbage, salt, and pepper. Toss to coat and cook until wilted and limp, 5 to 7 minutes, stirring constantly.

Remove from the heat, stir in the bacon bits, and serve.

YIELD: 8 servings

CORNBREAD-STUFFED POBLANOS

You get the goodness of carbs and a clear conscience by packing
it all in a vegetable, too! Munch on; you can thank us later.

INGREDIENTS:

2 poblano peppers, halved,
seeded, cleaned, and patted dry

½ cup (112 g) reduced-fat vegan mayonnaise or
(120 g) nondairy sour cream,
store-bought or homemade (page 211)

½ cup (120 ml) salsa verde,
store-bought or homemade (page 206)

1 tablespoon (21 g) agave nectar

½ cup (70 g) cornmeal

½ cup (63 g) all-purpose flour

1 teaspoon granulated onion

½ teaspoon sea salt

1 teaspoon baking powder

Nondairy milk, as needed

¼ cup (28 g) shredded vegan cheddar cheese (optional)

Pico de gallo, store-bought or homemade (page 206), or
more salsa verde, for serving

DIRECTIONS:

Preheat the oven to 375°F (190°C, or gas mark 5). Lightly
grease a baking sheet with oil or cooking spray. Place the
poblanos on the prepared sheet.

In a large bowl, combine the mayonnaise, salsa, and
agave. Add the cornmeal, flour, granulated onion, salt,
and baking powder. Stir until combined. Add the milk as
needed if the batter is too thick.

Spoon the mixture into the poblanos and smooth the top.
Bake for 30 minutes, or until the poblanos are tender and
a toothpick inserted into the cornbread comes out clean.
Sprinkle 1 tablespoon (7 g) of the cheese on each poblano
half during the last 5 minutes of baking. Serve topped
with pico de gallo, salsa verde, or a dollop of nondairy
sour cream.

YIELD: 2 servings

RECIPE NOTE

If you cannot find poblano peppers, consider using
regular green bell peppers. Keep in mind that they are
usually larger and wider than poblanos, so try to find
the smallest ones available at the market.

CHAPTER 5

The Bottomless Bread Basket

Worth-your-while yeast breads, biscuits, and other flour-ishing goods.

We love our carbohydrates, and we're not afraid to say it! If you are brand new to working with yeast, fear not! Just follow these tips and you will be a pro in no time:

- Be sure to bring ingredients to room temperature.

- Proof the yeast by adding it to the liquid and sweetener. To do so, simply heat the liquid to luke-warm (about 100°F [38°C]), then stir in the yeast and sweetener. Let stand for a few minutes until bubbles and foam form, then proceed with the recipe directions. If the yeast does not bubble and foam, start again with a newer package of yeast.

- Consider adding 2 tablespoons (18 g) vital wheat gluten per 4 cups (480 g) flour to yeast breads, especially when using whole wheat flour. It makes for a better elasticity and a lighter texture.

- If your dough springs back and is impossible to shape when you deflate it after the first rise, give it an additional 5 to 10 minutes of resting time so that it becomes a bit more cooperative.

- Check for doneness by wearing oven mitts, carefully inverting the loaf or rolls, and tapping the bottom: a hollow sound means the bread is ready to be taken out of the oven. Alternatively, use an instant-read thermometer and check that the temperature in the center of the bread is approximately 200°F (93°C).

CINNAMON SWIRL BREAD

This sweet bread is fantastic for breakfast, and serves as an amazing base for French toast.

FOR THE DOUGH:

1 cup (235 ml) soymilk, heated to lukewarm

¼ cup (60 ml) water, heated to lukewarm

⅓ cup (67 g) evaporated cane juice or granulated sugar, divided

1½ teaspoons active dry yeast

2 tablespoons (30 ml) plus ½ teaspoon vegetable oil, divided

3 cups (375 g) all-purpose flour, plus more as needed

¼ cup (36 g) vital wheat gluten flour

½ teaspoon ground cinnamon

¼ teaspoon salt

FOR THE SWIRL:

⅓ cup (73 g) packed brown sugar

2 teaspoons ground cinnamon

3 tablespoons (42 g) nondairy butter, melted

DIRECTIONS:

To make the dough: Combine the soymilk, water, and 1 tablespoon (13 g) of the sugar in a small bowl. Stir in the yeast and let sit for a few minutes until bubbles appear, to ensure the yeast is active. Add 2 tablespoons (30 ml) of the oil to the mixture.

In a large bowl, combine the flours, cinnamon, remaining sugar, and salt. Stir the wet ingredients into the dry, mixing until combined.

Turn out onto a lightly floured surface and knead for 8 minutes, until the dough is smooth and pliable, adding more flour as needed if the dough is too sticky. This is a dry, stiff dough, but it should still be workable.

Lightly coat a large bowl with the remaining ½ teaspoon oil. Place the dough in the bowl and gently turn to coat. Cover tightly with plastic wrap and let rise until doubled in size, 60 to 90 minutes.

To make the swirl: Combine the swirl ingredients into a paste. Set aside.

Gently deflate the dough and place on a lightly floured surface. Knead for 3 to 5 minutes.

Roll the dough into a rectangle 8 inches (20 cm) wide by 24 inches (60 cm) long. Spread the cinnamon paste thinly and evenly onto the dough. Starting at the short end, tightly roll up the dough. Place the rolled-up dough, seam side down, into an 8 × 4-inch (20 × 10-cm) loaf pan. Let rise for 30 minutes.

Preheat the oven to 350°F (180°C, or gas mark 4).

Bake for 25 to 30 minutes, or until the outer crust is golden brown and hard to the touch. Let cool on a wire rack before slicing.

YIELD: 1 loaf

RECIPE NOTE

Interested in taking this bread to the next level of awesomeness? Simply press down ½ cup (80 g) raisins and/or ½ cup (54 g) chopped pecans into the rolled-out dough, fold it into thirds lengthwise to cover the raisins and nuts, and use a rolling pin to roll it back into approximately the original rectangle size. Then proceed with the instructions to spread the cinnamon paste onto the dough and roll up.

JULIETTE BRIOCHE

SOY FREE

Buttery, light, and reminiscent of brioche, this coconut-based bread will have you coming back for more. And more. The good news is that the flavor of coconut is barely noticeable, for all you coconut haters of the world. We know you're out there.

INGREDIENTS:

⅔ cup (160 ml) coconut cream, heated to lukewarm (see note)

⅓ cup (80 ml) water, heated to lukewarm

¼ cup (48 g) Sucanat

2 teaspoons active dry yeast

3 cups (375 g) all-purpose flour, divided, plus more as needed

1 teaspoon fine sea salt

½ teaspoon oil

DIRECTIONS:

Combine the coconut cream and water in a medium-size bowl. Add the Sucanat and yeast and stir to combine. Let sit for a few minutes until bubbles appear, to ensure the yeast is active.

In a large bowl, combine 2 cups (250 g) of the flour and the salt. Stir the wet ingredients into the dry. Add the remaining 1 cup (125 g) flour as needed.

Turn out onto a lightly floured surface and knead for 8 to 10 minutes, until the dough is smooth and pliable, adding more flour, a little at a time, if the dough is too sticky. Alternatively, use a stand mixer fitted with the dough hook. The kneading time will be the same, until the dough forms a ball.

Lightly coat a large bowl with the oil. Place the dough in the bowl and gently turn to coat. Cover tightly with plastic wrap, and let rise for 90 minutes.

Lightly coat an 8 × 4-inch (20 × 10-cm) loaf pan with cooking spray. Gently deflate the dough. Place the dough in the pan. Let rise in a warm place for 1 hour.

Preheat the oven to 375°F (190°C, or gas mark 5).

Bake for 35 minutes, or until golden brown on top. Remove from the pan and let cool on a wire rack. Best when eaten on baking day.

YIELD: 1 loaf

RECIPE NOTE

If you cannot find coconut cream, replace it and the water with regular or even light coconut milk.

SUPER-TENDER WHOLE WHEAT BAGELS

SOY FREE

The hemp seeds provide a bit of crunch in the super-tender crumb of this bread.

INGREDIENTS:

14 ounces (414 ml) light coconut milk, heated to lukewarm

2 tablespoons (30 ml) pure maple syrup

1 tablespoon (15 g) maca powder

2 teaspoons active dry yeast

3½ cups (420 g) white whole wheat flour, plus more as needed

¼ cup (40 g) shelled hemp seeds

1 teaspoon fine sea salt

½ teaspoon oil

8 cups (1.9 l) water, for boiling bagels

½ cup (110 g) baking soda

DIRECTIONS:

Combine the coconut milk, syrup, maca powder, and yeast in a bowl. Let sit for a few minutes until bubbles appear, to ensure the yeast is active.

Combine the 3½ cups (420 g) flour, seeds, and salt in a large bowl. Stir the wet ingredients into the dry.

Turn out onto a lightly floured surface and knead for 8 to 10 minutes, adding more flour as needed, until the dough is smooth and pliable. Alternatively, use a stand mixer fitted with the dough hook. The kneading time will be the same, until the dough forms a ball.

Lightly coat a large bowl with the oil. Place the dough in the bowl and gently turn to coat. Cover tightly with plastic wrap, and let rise until doubled in size, 60 to 90 minutes.

Gently deflate the dough. Divide it into 8 equal portions; shape into rounds by pulling at the dough from the sides onto the bottom. Insert your thumb into the center of each dough ball, and twirl the dough around it until the hole reaches about 1½ inches (3.8 cm) in size. Let rest for 15 minutes.

Bring the water to a boil in a large pot. Add the baking soda slowly: the mixture will bubble up. Lower the heat to a gentle boil.

Preheat the oven to 400°F (200°C, or gas mark 6). Line 2 large baking sheets with parchment paper or silicone baking mats.

Place 4 bagels at a time in the saucepan and simmer for 1 minute, using a spoon to gently submerge the bagels occasionally.

Scoop out the bagels with a slotted spoon. Place on a wire rack to drain. Repeat with the remaining 4 bagels. Transfer to the prepared baking sheets.

Bake for 20 minutes, or until the bagels are golden brown and sound hollow when the bottom is tapped. Let cool on a wire rack.

YIELD: 8 bagels

KALE BAGELS

These green-speckled bagels make it easy to add a little extra roughage to your diet.
Even the veggie haters of the household will find themselves smitten with these.

INGREDIENTS:

1 cup (235 ml) water, heated to lukewarm

1 tablespoon (12 g) active dry yeast

2 cups (225 g) packed Kale with a Kick (page 172)

6 cups (720 g) bread flour, divided

1½ teaspoons fine sea salt

½ teaspoon oil

8 cups (1.9 l) water, for boiling bagels

½ cup (110 g) baking soda

DIRECTIONS:

Combine the water and yeast in a medium-size bowl. Let sit for a few minutes until bubbles appear, to ensure the yeast is active. Stir in the kale.

In a large bowl, combine 4 cups (480 g) of the flour and the salt. Stir in the kale mixture. Turn out onto a lightly floured surface and knead for 8 to 10 minutes, adding the remaining 2 cups (240 g) flour as needed, until the dough is smooth and pliable. Alternatively, use a stand mixer fitted with the dough hook. The kneading time will be the same, until the dough forms a ball.

Lightly coat a large bowl with the oil. Place the dough in the bowl and gently turn to coat. Cover tightly with plastic wrap, and let rise until doubled in size, 60 to 90 minutes.

Gently deflate the dough. Divide into 8 equal portions; shape into rounds by pulling at the dough from the sides onto the bottom. Insert your thumb into the center of each dough ball, and twirl the dough around it until the hole reaches about 1½ inches (3.8 cm) in size. Let rest for 15 minutes.

Bring the water to a boil in a large pot. Add the baking soda slowly: the mixture will bubble up. Lower the heat to a gentle boil.

Preheat the oven to 375°F (190°C, or gas mark 5). Line 2 large baking sheets with parchment paper or silicone baking mats.

Place 4 bagels at a time in the pot and simmer for 1 minute, using a spoon to gently submerge the bagels occasionally. Scoop out the bagels with a slotted spoon. Place on a wire rack to drain. Repeat with the remaining 4 bagels. Transfer to the prepared baking sheets.

Bake for 24 minutes, or until the bagels are golden brown and sound hollow when the bottom is tapped. Let cool on a wire rack.

YIELD: 8 bagels

SWEET WHOLE-WHEAT RYE BREAD

SOY FREE   LOW FAT

Why buy boring sandwich bread when you can bake your own?
Turn everyday brown bag lunches into something homemade with love!

INGREDIENTS:

1½ cups (355 ml) water, heated to lukewarm, divided

2 tablespoons (25 g) evaporated cane juice or granulated sugar

1½ teaspoons active dry yeast

2 tablespoons (44 g) molasses

2 tablespoons (42 g) agave nectar

2 cups (240 g) white whole wheat flour, plus more as needed

2 cups (240 g) dark rye flour

1 teaspoon salt

½ teaspoon olive oil

RECIPE NOTE

For supersoft bread, place the loaf inside a plastic bag while still warm. The outer crust will turn soft and pliable.

DIRECTIONS:

Combine 1 cup (235 ml) of the water and sugar in a small bowl. Stir in the yeast and let sit for a few minutes until bubbles appear, to ensure the yeast is active. Add the molasses and agave to the yeast mixture.

In a large bowl, combine the flours and salt. Stir the wet ingredients into the dry, mixing until combined, adding the remaining ½ cup (120 ml) water as needed, 1 tablespoon (15 ml) at a time, until the dough comes together.

Turn out the dough onto a lightly floured surface and knead for 8 minutes, until the dough is smooth and pliable, adding more white whole wheat flour as needed if the dough is too sticky. Alternatively, use a stand mixer fitted with the dough hook. The kneading time will be the same, until the dough forms a ball.

Lightly coat a large bowl with the oil. Place the dough in the bowl and gently turn to coat. Cover tightly with plastic wrap and let rise until doubled in size, 60 to 90 minutes.

Line a baking sheet with parchment paper or a silicone baking mat. Gently deflate the dough and place on a lightly floured surface. Knead for 3 to 5 minutes. Shape the dough into an oblong loaf and place on the prepared baking sheet. Let rise for 30 minutes. Using a sharp knife, carefully cut a few slits into the top of the loaf.

Preheat the oven to 350°F (180°C, or gas mark 4).

Bake for 35 to 40 minutes, or until the outer crust is dark golden brown and hard to the touch. Let cool completely before cutting into slices fit for sandwiches.

YIELD: 1 loaf

IRISH SODA BREAD

The problem with large soda breads is that it can be tricky to enjoy them
while they're still fresh. Individual soda breads to the rescue! The outer crust
allows the breads to remain fresher, but you will most likely not get to notice because
these babies will fly off the table faster than you can say, "Kiss me, I'm Irish."

INGREDIENTS:

¾ cup (180 ml) unsweetened soymilk,
plus more as needed

1 tablespoon (15 ml) white balsamic vinegar

2⅔ cups (320 g) white whole wheat flour

1 tablespoon (8 g) cornstarch

1 tablespoon (7 g) caraway seeds

3 tablespoons (42 g) nondairy butter

1 teaspoon fine sea salt, or to taste

2 teaspoons (9 g) baking soda

DIRECTIONS:

Preheat the oven to 425°F (220°C, or gas mark 7).
Line a baking sheet with parchment paper or a silicone
baking mat.

In a small bowl, combine the soymilk and vinegar: it will
curdle and become like buttermilk.

In a large bowl, using a fork, combine the flour, cornstarch, caraway seeds, butter, salt, and baking soda. Stir
in the buttermilk mixture. If the dough is too dry, add a
little extra milk until it is more manageable.

Turn out onto a lightly floured surface and knead a little
to assemble. Divide the dough into 4 equal portions.
Pat down with dampened hands, if needed. Place on
the prepared baking sheet; lightly coat the tops with
cooking spray.

Bake for 16 minutes, or until the breads are golden brown
and sound hollow when the bottom is tapped. Let cool on
wire rack.

YIELD: 4 small breads

RECIPE NOTE

Serve these individual soda breads alongside any soup
or salad, or with Colcannon Patties (page 100) and a
cold (vegan) brew.

BACON ONION BISCUITS

The usual biscuit-making guidelines are in force here: Use cold ingredients,
do not overwork the dough, do eat a whole batch by yourself . . .

INGREDIENTS:

½ cup (120 ml) cold unsweetened plain soymilk

1½ teaspoons white balsamic vinegar

1½ cups (180 g) cold all-purpose flour,
plus more as needed

1 tablespoon (5 g) imitation bacon bits,
store-bought or homemade (page 216)

1 tablespoon (8 g) granulated onion

¼ to ½ teaspoon fine sea salt, or to taste

2 teaspoons baking powder

1 teaspoon baking soda

⅓ cup (75 g) cold nondairy butter

¼ cup (28 g) shredded mozzarella-type vegan cheese,
such as Daiya (optional)

DIRECTIONS:

Preheat the oven to 400°F (200°C, or gas mark 6).
Line a baking sheet with parchment paper or a silicone
baking mat.

In a small bowl, combine the milk and vinegar: it will
curdle and become like buttermilk. Set aside.

In a large bowl, combine the 1½ cups (180 g) flour, bacon,
onion, salt, baking powder, and baking soda. Using your
fingertips or a fork, quickly cut in the butter. Add the buttermilk mixture and stir with a fork until just combined.

Turn out the dough onto a lightly floured counter and
add up to 3 tablespoons (23 g) extra flour on top of the
dough, kneading a few times until just incorporated and
not too sticky. Pat down to about 1 inch (2.5 cm) thick. Cut
out six 2-inch (5-cm) wide biscuits. Place the biscuits on
the prepared baking sheet. Sprinkle with the cheese.

Bake for 12 minutes, or until golden brown. Let cool on
a wire rack.

YIELD: 6 biscuits

RECIPE NOTE

Serve these freshly baked and still warm alongside a
big bowl of your favorite comforting vegetable- and
therefore vitamin-filled soup.

SOFT PEANUT BUTTER PRETZELS

Shape these babies whichever way you prefer: It's fun, exciting, and most important, delicious! Dip them in Mustard Sauce (page 207) for added oomph.

INGREDIENTS:

1 cup (235 ml) nondairy milk, heated to lukewarm

1 tablespoon (12 g) evaporated cane juice or granulated sugar

½ cup (128 g) natural creamy peanut butter

1½ teaspoons active dry yeast

2 cups (250 g) all-purpose flour, divided

1 cup (120 g) white whole wheat flour, plus more as needed

1 teaspoon fine sea salt

½ teaspoon oil

8 cups (1.9 l) water, for boiling pretzels

½ cup (110 g) baking soda

Coarse kosher salt, for sprinkling

DIRECTIONS:

In a medium-size bowl, combine the milk, sugar, and peanut butter until emulsified. Stir in the yeast and let sit for a few minutes until bubbles appear, to ensure the yeast is active.

Combine 1¾ cups (219 g) of the all-purpose flour, the 1 cup (120 g) whole wheat flour, and salt in a large bowl. Stir the wet ingredients into the dry.

Turn out onto a lightly floured surface and knead for 8 to 10 minutes, until the dough is smooth and pliable, adding the remaining ¼ cup (31 g) all-purpose flour as needed until the dough is smooth and pliable. Add even more whole wheat flour, a little at a time, if the dough is too sticky. Alternatively, use a stand mixer fitted with the dough hook. The kneading time will be the same, until the dough forms a ball.

Lightly coat a large bowl with the oil. Place the dough in the bowl and gently turn to coat. Cover tightly with plastic wrap, and let rise until doubled in size, 60 to 90 minutes.

Line a baking sheet with parchment paper or a silicone baking mat. Gently deflate the dough; divide into 6 equal portions. Roll each portion into a long rope (about 15 inches, or 46 cm) and twist into a traditional or more creative pretzel shape. Place the pretzels on the prepared baking sheet. Cover with plastic wrap and let rest for 30 minutes.

Preheat the oven to 375°F (190°C, or gas mark 5).

Bring the water to a boil in a large pot. Add the baking soda slowly: the mixture will bubble up. Lower the heat to medium. Place 2 pretzels at a time in the saucepan, and let boil for 1 minute, using a spoon to gently submerge the pretzels occasionally. Scoop out the pretzels with a slotted spoon. Place on a wire rack to drain. Repeat with the remaining 4 pretzels. Transfer to the prepared baking sheet. Sprinkle with the salt.

Bake for 14 minutes, or until the pretzels are golden brown and sound hollow when the bottom is tapped. Best enjoyed fresh. Toast any leftovers before enjoying.

YIELD: 6 pretzels

AVOCADO ROLLS

SOY FREE

The avocado flavor is rather subtle in these bunlike rolls (perfect for Mexican-style burgers!), and the guacamole gives a beautiful texture to this fluffy bread. Simply bypass the hot sauce and garlic if you want to use this recipe in sweet applications.

INGREDIENTS:

½ cup (120 g) prepared guacamole

1½ teaspoons active dry yeast

1 cup (235 ml) water, heated to lukewarm

3 tablespoons (63 g) agave nectar

2½ teaspoons (12.5 ml) hot sauce (optional)

2 cloves garlic, minced

Zest of 1 lemon

1 teaspoon fine sea salt

4 cups (500 g) all-purpose flour, divided, plus more as needed

½ teaspoon oil

DIRECTIONS:

Combine the guacamole, yeast, water, and agave in a medium-size bowl. Let sit for a few minutes until bubbles appear, to ensure the yeast is active. Add the hot sauce, garlic, and lemon zest and stir to combine.

In a large bowl, combine the salt and 3 cups (375 g) of the flour. Add the wet ingredients to the dry, and start mixing. Add the remaining 1 cup (125 g) flour as needed.

Turn out onto a lightly floured surface and knead for 8 to 10 minutes, until the dough is smooth and pliable, adding more flour, a little at a time, if the dough is too sticky. Alternatively, use a stand mixer fitted with the dough hook. The kneading time will be the same, until the dough forms a ball.

Lightly coat a large bowl with the oil. Place the dough in the bowl and gently turn to coat with oil. Cover tightly with plastic wrap and let rise until doubled in size, 60 to 90 minutes.

Line a baking sheet with parchment paper or a silicone baking mat. Gently deflate the dough. Divide into 6 equal portions. Shape into rolls. Place on the prepared baking sheet, loosely cover with plastic wrap, and let rise for 45 minutes.

Preheat the oven to 375°F (190°C, or gas mark 5).

Remove the plastic wrap from the rolls. Bake for 26 minutes, or until the rolls are golden brown and sound hollow when the bottom is tapped. Let cool on a wire rack.

YIELD: 6 rolls

SCARBOROUGH FAIR BUNS

SOY FREE

These buns are the perfect size for paninis and burgers, and of course for enjoying
while dancing around the house to your favorite Simon and Garfunkel records.

INGREDIENTS:

1½ cups (355 ml) water, heated to lukewarm, divided

1 tablespoon (12 g) evaporated cane juice or granulated sugar

4½ teaspoons (14 g) active dry yeast

3 tablespoons (45 ml) olive oil, divided

4 cups (500 g) all-purpose flour, plus more as needed

2 teaspoons (12 g) salt

1 tablespoon (2 g) dried parsley

1 tablespoon (2 g) dried sage

1 tablespoon (2 g) dried rosemary

1 tablespoon (2 g) dried thyme

1 tablespoon (7 g) garlic powder

DIRECTIONS:

Combine 1 cup (235 ml) of the water and the sugar in a small bowl. Stir in the yeast and let sit for a few minutes until bubbles appear, to ensure the yeast is active. Stir in 2 tablespoons (30 ml) of the oil and the remaining ½ cup (120 ml) water.

In a large bowl, combine the 4 cups (500 g) flour, salt, parsley, sage, rosemary, and thyme. Stir the wet ingredients into the dry, mixing until combined.

Turn out onto a lightly floured surface and knead for 8 minutes, until the dough is smooth and pliable, adding more flour as needed if the dough is too sticky. Alternatively, use a stand mixer fitted with the dough hook. The kneading time will be the same, until the dough forms a ball.

Lightly coat a large bowl with ½ teaspoon of the oil. Place the dough in the bowl and gently turn to coat. Cover tightly with plastic wrap and let rise until doubled in size, 60 to 90 minutes.

Preheat the oven to 350°F (180°C, or gas mark 4). Line a baking sheet with parchment paper or a silicone baking mat.

Gently deflate the dough and tun out onto a lightly floured surface. Knead for 3 to 5 minutes.

Divide the dough into 8 equal pieces. Roll each piece into a ball, and then flatten into a disk shape about 4 inches (10 cm) wide × 1 inch (2.5 cm) thick. Place on the prepared baking sheet. Brush the top of each bun with the remaining 2½ teaspoons olive oil and then sprinkle with the garlic powder.

Bake for 20 to 25 minutes or until golden brown. Let cool on a wire rack.

YIELD: 8 buns

WHITE PANINI ROLLS

SOY FREE   **LOW FAT**

These rolls are plain and simple—a nice neutral backdrop for the delicious
flavors you will sandwich between them. They work perfectly in place of a bun
for veggie burgers, and turn an everyday PB & J into a gourmet masterpiece.

INGREDIENTS:

1½ cups (235 ml) water, heated to lukewarm, divided

1 tablespoon (12 g) evaporated cane juice or granulated sugar

3 envelopes (each ¼ ounce, or 7g) active dry yeast

4 cups (500 g) all-purpose flour, plus more as needed

2 teaspoons salt

½ teaspoon olive oil

DIRECTIONS:

Combine 1 cup (235 ml) of the water and the sugar in a small bowl. Stir in the yeast and let sit for a few minutes until bubbles appear, to ensure the yeast is active.

In a large bowl, combine the 4 cups (500 g) flour and salt. Stir in the yeast mixture, mixing until combined, adding the remaining ½ cup (120 ml) warm water as needed, 2 tablespoons (30 ml) at a time.

Turn out onto a lightly floured surface and knead for 8 minutes, until the dough is smooth and pliable, adding more flour as needed if the dough is too sticky. Alternatively, use a stand mixer fitted with the dough hook. The kneading time will be the same, until the dough forms a ball.

Lightly coat a large bowl with the oil. Place the dough in the bowl and gently turn to coat. Cover tightly with plastic wrap and let rise until doubled in size, 60 to 90 minutes.

Preheat the oven to 350°F (180°C, or gas mark 4). Line a baking sheet with parchment paper or a silicone baking mat.

Gently deflate the dough and turn out onto a lightly floured surface. Knead for 3 to 5 minutes.

Transfer the dough to the prepared baking sheet and shape into a rectangle about 8 × 14 inches (20 × 35 cm). Using a pizza roller or a pastry cutter, cut into 6 or 8 even pieces (depending on the size you want) but do not separate. Dust lightly with flour. Cover loosely with a dish towel and let rest for 20 minutes.

Bake for about 25 minutes, or until just beginning to turn golden.

YIELD: 6 to 8 rolls

PINTO BEAN TORTILLA ROLLS

SOY FREE

You'll probably want to eat these scrumptious rolls with a nice scoop
of chili—just beware of the beans striking back with a vengeance!

INGREDIENTS:

Scant 4 cups (110 g) tortilla chips

1 can (15 ounces, or 425 g) pinto beans,
drained and rinsed

1 tablespoon (15 ml) adobo sauce

1 tablespoon (15 g) chopped chipotle chile

1 teaspoon salt

1 cup (235 ml) water, heated to lukewarm

1 tablespoon (7 g) granulated onion

2 tablespoons (30 ml) peanut oil

1 heaping teaspoon active dry yeast

2 cups (250 g) all-purpose flour, divided

1 cup (120 g) white whole wheat flour

DIRECTIONS:

Combine the chips, beans, adobo sauce, and chipotle in
a food processor. Process until mostly ground. Transfer
to a large bowl.

Add the salt, water, onion, oil, and yeast. Stir and let sit
for a few minutes until bubbles appear, to ensure the
yeast is active.

Add 1 cup (125 g) of the all-purpose flour and the whole
wheat flour; stir with a rubber spatula, "stabbing" at
the dough for about 4 minutes, adding the remaining
1 cup (125 g) all-purpose flour as needed. The dough
will become a bit less sticky as you do this. Cover and
let rise for 2 hours.

Line a baking sheet with parchment paper or a silicone
baking mat. Gently deflate the dough and divide into
6 equal portions. Shape into rolls. Place the rolls on the
prepared sheet. Let rise for 1 hour.

Preheat the oven to 375°F (190°C, or gas mark 5). Bake
for 30 minutes, or until the rolls sounds hollow when the
bottom is tapped. Let cool on a wire rack.

YIELD: 6 rolls

SPELT FLOUR TORTILLAS

Who needs store-bought flour tortillas when it's such a breeze to make them yourself?
Find out how to turn these into chips in the Mucho Macho Nachos (page 148) recipe.

INGREDIENTS:

2 cups (240 g) light spelt flour, plus more as needed

2 teaspoons (9 g) baking powder

½ cup (120 ml) nondairy creamer or coconut milk, heated to lukewarm

¼ cup (60 ml) water, heated to lukewarm

1 tablespoon (15 ml) peanut oil

½ teaspoon fine sea salt

½ teaspoon red pepper flakes or ¼ teaspoon ground pepper, or to taste (optional)

DIRECTIONS:

Combine the 2 cups (240 g) flour and baking powder in a large bowl. Add the remaining ingredients, stirring with a fork. Switch to using a rubber spatula and gather the dough in the center of the bowl. Cover and let rest for 15 minutes.

Turn out onto a lightly floured surface, gather the dough into a ball, and knead gently about 10 times, adding more flour as needed. You should need about ¼ cup (30 g), but that will depend on humidity and flour quality. Divide into 12 equal portions, cover with a plastic wrap, and let rest for 10 minutes.

Sprinkle more flour (a little at a time) onto the counter, each piece of dough, and the rolling pin, as needed. You may have to add more flour on each side as you roll out the dough. You don't want big pockets of flour, so apply flour evenly a little at a time. Roll out the dough from the center outward, 1 piece at a time. You want it to be very thin and about 8 inches (20 cm) in diameter.

Heat a dry 10-inch (25-cm) skillet over medium heat. Carefully transfer 1 rolled-out tortilla to the skillet. Cook for 45 seconds on each side: the tortilla will bubble up a bit. Keep a close eye on it and adjust the temperature and cooking time accordingly. While it is cooking, roll out another tortilla, remove the cooked one from the pan, and slide in the freshly rolled tortilla. Repeat the rolling-out and cooking process until all the tortillas are cooked.

YIELD: 12 small tortillas

SKILLET CORNBREAD

Onions, herbs, and garlic take already hearty cornbread to a whole new savory place we never want to leave. We're happy and hungry that way!

INGREDIENTS:

1 cup (235 ml) unsweetened plain soymilk

¼ cup (56 g) nondairy butter, melted and cooled, plus 1 extra tablespoon (14 g) for the skillet

½ teaspoon fine sea salt

¼ cup (5 g) chopped fresh cilantro

1 tablespoon (7 g) granulated onion

½ cup (120 g) nondairy sour cream, store-bought or homemade (page 211), or plain soy yogurt

½ teaspoon pepper

2 cloves garlic, minced

1½ cups (180 g) all-purpose flour

¾ cup (105 g) cornmeal

1 tablespoon (12 g) baking powder

DIRECTIONS:

Preheat the oven to 400°F (200°C, or gas mark 6). Place a dry 8-inch (20-cm) cast-iron skillet in the oven as it preheats.

Combine the milk, melted butter, salt, cilantro, onion, sour cream, pepper, and garlic in a large bowl. Sift the flour, cornmeal, and baking powder on top. Stir until just combined.

Place the remaining 1 tablespoon (14 g) butter in the hot skillet, brushing it all over. Pour the batter into the skillet.

Bake for 30 minutes, or until a toothpick inserted into the center comes out clean. Remove from the skillet. Let cool on wire rack.

YIELD: 6 to 8 servings

GARLIC KNOTS

For great pizza recipes using this dough as the crust, see Roasted Broccoli and Garlic Pizza (page 143), Deep-Dish Pizza Pie (page 144), and Pesto con Gusto Pizza (page 145). Consider swapping out the garlic powder for onion powder in pizza crusts, too.

INGREDIENTS:

1 cup (235 ml) water, heated to lukewarm

1 tablespoon (12 g) evaporated cane juice or granulated sugar

1½ teaspoons (6 g) active dry yeast

2½ to 3 cups (312 to 375 g) all-purpose or bread flour, plus more as needed

1 teaspoon salt

2 tablespoons (16 g) garlic powder, divided

2 tablespoons (30 ml) olive oil

2 tablespoons (28 g) nondairy butter, softened, plus 2 tablespoons (28 g), melted

2 tablespoons (15 g) minced garlic

¼ teaspoon dried basil

¼ teaspoon paprika

DIRECTIONS:

Combine the water and sugar in a small bowl. Stir in the yeast and let sit for a few minutes until bubbles appear, to ensure the yeast is active.

In a large bowl, combine 2½ cups (312 g) of the flour, salt, and 1 tablespoon (8 g) of the garlic powder. Add the yeast mixture and olive oil and mix until combined.

Turn out onto a lightly floured surface (or use a stand mixer fitted with the dough hook) and knead for 8 minutes, until the dough is smooth and pliable, adding more flour as needed if the dough is too sticky. Place the dough in a large, oiled bowl and gently turn to coat. Cover tightly with plastic wrap and let rise until doubled in size, 60 to 90 minutes.

Gently deflate the dough. On a well-floured or nonstick surface, roll the dough into a 8 × 12-inch (20 × 30-cm) rectangle. Spread the softened butter evenly over the dough, then sprinkle on the minced garlic, dried basil, and paprika.

Using a sharp knife or pizza cutter, cut the rectangle into twelve 1 × 8-inch (2.5 × 20-cm) strips. Carefully tie each strip into a simple knot, keeping the buttered side inside. Place on a baking sheet lined with parchment paper or a silicone baking mat and cover loosely with plastic wrap. Let rise for 30 minutes. Meanwhile, preheat the oven to 375°F (190°C, or gas mark 5).

Bake for 15 minutes. Carefully remove from the oven and brush each knot with the melted butter and sprinkle with the remaining 1 tablespoon (8 g) garlic powder. Bake for 5 to 6 minutes longer, or until golden. Let cool on a wire rack.

YIELD: 12 knots

RECIPE NOTE

Use bread flour in this recipe for a great pizza crust; just add up to 1 extra cup (125 g) flour until the dough is smooth and pliable. Let rise for 60 minutes.

Gently deflate the dough and shape into a large rectangle, then and place on a lightly greased baking sheet. Top with the desired pizza toppings, and bake for 20 to 24 minutes in a 400°F (200°C, or gas mark 6) oven, or until the edges are golden brown.

SUN-DRIED TOMATO, GARLIC, AND BASIL FLATBREAD

SOY FREE

Bake this flatbread and cut it into sandwich-size squares. It makes a mean panini, an even meaner grilled cheese, and the meanest pizza crust!

INGREDIENTS:

1 cup (235 ml) water, heated to lukewarm

1 tablespoon (12 g) evaporated cane juice or granulated sugar

1½ teaspoons (6 g) active dry yeast

¼ cup (60 g) finely diced sun-dried tomatoes, packed in oil

1 tablespoon (15 g) minced garlic

6 tablespoons (90 ml) plus 1 teaspoon olive oil, divided

2 cups (250 g) all-purpose flour, plus more as needed

½ teaspoon salt

⅛ teaspoon freshly cracked pepper

6 leaves fresh basil, finely chopped

DIRECTIONS:

Combine the water with sugar in a small bowl. Stir in the yeast and let sit for a few minutes until bubbles appear, to ensure the yeast is active. Stir in the sun-dried tomatoes, garlic, and 2 tablespoons (30 ml) of the olive oil.

In a large bowl, combine the 2 cups (250 g) flour, salt, pepper, and basil. Stir the wet ingredients into the dry, mixing until combined.

Turn out the dough onto a lightly floured surface and knead for 8 minutes, until the dough is smooth and pliable, adding more flour as needed if the dough is too sticky. Alternatively, use a stand mixer fitted with the dough hook. The kneading time will be the same, until the dough forms a ball.

Lightly coat a large bowl with ½ teaspoon of the oil. Place the dough in the bowl and gently turn to coat. Cover tightly with plastic wrap and let rise until doubled in size, 60 to 90 minutes.

Gently deflate the dough and place on a lightly floured surface. Knead for 3 to 5 minutes.

Press the dough out into a rectangle about 10 × 16 inches (25 × 60 cm) and about ⅜ inch (1 cm) thick, using your fingertips. (Or into a rectangle that will fit on your baking sheet.) Let rest for 20 to 30 minutes.

Preheat the oven to 400°F (200°C, or gas mark 6). Line a baking sheet with parchment paper or a silicone baking sheet.

Brush 2 tablespoons (30 ml) of the olive oil evenly all over the dough. Place the oiled side of the bread face down on the baking sheet, and brush the remaining 2 tablespoons (30 ml) oil onto the other side.

Bake for 18 to 22 minutes, or until firm and just beginning to brown. Let cool completely before cutting into squares.

YIELD: 8 squares

CHAPTER 6

Condiments, Sauces, and Other Staples

Luscious items, indispensable odds and ends, all united and eager to give a little extra *je ne sais quoi* to your dishes.

Although some of these recipes may appear to be (and are) pretty basic, you will find that the resulting flavors prove themselves to be anything but. What better way is there to add pizzazz to your dishes than by preparing favorites such as salsa, pico de gallo, and even mozzarella (pictured at top right) in the comfort of your own home? And if you thought that the only way to enjoy your vegan chorizo or pepperoni was to buy them ready-made at the store, rest assured that it takes neither special skills nor complicated ingredients—and next to no time—to whip up a batch to complement tacos or pizza the best way we know how.

SALSA VERDE

SOY FREE   GLUTEN FREE

Please use caution when handling chile peppers! Do not touch your eyes and wear gloves, if possible. Only use the habanero if you want mega heat. Use a second jalapeño if you want a little extra heat but aren't ready to deal with that traitor, the habanero. Most important: Be sure to dig in, chip planted firmly in hand.

INGREDIENTS:

10 tomatillos, papery skins removed, rinsed, and halved

6 scallions, white and green parts, cleaned and trimmed

½ a lime

1 jalapeño pepper, left whole to roast

1 habanero pepper, left whole to roast (optional) for extra, EXTRA heat

½ teaspoon coarse sea salt

1 tablespoon (15 ml) peanut oil

½ cup (8 g) fresh cilantro

DIRECTIONS:

Preheat the oven to 400°F (200°C, or gas mark 6). Place the tomatillos, cut side down, scallions, and peppers, cut side down, on a large baking sheet. Sprinkle with the salt and drizzle with the oil until well coated. Roast for 15 minutes. Remove from the oven and let cool before handling.

Squeeze the juice of the lime into a blender jar. Carefully remove the ribs and seeds from the jalapeño and habanero. Add the cilantro and process until no large chunks remain. Store in an airtight container in the refrigerator for up to 4 days.

YIELD: 2 cups (470 ml)

PICO DE GALLO

LOW FAT   GLUTEN FREE   SOY FREE

We are of the firm belief that because this condiment is packed with veggies, it is more acceptable to munch on an honest amount of Mucho Macho Nachos (page 148).

INGREDIENTS:

4 ounces (113 g) fire-roasted diced green chiles or 1 small seeded and chopped jalapeño

1 pound (454 g) Roma tomatoes, finely diced

1 can (15 ounces, or 425 g) black beans, drained and rinsed

1 large clove garlic, minced

½ teaspoon ground cumin

Juice of ½ lime

Salt and pepper, to taste

4 scallions, chopped

⅓ cup (5 g) chopped fresh cilantro

DIRECTIONS:

Combine all the ingredients in a large bowl. Let stand for at least 1 hour in the refrigerator, for the flavors to meld. Store in an airtight container in the refrigerator for up to 4 days.

YIELD: 4 cups (960 g)

MEXICAN-STYLE DIPPING SAUCE FOR CORN

QUICK AND EASY   GLUTEN FREE

Grilled corn is a treat all on its own. Add this deliciously devilish Mexican-style dip (pictured on page 96) to take your corn on the cob to a whole new level!

INGREDIENTS:

1 cup (224 g) vegan mayonnaise, store-bought or homemade (page 211)

½ cup (120 g) nondairy cream cheese

2 tablespoons (30 ml) lime juice

½ teaspoon chipotle chile powder

½ teaspoon dried dill or 1½ teaspoons, fresh

DIRECTIONS:

Whisk all the ingredients together (or blend in a blender) and keep refrigerated until ready to serve. Serve in a tall, wide-mouth glass for easy dipping.

YIELD: 1½ cups (365 g)

MUSTARD SAUCE

QUICK AND EASY

A zippy sauce that is great as a dressing for potatoes or to dip Soft Peanut Butter Pretzels (page 193) into!

INGREDIENTS:

⅔ cup (160 g) nondairy unsweetened plain yogurt

2 tablespoons (30 ml) extra-virgin olive oil

1 tablespoon (15 ml) apple cider vinegar

2 tablespoons (30 g) mustard

1 tablespoon (21 g) agave nectar

½ teaspoon granulated onion

Salt and pepper, to taste

Pinch of fresh or dried dill (optional)

DIRECTIONS:

Whisk all the ingredients together in a medium-size bowl. Store in an airtight container in the refrigerator for up to 1 week.

YIELD: ¾ cup (180 ml)

MAMOU'S MAGICAL VINAIGRETTE

There is no vegetable that doesn't like being doused with the vinaigrette Celine's mom has always made to dress her salads. It is also delicious on rice or potatoes. You may need to double the recipe depending on the vegetable or grain it goes on to.

INGREDIENTS:

2 tablespoons (10 g) chopped scallion

1 clove garlic, pressed (optional; adjust to taste, as this quantity makes for quite a garlicky flavor)

¼ teaspoon ground white pepper

Pinch of salt

1 teaspoon any mustard

1 tablespoon (15 ml) white balsamic vinegar

1 tablespoon (15 ml) extra-virgin olive oil

1 tablespoon (15 ml) flaxseed, grapeseed, or more olive oil

¼ cup (6 g) chopped fresh parsley (optional)

DIRECTIONS:

Combine the scallion, garlic, pepper, salt, and mustard in a small bowl, stirring with salad servers. Be sure to crush the scallions while stirring to squeeze out all the flavor.

Emulsify with vinegar by drizzling it in while constantly stirring. Slowly drizzle in the oils, stirring constantly, until the vinaigrette is creamy.

If not using wilt-prone salad leaves, let marinate a bit so the flavors develop. Store in a jar in the refrigerator for up to 1 week.

YIELD: ¼ cup (60 ml)

SUPER EASY MARINADE

This marinade works well on all sorts of things, from broccoli to tempeh, and makes an easy task of quick and simple weeknight dinners.

INGREDIENTS:

2 tablespoons (30 ml) soy sauce

¼ cup (60 ml) extra-virgin olive oil

¼ teaspoon liquid smoke

2 tablespoons (30 g) Dijon mustard

1 teaspoon prepared horseradish

1 tablespoon (15 ml) apple cider vinegar

1 tablespoon (21 g) agave nectar

¼ teaspoon freshly ground black pepper

½ teaspoon garlic powder

1 teaspoon onion powder

DIRECTIONS:

Whisk all the ingredients together. Store in an airtight container in the refrigerator until ready to use, up to 1 week. To use, pour over items to be marinated, toss to coat, and let sit for at least 20 minutes or up to overnight.

YIELD: ½ cup (120 ml)

WHISKEY BARBECUE SAUCE

Tangy and sassy and all that a barbecue sauce should be! If you are
not a fan of whiskey, feel free to substitute with white vinegar.

INGREDIENTS:

2 tablespoons (30 ml) olive oil

1 medium-size yellow onion, roughly chopped

4 cloves garlic, minced

1 can (16 ounces, or 448 g) tomato sauce

2 tablespoons (33 g) tomato paste

¼ cup (80 g) grape jelly

½ cup (110 g) packed brown sugar

2 teaspoons sambal oelek or Sriracha sauce

¼ cup (60 ml) whiskey

1 tablespoon (15 ml) liquid smoke

2 tablespoons (30 g) Dijon mustard

Salt and pepper, to taste

DIRECTIONS:

Heat the oil in a medium-size pot over medium-high heat.
Add the onion and garlic and sauté for about 5 minutes,
or until fragrant and translucent.

Add the tomato sauce, tomato paste, jelly, brown sugar,
sambal oelek, whisky, liquid smoke, mustard, salt, and
pepper. Stir to combine.

Bring to a boil, reduce the heat to a simmer, cover, and
simmer over low heat for 30 minutes. Uncover and simmer for 5 to 10 minutes longer, until thick and saucy.

Store in an airtight container in the refrigerator for up
to 3 weeks.

YIELD: 3 cups (864 g)

SPINACH PESTO

SOY FREE   GLUTEN FREE

Put this green wonder to the test in our Pesto, Farro, and Fagioli (page 136) or
Tempeh, Pepper and Spinach-Pesto Sandwich (page 84), to name but a few.

INGREDIENTS:

⅓ cup (53 g) dry-roasted whole almonds

3¾ cups (113 g) fresh baby spinach leaves

¼ cup (6 g) fresh basil

Salt and pepper, to taste

4 cloves garlic, minced

¼ to ⅓ cup (60 to 80 ml) extra-virgin olive oil

DIRECTIONS:

Grind the almonds in a food processor. Add the spinach,
basil, salt, pepper, and garlic. Pulse until no whole leaves
are left. Slowly drizzle in the oil while the machine is running until the desired consistency is reached. Store in an
airtight container for up to 1 week.

YIELD: 1 cup (240 g)

TOFU MAYO

No need to worry if your local market doesn't carry egg-free mayo—just whip up some of your own. This recipe works very well as a sandwich spread or in any of the mayonnaise-based dressings right here in this book. As long as you use gluten-free vinegar, this mayo is indeed gluten free.

INGREDIENTS:

7 ounces (198 g) extra-firm tofu, drained and pressed

¼ cup (35 g) finely ground raw cashews

1 tablespoon (15 ml) freshly squeezed lemon juice

1 tablespoon (12 g) raw sugar or (21 g) agave nectar

1½ teaspoons brown or Dijon mustard

1 teaspoon apple cider vinegar or rice wine vinegar

½ teaspoon sea salt

6 tablespoons (90 ml) canola oil

DIRECTIONS:

Place the tofu, cashew powder, lemon juice, sugar, mustard, vinegar, and salt in a blender or food processor and whirl away. Slowly drizzle in the oil while the machine is running until you reach the desired consistency. Store in an airtight container in the refrigerator for up to 2 weeks.

YIELD: Almost 2 cups (470 ml)

TOFU SOUR CREAM

Although nondairy versions of traditionally dairy products are becoming more readily available, you may occasionally need to whip up a delicious batch of your own.

INGREDIENTS:

7 ounces (198 g) extra-firm tofu, drained well and pressed

¼ cup (28 g) finely ground raw cashews

1 tablespoon (15 ml) white rice vinegar

1 tablespoon (15 ml) freshly squeezed lemon or lime juice

1 tablespoon (18 g) white miso

1 tablespoon (15 ml) canola oil

DIRECTIONS:

Place all the ingredients in a blender or food processor and blend until very, very smooth and creamy. Keep in an airtight container in the refrigerator until ready to use. Should last up to 1 week.

YIELD: About 1½ cups (355 ml)

CREAMY CHEESY SAUCE

If you find the cost of good shredded vegan cheese a bit too steep for your pocketbook, here's how to make it last a bit longer and even improve its taste. This deliciously rich and decadent sauce goes perfectly on top of pizzas, baked potatoes, and steamed veggies, and even stirred into chili or baked beans.

INGREDIENTS:

1 cup (112 g) shredded mozzarella- or cheddar-type (flavor depending on use) vegan cheese, such as Daiya

1 cup (235 ml) unsweetened soymilk

1 to 2 tablespoons (8 to 16 g) cornstarch, to desired thickness

1 tablespoon (15 g) maca powder

¼ teaspoon ground pepper, or to taste

1 clove garlic, minced

¼ cup (56 g) nondairy butter, melted

Salt, to taste (optional)

DIRECTIONS:

Combine the cheese, soymilk, cornstarch, maca powder, pepper, garlic, and butter in a microwave-safe dish. Using an immersion blender, blend until smooth and combined.

Microwave for 2 minutes, stir with a fork, and season with salt. Alternatively, combine the blended ingredients in a medium-size saucepan and cook over medium-high heat for 3 minutes, or until thickened, whisking constantly. Store in an airtight container in the refrigerator for up to 4 days. Gently reheat in a small saucepan before using.

YIELD: 1½ cups (355 ml)

WALNUT PARMESAN SPRINKLES

Make these and store them in a shaker jar to sprinkle on pasta, pizza, salads, or anywhere you'd sprinkle on some grated Parmesan cheese.

INGREDIENTS:

½ cup (60 g) walnut pieces

½ cup (60 g) nutritional yeast

½ cup (40 g) panko bread crumbs

½ teaspoon dried basil

¼ to ½ teaspoon salt, or to taste

DIRECTIONS:

Add all the ingredients to a blender or food processor and pulse until the walnut pieces have been ground into a powder.

YIELD: About 1½ cups (126 g)

HEMP ALMOND PARMESAN

QUICK AND EASY   GLUTEN FREE

You might find yourself grabbing a spoon and making a dent in this buttery parmesan as is, instead of putting it to good use in meatloaf (page 101), Panzanella Sandwiches (page 82), and anywhere Parmesan cheese would be needed.

INGREDIENTS:

1 cup (160 g) dry-roasted whole almonds

¾ cup (120 g) hemp seeds or (108 g) sesame seeds

Pinch of fine sea salt

2 cloves garlic, minced

1 tablespoon (15 g) maca powder

¼ cup (30 g) nutritional yeast

¼ cup (28 g) coconut flour

1 tablespoon (9 g) white miso

DIRECTIONS:

Combine all the ingredients in a food processor and process until the almonds are ground and a Parmesan-like appearance is obtained. Store in an airtight container in the refrigerator for up to 2 weeks.

YIELD: 3 cups (305 g)

SMOKY PUB CHEESE

SOY FREE   QUICK AND EASY

This thick spreadable cheese is open to all kinds of adaptations. The different flavors you can make are only limited by your imagination. Try it on crackers, a sandwich, or the Ultimate Patty Melt (page 95).

INGREDIENTS:

1 cup (235 ml) vegetable broth or water

2 tablespoons (32 g) tahini

2 to 4 tablespoons (15 to 30 g) nutritional yeast, to taste

¼ teaspoon salt

1 teaspoon onion powder

½ teaspoon sugar

1 cup (78 g) quick-cooking oats

3 tablespoons (45 ml) canola or other mild-flavored vegetable oil

1 tablespoon (12 g) diced pimiento or piquante or Peppadew peppers

1 teaspoon liquid smoke

DIRECTIONS:

Combine the water, tahini, nutritional yeast, salt, onion powder, and sugar in a pot and bring to a boil. Stir in the oats, oil, pimiento, and liquid smoke. Remove from the heat, cover, and let sit for 10 to 15 minutes to cool.

Using an immersion blender, or transferring to a tabletop blender, process until silky smooth. The consistency will be that of thick peanut butter.

Alternatively, place all the ingredients in a blender, and process until smooth. Transfer to a microwave-safe dish. Microwave on High for 1 minute. Stir. Heat at additional 20-second intervals until thick and creamy.

Store in an airtight container in the refrigerator for up to 2 weeks. Enjoy cold, or heat up for a thinner sauce.

YIELD: 1½ cups (336 g)

MOZZARELLA ▶

A firmer version than the recipe that appears in Pesto con Gusto Pizza (page 145), the coconut oil gives this mozzarella a wonderfully buttery taste. Adjust the seasonings and spices to your liking.

INGREDIENTS:

¾ cup (180 ml) unsweetened soymilk

1 tablespoon (15 ml) white vinegar or freshly squeezed lemon juice

¼ cup (60 ml) melted coconut oil

Heaping ¼ teaspoon fine sea salt

¼ teaspoon freshly ground black pepper

¼ teaspoon garlic powder

Heaping ¼ teaspoon onion powder

2 tablespoons (16 g) cornstarch

DIRECTIONS:

Combine all the ingredients in a microwave-safe glass measuring cup. Using an immersion blender, blend until foamy and perfectly combined.

Heat in the microwave for 2 minutes, making sure the mixture doesn't foam up and overflow. The preparation should have the consistency of a thick yogurt, but if it is still extremely liquid, microwave again. Stir with a fork.

Let cool before using. It gets firmer to the point of being a soft block (see top-right photo on page 205) once refrigerated for a few hours. Store in the refrigerator, tightly wrapped, for up to 4 days.

YIELD: 1 cup (240 g)

TVP PEPPERONI ▶

This is perfect on top of pizza (pictured) or in Crispy Pepperoni Bites (page 162).

INGREDIENTS:

¼ teaspoon freshly ground black pepper

¼ teaspoon fine sea salt

1 tablespoon (7 g) paprika

1 tablespoon (8 g) garlic powder

¼ to ½ teaspoon red pepper flakes

1 teaspoon dried basil

¼ to ½ teaspoon cayenne pepper, or to taste

1 teaspoon Sucanat or other dry sweetener

2 tablespoons (30 ml) olive oil

1 tablespoon (15 ml) liquid smoke

1 cup (96 g) TVP granules

1 cup (235 ml) boiling water

DIRECTIONS:

Combine the spices and Sucanat in a medium-size bowl. Stir in the oil and liquid smoke. Place the TVP on top. Pour the boiling water on top and stir with a fork. Cover with plastic wrap and let stand for 10 minutes. Fluff with a fork. Store in an airtight container in the refrigerator for up to 4 days.

YIELD: 12 ounces (340 g)

TVP CHORIZO

QUICK AND EASY

Use this recipe in Chorizo Flautas (page 164), Chorizo and Egg Frittata (page 42), and anywhere chorizo is called for.

INGREDIENTS:

3 tablespoons (24 g) nutritional yeast

¾ teaspoon fine sea salt

1½ teaspoons ground cumin

¼ teaspoon cayenne pepper

¾ teaspoon paprika

1 tablespoon (8 g) chili powder

1 teaspoon granulated onion

1½ tablespoons (23 ml) apple cider vinegar

3 tablespoons (51 g) ketchup or tomato paste

1½ tablespoons (23 ml) extra-virgin olive oil

¾ cup (72 g) TVP granules

6 tablespoons (90 ml) boiling water

DIRECTIONS:

Combine all the spices, vinegar, ketchup, and oil in a medium-size bowl. Stir in the TVP. Pour the boiling water on top and stir well. Cover with plastic wrap and let stand for 10 minutes to reconstitute the TVP.

Brown in a pan before using, if desired. Store in an air-tight container in the refrigerator for up to 4 days.

YIELD: 12 ounces (340 g)

IMITATION BACON BITS

GLUTEN FREE

Sprinkle on top of baked potatoes, in tofu scrambles, or anywhere you would use bacon bits.

INGREDIENTS:

1 to 2 tablespoons (15 to 30 ml) liquid smoke, or to taste

1 scant cup (205 ml) water

1 cup (96 g) TVP granules

¼ teaspoon salt

A few drops red food coloring (optional)

3 tablespoons (45 ml) canola or other vegetable oil

DIRECTIONS:

To a measuring cup, add the liquid smoke, then fill with water to get 1 cup (235 ml). Combine the liquid smoke mixture with TVP, salt, and food coloring in a microwave-safe dish. Cover tightly with plastic wrap and microwave on High for 5 minutes. Carefully remove the wrap.

Heat the oil in a frying pan over medium-high heat. Add the reconstituted TVP and toss to coat with oil. Panfry until desired crispness, stirring often. You don't necessarily want to "brown" them, but rather dry them out, about 10 minutes. Let cool completely.

Refrigerated, these should last at least a week, but probably much longer.

YIELD: About 1 cup (100 g)

CAULIFLOWER AND ONION PICKLES

SOY FREE **LOW FAT** **GLUTEN FREE**

Although it's typically called giardiniera and contains carrots and other pickled veggies, we find that cauliflower and onion are the tastiest of the bunch. The longer you let them marinate in the refrigerator, the better.

INGREDIENTS:

3 cups (705 ml) white vinegar

3 cups (705 ml) water

1 jalapeño, ribs and seeds removed if you want less heat, sliced (optional)

10 ounces (283 g) pearl onions

1 small head cauliflower, separated into small florets

2 tablespoons (25 g) evaporated cane juice or granulated sugar

1 tablespoon (18 g) fine sea salt

DIRECTIONS:

Combine all the ingredients in a 4-quart (3.8-l) Pyrex bowl with a lid, or in several pickle jars. The veggies need to be completely immersed in the liquid: if the liquid measurements above are not enough for the quantity/size of veggies, add extra water and vinegar in equal amounts. Stir with a spoon, cover with the lid, and marinate in the refrigerator for at least 4 days before enjoying. Store in an airtight container in the refrigerator for up to 3 weeks.

YIELD: About 2 quarts (1.9 l)

PICKLED PEPPERS

SOY FREE **LOW FAT** **GLUTEN FREE**

This recipe is a variation of one given to Joni by her coworker Miguel. They last forever in a big ol' jar, and only get better over time. Keep in mind that these spicy devils are very vinegary and pack a mean punch. They also look great packaged in jars and given as gifts! Oh, and on top of nachos . . . killer!

INGREDIENTS:

6 cups (1.4 l) white vinegar

20 jalapeños, stems removed and sliced into rounds

5 jalapeños, left whole

5 carrots, peeled and sliced into rounds

10 radishes, thinly sliced

1 large white onion, julienned

1 tablespoon (18 g) sea salt

DIRECTIONS:

Combine all the ingredients in a large container with a lid. Marinate overnight in the refrigerator.

YIELD: 2 quarts (1.9 l)

RECIPE NOTE

Other nice additions to this mix include chopped celery, chopped red bell pepper, fresh cilantro, whole garlic cloves, and whole black peppercorns.

CHESTNUT CREAM SPREAD

GLUTEN FREE   SOY FREE

It is uncanny how similar to honey this spread is. However, it is slightly less sweet
than what is commonly enjoyed as a dessert item, and it makes a perfect and unusual
spread to use on bread. Try it as is once, then adjust the amount of sweetener if needed.

INGREDIENTS:

4 packages (each 3½ ounces, or 100 g)
prepared roasted chestnuts

14 ounces (414 ml) light coconut milk

½ cup (100 g) evaporated cane juice or granulated sugar

1½ teaspoons (7.5 ml) pure vanilla extract

DIRECTIONS:

Combine the chestnuts, milk, and sugar in a medium-size
saucepan. Bring to a low boil; simmer, uncovered, for
20 minutes. Remove from the heat and add the vanilla.
Using a blender, process until smooth. Store in an airtight
container in the refrigerator for up to 2 weeks.

YIELD: 3 cups (755 g)

ALTELLA SPREAD

GLUTEN FREE

We were longing for an almond-based version of the rich, world-famous chocolate and hazelnut
spread that would still be ready to use right out of the refrigerator. Mission accomplished!

INGREDIENTS:

½ cup (60 g) powdered sugar, sifted

½ cup plus 2 tablespoons (110 g) vegan
semisweet chocolate chips

½ cup (120 ml) any nondairy milk

¾ cup (120 g) dry-roasted whole almonds

DIRECTIONS:

Combine the sugar, chocolate chips, and milk in a microwave-safe bowl. Heat until the chocolate melts, about
1 minute, stirring occasionally. Alternatively, use a double
boiler. Set aside to cool.

In a food processor, grind the almonds until a paste
forms. Slowly drizzle in the chocolate mixture and process until perfectly smooth and combined, scraping
down the sides occasionally.

Store in an airtight container in the refrigerator for up
to 2 weeks.

YIELD: 1 cup (320 g)

RECIPE NOTE

If you'd rather work with ready-made natural nut butter
instead of grinding whole nuts, process 6 tablespoons
(96 g) nut butter with the melted chocolate mixture.
Any nut butter (and any nut!) works well here.

CHAPTER 7

Ooey, Gooey, and Downright Sinful Sweets

An irresistible selection of cookies, ice creams, and other indulgences.

If you happen to be well known for having a mega sweet tooth and bear a striking resemblance to Monsieur Cookie Monster, the following pages might very well become the most worn out of the cookbook. And there's absolutely no shame in that!

No matter what, please heed this much-needed warning: you must make sure you have a nice tall glass of cold nondairy milk at hand, because you'll definitely need it to wash down all the goods you'll find here. Think your taste buds can handle it? It's time to put them to the test.

CAKE BATTER ICE CREAM

Celine couldn't take any more begging from her husband to mimic his favorite ice cream, which is served at a popular creamery where add-ins are, well, added into the ice cream upon a granite stone right in front of your drooling self. Behold! Now you can have your cake, and ice cream, too.

INGREDIENTS:

1 cup (120 g) vegan yellow cake mix, such as Cherrybrook Kitchen

¼ to ½ cup (50 to 100 g) evaporated cane juice or granulated sugar, depending on cake mix used and personal preference (dip a finger in the batter to try)

2 cups (470 ml) nondairy creamer

½ cup (120 ml) any thick and rich nondairy milk

1 teaspoon pure vanilla extract

Pinch of salt

DIRECTIONS:

Remember to place the bowl of your ice cream maker in the freezer at least 24 hours prior to making the dessert.

Using a blender, combine all the ingredients until smooth.

Prepare the ice cream following the manufacturer's instructions. Return to the freezer to firm up, if desired.

YIELD: 4 servings

RECIPE NOTE

For some extra fun, cut the cake into thin slices, pile a scoop of the softened ice cream between 2 slices, and you have a Cake Batter Ice Cream cake sandwich. Or add pieces of baked cake to the ice cream during the last 5 minutes of churning. Or throw in chopped pieces of your favorite fruit (we like cherries or Marinated Strawberries [page 230]) along with a few pieces of dark chocolate, for extra crunch, as seen in the Banana Split Waffle picture (page 28).

COFFEE BEAN ICE CREAM

If you are like Celine's husband and walk around with a coffee IV drip all day long, this should please you and keep you buzzing for days on end. Or for a few minutes at least.

INGREDIENTS:

2 cups (470 ml) nondairy creamer

1 cup (235 ml) thick nondairy milk

¾ cup (180 ml) Coffee Syrup (recipe below)

1½ teaspoons pure vanilla extract

Pinch of salt

2 tablespoons (16 g) cornstarch

⅓ cup (53 g) vegan dark chocolate-covered coffee beans, coarsely chopped

DIRECTIONS:

Combine the creamer, milk, syrup, vanilla, salt, and cornstarch in a blender and process until smooth. Place in a saucepan, bring to a low boil, lower the heat, and cook until slightly thickened, whisking constantly, about 4 minutes. Let cool and chill for a few hours or overnight.

Prepare the ice cream following the manufacturer's instructions. Add the coffee beans during the last 5 minutes of churning.

YIELD: 4 servings

BONUS RECIPE

COFFEE SYRUP

You will need to prepare the coffee syrup prior to making the ice cream, but the good news is it's multi-purpose. Make a double batch and save the leftovers for making iced coffees: simply stir a spoonful into a cup of your favorite nondairy milk and pour over ice.

Ingredients:

1¼ cups (295 ml) strong brewed coffee (brewed from 1¼ cups [295 ml] water and ¼ cup [20 g] ground coffee)

1 cup (200 g) evaporated cane juice or granulated sugar

Tiny pinch of salt

½ teaspoon pure vanilla extract

Directions:
Combine the coffee, sugar, and salt in a saucepan. Simmer over medium heat for 30 minutes, stirring occasionally, until reduced to ³/₄ cup (180 ml). Keep a close eye so the coffee doesn't scorch. Remove from the heat and let cool. Stir in the extract and chill overnight; the syrup will thicken once refrigerated.

Yield: ¾ cup (180 ml)

PEANUT BUTTER ICE CREAM

This concoction tastes super caramel-ly thanks to the use of Sucanat. It is best to use an immersion blender to get the fluffiest results. Consider adding bits of Peanut Butter Cups (page 232) or any other add-in during the last 5 minutes of churning.

If you use gluten-free vanilla, then this recipe is indeed gluten free.

INGREDIENTS:

¾ cup (192 g) natural creamy or crunchy peanut butter

4 ounces (113 g) extra-firm silken tofu

6 ounces (170 g) nondairy cream cheese

3 tablespoons (63 g) agave nectar

3 tablespoons (36 g) Sucanat or brown sugar

Pinch of sea salt

2 teaspoons (10 ml) pure vanilla extract

¼ cup (60 ml) nondairy milk, plus more as needed

DIRECTIONS:

In a large bowl, combine all the ingredients with an immersion blender, using an up and down motion to "fluff up" the mixture. If the thickness gives your blender too hard a time, add a little extra milk to make it more manageable. Dip a finger into the mixture to have a taste and adjust the level of sweetness if needed.

Prepare the ice cream following the manufacturer's instructions. Chill just a little bit longer, about 30 minutes, before serving, until the desired firmness is reached.

YIELD: 4 servings

PEANUT BUTTER MOLASSES SHAKE ▶

Tired of the usual vanilla, chocolate, and strawberry shakes? We have just the thing for you, with this unusual and delectable combination of peanut butter and molasses, all rolled into one icy beverage that will make you go (optionally) bananas!

INGREDIENTS:

2 big scoops Peanut Butter Ice Cream (recipe above)

1 tablespoon (22 g) regular molasses, or to taste

½ frozen banana, cut into chunks (optional)

Pinch of sea salt

⅓ cup (80 ml) nondairy milk

DIRECTIONS:

Combine all of the ingredients in a blender, process until smooth, and enjoy.

SIMPLY VANILLA ICE CREAM

This simple vanilla ice cream boasts the richness of true vanilla bean.
If you use gluten-free vanilla, then this recipe is indeed gluten free.

INGREDIENTS:

3 cups (705 ml) vanilla soy creamer,
other nondairy creamer, or milk

1 cup (200 g) evaporated cane juice or granulated sugar

¼ cup (32 g) cornstarch

Scrapings from 1 vanilla bean

1 tablespoon (15 ml) pure vanilla extract

DIRECTIONS:

In a saucepan, combine the creamer, sugar, cornstarch, and vanilla bean scrapings. Bring to a boil, stirring often. As soon as it begins to boil, remove from the heat and stir in the vanilla extract.

Cover and place in the refrigerator to cool for an hour or so, then prepare the ice cream following the manufacturer's instructions.

YIELD: 4 servings

MINT CHIP ICE CREAM

Now, the trick here is to NOT use plain old chocolate chips. You will remember from your childhood that good mint chip ice cream has little flakes of chocolate in it, not big chunks!

If you use gluten-free extracts, then this recipe is indeed gluten free.

INGREDIENTS:

3 cups (705 ml) vanilla soy creamer,
other nondairy creamer, or milk

1 cup (200 g) evaporated cane juice or granulated sugar

¼ cup (32 g) cornstarch

1 tablespoon (15 ml) pure vanilla extract

2 tablespoons (30 ml) pure peppermint extract

A few drops green food coloring (optional)

⅓ cup (38 g) vegan chocolate shavings

DIRECTIONS:

In a saucepan, combine the creamer, sugar, and cornstarch. Bring to a boil, stirring often. As soon as it begins to boil, remove from the heat and stir in the vanilla extract, peppermint extract, and food coloring. Cover and place in the refrigerator to cool for at least an hour.

Stir in the chocolate shavings, then prepare the ice cream following the manufacturer's instructions.

YIELD: 4 servings

BUTTERSCOTCH ICE CREAM CAKE

We used to be first in line at the shop where they slap ice cream onto a frozen marble slab and mix in whatever strikes your fancy, such as pretzels, chocolate-covered coffee beans, nuts, and so on—only now we can make it at home!

FOR THE BUTTERSCOTCH SAUCE:

1 cup (192 g) Sucanat

Pinch of salt

¼ cup (60 ml) nondairy milk, plus more as needed

2 tablespoons (28 g) nondairy butter

1 teaspoon pure vanilla extract

FOR THE ICE CAKE:

1½ recipes Cake Batter Ice Cream (page 222), softened

½ cup (88 g) vegan mini semisweet chocolate chips

⅓ cup (50 g) dry-roasted salted peanuts

½ cup (53 g) chopped brownies (any recipe works!)

DIRECTIONS:

To make the sauce: Combine the Sucanat, salt, ¼ cup (60 ml) milk, and butter in a saucepan. Bring to a boil, lower the heat, and cook until the sugar dissolves, about 2 minutes. Remove from the heat. Stir in the vanilla and more milk as needed to reach the desired texture. Let cool.

To make the cake: Line a 9-inch (23-cm) spring-form pan with plastic wrap. Beat the ice cream in a large bowl until it softens even more. Add the remaining ingredients and beat until combined. Scrape into the prepared pan and press down, using the overhanging plastic wrap to push and shape into a cake.

Place in the freezer to firm up. Let thaw a few minutes before slicing, and serve with the butterscotch sauce or Chocolate Syrup (page 227).

YIELD: 10 servings, about ¾ cup (180 ml) butterscotch sauce

CHOCOLATE SYRUP

Stir this syrup into your favorite nondairy milk, or pour it on top of nondairy ice cream or waffles. Or directly into your mouth.

INGREDIENTS:

1 cup (80 g) Dutch-processed cocoa powder

2 cups (440 g) packed light brown sugar

1½ cups (355 ml) soymilk

1 teaspoon pure vanilla extract

DIRECTIONS:

Using a blender, combine the cocoa, brown sugar, and soymilk until perfectly smooth.

Transfer the mixture to a medium-size saucepan; bring to a boil. Lower the heat to medium and cook until the sugar dissolves, about 3 minutes, whisking occasionally. Remove from the heat and stir in the vanilla. Let cool completely. The syrup will thicken as it cools.

Transfer to an airtight glass bottle and store in the refrigerator. The sauce will keep for about 2 weeks.

YIELD: 3⅓ cups (785 ml)

AB AND C PUDDING

SOY FREE

One layer of nutty pudding, one dollop of compote, one more layer
of pudding. Try hard to find something wrong with this mouthwatering
concept; we bet you one layered pudding you won't be able to.

If you make sure to use gluten free vanilla, then this recipe is indeed gluten free.

FOR THE ALMOND BUTTER:

1 cup (160 g) dry-roasted whole almonds

1 teaspoon to 1 tablespoon (15 ml)
vegetable oil, as needed

FOR THE PUDDING:

1½ cups (355 ml) unsweetened almond milk

½ cup (100 g) evaporated cane juice or granulated sugar

Pinch of salt

2 tablespoons (16 g) cornstarch

1½ teaspoons pure vanilla extract

FOR THE COMPOTE:

2 pounds (908 g) fresh strawberries,
trimmed, cleaned, and quartered

¼ cup (50 g) evaporated cane juice or granulated sugar

2 tablespoons (30 ml) freshly squeezed lemon juice

Pinch of salt

DIRECTIONS:

To make the almond butter: Grind the almonds in a food
processor until a paste forms; this could take a few minutes, so patience is key. If the food processor refuses to
make butter out of your nuts, start by adding 1 teaspoon
of oil and go from there, until the consistency of nut butter is achieved.

To make the pudding: Using a blender, combine the nut
butter, milk, sugar, salt, cornstarch, and process until
smooth. Transfer to a saucepan, bring to a low boil, lower
the heat to medium-low, and cook, whisking constantly,
for approximately 4 minutes, until thickened. Stir in the
vanilla and set aside.

To make the compote: Combine the strawberries, sugar,
lemon juice, and salt in a large pot. Bring to a boil, lower
the heat to medium-high, and cook for 15 minutes, or
until most of the liquid is gone. Use a potato masher and
coarsely mash the fruit. Set aside to cool.

Whisk the pudding before placing about 3 tablespoons
(45 ml) of it in 4 small dessert dishes, add as much (1 to
2 tablespoons [15 to 30 ml]) compote as desired in the
center, and equally divide the rest of the pudding among
the dishes. Serve chilled. Store leftover compote in an
airtight container in the refrigerator; it will keep for about
1 week.

YIELD: 4 servings, approximately 4 cups (1 kg) compote

RECIPE NOTES

• Use any frozen or fresh fruit you want to make
the compote. Or use store-bought. There will be
leftovers with the compote recipe.

• Use store-bought natural roasted almond butter
instead of making your own. You will need ½ cup
(128 g) of it for the pudding.

FUNNEL CAKE

QUICK AND EASY

No need to travel to a state fair to enjoy a funnel cake! These are easier than you might think and whip up in less than 20 minutes! Unless you have mad skills with a real funnel, we suggest you use a plastic bag and snip off the corner. A deep fryer works well here, but if you don't have one, a pot filled with about 3 inches (7.5 cm) of oil will do the trick nicely.

INGREDIENTS:

Vegetable oil, for frying

1¼ cups (156 g) all-purpose flour

2 tablespoons (25 g) evaporated cane juice or granulated sugar

½ teaspoon baking soda

½ teaspoon baking powder

⅛ teaspoon salt

1 cup (235 ml) soymilk

1 teaspoon pure vanilla extract

Powdered sugar, for sprinkling

DIRECTIONS:

Preheat the oil in a deep fryer or pot to 350°F (180°C).

While the oil is heating, whisk together the flour, sugar, baking soda, baking powder, salt, soymilk, and vanilla in a medium-size bowl until smooth. It should be the consistency of a thin pancake batter.

Pour the batter into a resealable plastic bag. Snip off a corner of the plastic bag and quickly swirl about one-fourth of the batter into the oil.

Fry for 1 to 2 minutes, then carefully flip using a slotted spoon. Fry for 1 to 2 minutes longer, until golden and crispy. Carefully transfer to a plate lined with paper towels to absorb the excess oil. Repeat with the remaining batter.

While stil warm, sprinkle with powdered sugar and serve.

YIELD: 4 (4-inch, or 10 cm) funnel cakes

FRANGIPANE RICE PUDDING

Even the less enthusiastic rice pudding eaters out there will burst into song for more of this sweet dessert, created so that one of the flavors Celine's mom loves the most, frangipane, would get to be savored in a whole new way.

INGREDIENTS:

1 cup (185 g) uncooked brown or white jasmine or other rice (adjust water amount according to package directions)

2 cups (470 ml) water

1 cup (160 g) dry-roasted whole almonds

1½ teaspoons potato starch or cornstarch

⅓ cup (64 g) raw sugar

Pinch of fine sea salt

3 tablespoons (42 g) nondairy butter

1 teaspoon pure almond extract

1 cup (120 g) dried cherries

2 cups (470 ml) almond milk

DIRECTIONS:

Combine the rice with water in a saucepot. Bring to a boil, reduce the heat to medium-low, cover, and cook for 20 to 25 minutes, or until the water is absorbed. Alternatively, use a rice cooker.

Combine the almonds, potato starch, sugar, and salt in food processor. Process until the almonds are completely ground, about 1 minute. Add the butter and almond extract; process until thoroughly combined.

Combine the cooked rice, cherries, almond mixture, and almond milk in a saucepan. Bring to a boil, lower the heat to medium-low, and simmer for 20 minutes, or until thick and creamy, stirring occasionally.

Serve warm, at room temperature, or cold.

YIELD: 6 servings

MARINATED STRAWBERRIES

SOY FREE   LOW FAT

Perfect to enjoy on top of pancakes or waffles, as is, or in Fruity Creamsicle Whoopie Pies (page 242) or Strawberry Cream Pretzel Pie (page 239). Double or triple the recipe—it's that good.

INGREDIENTS:

1 cup (172 g) sliced fresh strawberries

1 tablespoon (12 g) evaporated cane juice or granulated sugar

Dash of balsamic vinegar

DIRECTIONS:

Combine the strawberries, sugar, and vinegar in a bowl. Cover and let macerate for 30 minutes before using in recipes, and enjoy immediately.

YIELD: 1 cup (172 g)

PEANUT BUTTER CUPS

If you, too, share your life with a peanut butter and chocolate fiend, you'll see that whipping up a batch of these delicious candies is guaranteed to put a grateful smile upon your sweetie's face.

FOR THE CHOCOLATE:

1½ cups (273 g) chopped vegan semisweet chocolate

2 tablespoons (32 g) natural creamy no-stir peanut butter

Pinch of salt

FOR THE FILLING:

12 tablespoons (¾ cup, or 192 g) natural creamy no-stir peanut butter

⅓ cup (67 g) evaporated cane juice or granulated sugar, packed light brown sugar, or sifted powdered sugar (for less crunchy results)

2 tablespoons (10 g) vegan graham cracker crumbs (optional)

Pinch of salt

DIRECTIONS:

Prepare a standard muffin tin with 12 paper liners.

To make the chocolate: Combine the chocolate, peanut butter, and salt in a microwave-safe bowl. Microwave in 1-minute increments until melted and smooth, keeping a close eye to avoid burning and stirring often. Alternatively, use a double boiler.

Place 2 teaspoons of the melted chocolate in each cupcake liner and with the back of a spoon carefully spread across the bottom and one-fourth of the way up the liner. Repeat with all 12 liners. Place the chocolate-covered liners on a plate and chill in the refrigerator until firm, about 20 minutes.

Meanwhile, prepare the filling: In a medium-size bowl, stir together the peanut butter, sugar, graham cracker crumbs, and salt.

Divide the peanut butter filling among the 12 liners, about 1 heaping tablespoon (20 g) per liner, pressing down gently to make sure the filling spreads out. Chill in the refrigerator until firm, about 20 minutes.

Top the filling with 2 teaspoons of the remaining melted chocolate, spreading carefully so that none of the peanut butter can be seen. Let the cups chill in the refrigerator for at least 1 hour before enjoying. Store in the refrigerator or freezer.

YIELD: 12 candies

PEANUT BUTTER FUDGE

GLUTEN FREE   SOY FREE

We wanted to have a recipe that made use of this fudge just so that you don't find yourself diving into it headfirst without even bothering to come up for air. It's that good. So try the Peanut Butter Fudge Cookies (page 247)!

INGREDIENTS:

1 cup (256 g) peanut butter

1 cup (200 g) evaporated cane juice or granulated sugar

½ cup (56 g) dry-roasted salted peanuts

¼ cup (60 ml) light coconut milk

DIRECTIONS:

Lightly coat a mini loaf pan (approximately 5 × 3 inches [13 × 8 cm]) with cooking spray or line it with parchment paper; please note the fudge will fill the pan to the top, so if you prefer thinner pieces of fudge, use a larger pan.

Combine the peanut butter, sugar, peanuts, and coconut milk in a medium-size saucepan. Bring to a boil. Once it starts boiling, let it roll for 1 minute, stirring constantly, until thickened. Transfer to the loaf pan and let cool before storing in the freezer for a few hours to set. Remove from pan and slice into 1-inch (2.5-cm) squares. Leftovers are best left stored in the freezer for the fudge to keep its optimal texture.

YIELD: 15 squares

BASIC PIE CRUST

As basic as they go, this makes for a delicious, foolproof crust that is perfect to use for both sweet and savory purposes.

INGREDIENTS:

2½ cups (313 g) all-purpose flour

½ cup plus 2 tablespoons (140 g) nondairy butter, cold

Heaping ¼ teaspoon sea salt

6 tablespoons plus 2 teaspoons (100 ml) water, as needed

DIRECTIONS:

Using a food processor, pulse together the flour, butter, and salt until combined. Slowly drizzle in the water with the machine running, pulsing until the dough comes together into a ball. Wrap in plastic and chill for 1 hour. Bake as directed in recipes.

YIELD: 2 crusts

S'MORE PIE

Gooey, sinful dessert, what would we ever do without you? Because an open fire isn't always handy to roast your marshmallows and build standard-size s'mores, we figured it was time to make a pie-shaped version of this traditional treat available during all seasons.

FOR THE CRUST:

1½ cups (170 g) vegan graham cracker crumbs

¼ cup (60 ml) melted nondairy butter or coconut oil

¼ cup (48 g) Sucanat

Pinch of fine sea salt

FOR THE FILLING:

1½ cups (176 g) vegan semisweet chocolate chips

¼ cup (84 g) light agave nectar

8 ounces (227 g) firm (not silken) tofu, drained, crumbled, and squeezed to get rid of excess liquid

4 ounces (113 g) nondairy cream cheese

2 tablespoons (10 g) Dutch-process cocoa

¼ cup (28 g) vegan graham cracker crumbs

1¼ cups (120 g) vegan marshmallow creme, such as Ricemellow Creme, divided

Pinch of fine sea salt

DIRECTIONS:

To make the crust: Preheat the oven to 350°F (180°C, or gas mark 4). Lightly coat a 9-inch (23-cm) pie plate with cooking spray.

Combine the graham cracker crumbs, butter, Sucanat, and salt in a medium-size bowl with a fork, or use a food processor. Press down into the prepared pan. Bake for 8 minutes, being careful not to burn. Let cool completely before adding the filling.

To make the filling: Combine the chocolate chips and agave in a double boiler, and heat until melted, stirring constantly.

Combine the tofu, cream cheese, cocoa, graham cracker crumbs, ¼ cup (24 g) marshmallow creme, and salt in a food processor. Process until smooth, scraping the sides occasionally. Add the melted chocolate and process until smooth, scraping the sides occasionally.

Scrape the filling evenly into the prepared crust. Chill for 2 hours.

Spread the remaining 1 cup (96 g) marshmallow creme evenly on top of the chilled pie. Using a kitchen torch, caramelize the marshmallows. Alternatively, use the broiler to just caramelize the top, but keep a close eye so it doesn't burn! Slice and serve.

YIELD: 8 to 10 servings

RECIPE NOTE

You will need 7 ounces (198 g) whole graham crackers in all. You can also use a store-bought vegan graham cracker crust, if you're in a hurry.

APPLE PIE WITH PECAN CRUST

We don't really make a point of eating our pi, er, pie at 3:14 a.m. or p.m.,
but one thing we always do is add ice cream on top, because life's too
short and our appetite for sweet goodness is pretty much endless.

FOR THE CRUST:

¾ cup (74 g) pecan halves

1½ cups (180 g) whole wheat pastry flour

¼ cup (55 g) packed light brown sugar

Pinch of fine sea salt

¼ cup (56 g) nondairy butter

¼ cup (60 ml) nondairy milk, plus more as needed

FOR THE FILLING:

4 large Granny Smith or other
good-for-baking apples, peeling optional, cored,
quartered, and cubed into bite-size pieces

2 tablespoons (28 g) nondairy butter

3 tablespoons (45 ml) nondairy milk or
freshly squeezed lemon juice, divided

½ cup (110 g) packed light brown sugar

2 teaspoons (4.6 g) ground cinnamon

2 teaspoons (10 ml) apple cider vinegar

Pinch of fine sea salt

1 tablespoon (8 g) cornstarch

DIRECTIONS:

Preheat the oven to 375°F (190°C, or gas mark 5). Lightly
coat a 9-inch (23-cm) pie plate with cooking spray.

To make the crust: Add the pecans, flour, brown sugar,
salt, and butter to a food processor. Pulse a few times to
grind the pecans and combine. Add the milk, a little at a
time, just until the dough sticks together when pinched.

Evenly crumble the dough into the prepared pie plate, and
press it down to cover the whole bottom and sides of the
plate. Make sure no cracks are left so that the filling has
no chance of seeping through. Alternatively, you can roll
out the crust. You can also reserve a generous handful of
the crust to crumble on top of the pie before baking.

Cover the crust with a piece of parchment paper and pie
weights. Prebake for 24 minutes.

In the meantime, make the filling: Combine the apples,
butter, 2 tablespoons (30 ml) of the milk, brown sugar,
cinnamon, vinegar, and salt in a pot. Bring to a boil, lower
the heat to medium, and cook for 14 minutes, stirring
often, or until the syrup is rather thick and the apples
are just barely tender without falling apart.

Combine the remaining 1 tablespoon (15 ml) milk and
the cornstarch in a small bowl. Add to the apple mixture,
stirring well, and cook for 2 minutes longer, or until
thickened.

Scrape the filling evenly into the crust. Bake for 24 minutes,
or until the edges of the crust are golden brown. Place on
a wire rack to cool.

YIELD: 8 servings

CREAMY BANANA PIE

A super-intense chocolate crust creates the tastiest partnership with white chocolate and fruity goodness. Consider making it with semisweet chocolate if the vegan white chocolate chips are really too hard to locate.

FOR THE CRUST:

1 cup (120 g) whole wheat pastry flour

⅓ cup (58 g) vegan semisweet chocolate chips

¼ cup (20 g) unsweetened cocoa powder

¼ cup (48 g) raw sugar

¼ teaspoon baking powder

¼ teaspoon salt

¼ cup (60 ml) peanut oil

½ teaspoon pure vanilla extract

3 tablespoons (45 ml) nondairy milk

FOR THE FILLING:

12 ounces (340 g) vacuum-packed extra-firm silken tofu

1 package (3¾ ounces, or 105 g) vegan vanilla pudding mix, such as Mori Nu

1 cup (256 g) crunchy almond butter

¾ cup (151 g) vegan white chocolate chips, melted

FOR THE BANANAS:

1½ tablespoons (21 g) nondairy butter

4 medium-size bananas, cut diagonally into ½-inch (1.3-cm) slices

1 tablespoon (15 ml) freshly squeezed lemon juice

DIRECTIONS:

To make the crust: Preheat the oven to 350°F (180°C, or gas mark 4). Lightly coat an 8-inch (20-cm) round pie plate with cooking spray.

Combine the flour, chocolate chips, cocoa powder, sugar, baking powder, and salt in a food processor. Process until ground. Add the oil and vanilla, and pulse until just combined. Add the milk, 1 tablespoon (15 ml) at a time, until the dough sticks together when pinched.

Crumble the dough evenly into the prepared pie plate, and press down on the bottom and edges of the pan. Cover with foil and pie weights. Bake for 20 minutes.

Remove the foil and bake for 5 to 10 minutes longer, or until the crust is dry, being careful not to burn. Let cool for 10 minutes in the pan. Remove from the pan and let cool completely on a wire rack.

To make the filling: Place the tofu in a food processor and pulse a few times until blended. Add the pudding mix and pulse a few more times. Add the almond butter and melted chips, and process until smooth. It will take a few minutes to reach the proper thickness. Set aside.

To make the bananas: Heat the butter in a large skillet over medium heat until melted. Add the banana slices (you might have to do this in several batches to avoid crushing the banana slices when flipping them over) and lemon juice; cook until brown and tender, carefully turning once. Set aside and let cool.

Scrape half of the filling into the cooled crust and spread evenly. Cover with half of the banana preparation. Spread the remaining filling on top of the bananas and smooth evenly. Decorate the top with the remaining banana preparation.

Let chill or freeze overnight before slicing. If frozen, thaw for a couple of hours in the refrigerator before enjoying.

YIELD: 10 servings

STRAWBERRY CREAM PRETZEL PIE

We sacrificed ourselves to make sure this decadent, supersweet, almost cookielike dessert would hit the spot by serving it several times over the course of a week, and while we're 110 percent satisfied with the outcome, we're just going to make it one more time to be 120 percent sure of it. Yes.

FOR THE CRUST:

4½ ounces (128 g) thin pretzels

⅓ cup (75 g) nondairy butter, melted

¼ cup (48 g) raw sugar

¾ cup (132 g) vegan semisweet chocolate chips

FOR THE FILLING:

8 ounces (227 g) nondairy cream cheese

1 cup (120 g) powdered sugar, sifted

1 recipe Marinated Strawberries (page 230), thoroughly drained, divided

6 tablespoons (42 g) coconut flour

1 teaspoon pure vanilla extract

DIRECTIONS:

To make the crust: Preheat the oven to 325°F (170°C, or gas mark 3). Lightly coat a 9-inch (23-cm) pie plate with cooking spray.

Using a food processor, finely grind the pretzels. Add the melted butter and raw sugar and pulse to combine. Press down into the prepared pan. Bake for 10 minutes just to set the crust. Transfer to a wire rack and let cool for 10 minutes.

Sprinkle the chocolate chips in an even layer on the crust, and place back in the oven, using the residual heat to let the chocolate melt, about 2 minutes. Carefully spread with an offset spatula. Chill in the refrigerator until the chocolate sets, about 20 minutes.

To make the filling: Using an electric mixer, combine the cream cheese and powdered sugar. Beat ¼ cup (40 g) of the marinated strawberries into the preparation: do not worry about crushing them; you want them to turn the filling pink. Add the coconut flour and vanilla, and beat until incorporated.

Spread the filling over the chocolate layer on the crust, using an offset spatula. Chill in the freezer for 1 hour to make slicing easier. Storing it in the freezer and thawing for 15 minutes before enjoying is best. Top with the remaining ¾ cup (120 g) marinated strawberries upon serving.

YIELD: 12 servings

GRASSHOPPER PIE

In a complete role reversal, this pie was invented after an alcoholic beverage of the same name. Keep a few extra cookies on hand to crumble on top for decoration and extra cookie goodness.

FOR THE CRUST:

24 creme-filled chocolate cookies, such as Newman O's or Joe-Joe's

½ cup (112 g) nondairy butter, melted

FOR THE FILLING:

¼ cup (56 g) nondairy butter

16 ounces (454 g) nondairy cream cheese

½ cup (100 g) evaporated cane juice or granulated sugar

10 ounces (280 g) vegan marshmallows, such as Dandies

1 teaspoon pure vanilla extract

1 tablespoon (15 ml) pure peppermint extract

A few drops green food coloring (optional)

DIRECTIONS:

To make the crust: Add cookies and melted butter to a food processor and process until a fine crumb is formed. Press into a 9-inch (23 cm) pie plate. Set aside.

To make the filling: In a saucepot, heat the butter, cream cheese, and sugar over medium heat until the sugar is completely dissolved and the mixture is creamy and silky smooth, stirring constantly. Stir in the marshmallows and cook until melted and smooth. Remove from the heat. Stir in the vanilla, peppermint extract, and food coloring.

Pour the mixture into the crust and smooth out the top. Place in the refrigerator to set. It should set within an hour, but this pie tastes best cold, so wait at least 2 hours before slicing to enjoy.

YIELD: 8 servings

RECIPE NOTE

To make a Grasshopper cocktail, add equal parts Creme de Menthe, white Creme de Cacao, and vanilla nondairy creamer to a cocktail shaker filled with ice. Shake and strain into a cocktail glass and serve.

PECAN PEACH GOBBLE-R À LA MODE

Feel free to make half a recipe of Basic Pie Crust (page 234) instead of the crust used here. But be absolutely sure to serve the "gobble-r" still warm with a melting, big scoop of Cake Batter Ice Cream (page 222) and sprinkled with the pecans!

FOR THE CANDIED PECANS:

½ cup (50 g) pecan halves

1½ tablespoons (23 ml) pure maple syrup

Pinch of salt

FOR THE CRUST:

4 ounces (113 g) nondairy cream cheese

½ teaspoon lemon zest

1¼ cups (156 g) all-purpose flour

¼ teaspoon fine sea salt

¼ cup (60 ml) cold water

FOR THE FILLING:

1 tablespoon (14 g) nondairy butter

2 pounds (908 g) fresh or frozen sliced peaches, thawed and drained if using frozen

⅓ cup (67 g) evaporated cane juice or granulated sugar

3 tablespoons (45 ml) water mixed with 3 tablespoons (24 g) cornstarch to form a slurry

2 teaspoons (2.2 g) nondairy butter, melted

1 tablespoon (12 g) evaporated cane juice or granulated sugar or raw sugar

DIRECTIONS:

To make the candied pecans: Combine the pecans, maple syrup, and salt in a dry skillet. Cook over medium-high heat, stirring often, until the syrup caramelizes, about 3 minutes. Spread on a baking sheet to cool.

To make the crust: Place the cream cheese, zest, flour, and salt in a food processor. Pulse a few times until the cream cheese is mostly broken down. Drizzle in the water until a dough forms. Wrap in plastic and chill for 1 hour.

Preheat the oven to 400°F (200°C, or gas mark 6).

To make the filling: Melt the butter in a large skillet. Add the peaches and sugar, and cook for 2 minutes over medium-high heat. Add the slurry and cook for 5 minutes, carefully stirring occasionally until thickened. Set aside.

Turn out the dough onto a lightly floured surface and roll into a 9½-inch (23-cm) square.

Place the peaches in a 9-inch (23-cm) square baking dish. Carefully place the rolled-out crust on top of the peaches. Cut out a couple of air vents in the center of the crust with a pair of clean kitchen scissors. Lightly brush the crust with the melted butter. Sprinkle the sugar evenly on top.

Place the baking dish on a baking sheet to catch any drips. Bake for 55 minutes, or until the crust is golden brown. Serve with ice cream and top with the pecans.

YIELD: 6 servings

FRUITY CREAMSICLE WHOOPIE PIES

Supersweet, creamy, and fruity—whoop whoop! Feel free to use either cherries or strawberries here for the filling—both are outstanding. (Cherry filling is pictured.) Dried fruit works well, too!

FOR THE COOKIES:

1½ cups (300 g) evaporated cane juice or granulated sugar

½ cup (120 ml) vegetable oil

¾ cup (180 g) nondairy vanilla-flavored yogurt

1 tablespoon (15 ml) pure vanilla extract

2 teaspoons (10 ml) rose water if using strawberry filling
or
½ teaspoon pure almond extract if using cherry filling

½ teaspoon fine sea salt

4 cups (500 g) all-purpose flour

1 tablespoon plus 1 teaspoon (16 g) baking powder

2 teaspoons baking soda

FOR THE FILLING:

½ cup (120 g) nondairy cream cheese

¼ cup (56 g) nondairy butter

4 cups (480 g) powdered sugar, sifted

½ teaspoon pure almond extract if using cherry filling

32 cherries, quartered, pitted, and patted dry, or ½ recipe Marinated Strawberries (page 230), drained well

DIRECTIONS:

To make the cookies: Preheat the oven to 350°F (180°C, or gas mark 4). Line 2 baking sheets with parchment paper or silicone baking mats.

Combine the sugar, oil, yogurt, vanilla, rose water or almond extract, and salt in a large bowl. Add the flour, baking powder, and baking soda; stir until combined. Use your hands if you must; the dough can handle it.

Divide the dough into 16 equal portions of a scant ¼ cup (66 g) each. Shape into balls and flatten on top just a little. Transfer to the prepared baking sheets.

Bake for 15 minutes, or until set and golden brown. Let cool on the baking sheets for a few minutes before transferring to a wire rack once the cookies are firm enough. Let cool completely before filling.

To make the filling: Combine the cream cheese, butter, powdered sugar, and almond extract (if using cherries) in a large bowl. Using an electric mixer, beat just until fluffy; do not beat for too long or it will turn runny.

Either gently fold the fruit into the frosting and sandwich between 2 cookies or spread a thin layer of frosting on 2 cookies and place 4 quartered cherries or 1 tablespoon (11 g) drained strawberries in the middle. Repeat to make 8 cookie sandwiches in all.

These are best enjoyed promptly once prepared, or keep the cookies at room temperature and the filling in the refrigerator and prepare them just before serving, otherwise the juice that's inevitably left in the fruit will ooze into the cookies.

YIELD: 8 large whoopie pies

HANDHELD BLUEBERRY PIES

What could possibly make blueberry pie any better? When you can hold it in your hand, of course! A deep fryer works best here, but if you don't have one, a pot filled with 4 inches (10 cm) of oil will do the trick just fine.

FOR THE BLUEBERRY FILLING:

2 cups (290 g) fresh or frozen blueberries

⅓ cup (67 g) evaporated cane juice or granulated sugar

2 tablespoons (28 g) nondairy butter

FOR THE CRUST:

1½ cups (188 g) all-purpose flour

⅓ cup (67 g) evaporated cane juice or granulated sugar

1 teaspoon ground cinnamon

½ cup (112 g) cold nondairy butter, cubed

2 tablespoons (30 ml) soy or other nondairy milk

Vegetable oil, for frying

Powdered sugar, for sprinkling (optional)

DIRECTIONS:

To make the filling: Place all the ingredients in a saucepot and simmer over medium heat for about 10 minutes, stirring so that the mixture does not burn and stick to the bottom of the pot.

To make the crust: In a medium-size mixing bowl, sift together the flour, sugar, and cinnamon. Add the butter, and incorporate into the flour mixture with your fingertips. Add the milk, slowly, and knead together. Don't overwork the dough, or you will end up with a tough crust.

Divide the dough into 4 equal pieces. Turn out onto a lightly floured surface and roll each piece into a circle about 8 inches (20 cm) in diameter.

Place one-fourth of the filling in the center of each crust. Fold over the crust into a half circle. Seal the edges with the tines of a fork.

Heat the oil in a deep fryer or pot to 350°F (180°C). Carefully add 1 pie to the hot oil and fry for 3 to 4 minutes, flipping halfway through, until golden and crispy. Transfer to a paper towel-lined plate to absorb the excess oil. Repeat with the remaining 3 pies.

Sprinkle with powdered sugar. Let cool slightly before serving. That filling is HOT!

YIELD: 4 pies

CRISPY GLAZED CHERRY PIE BITES

If you thought puff pastry was tasty when it was baked, just wait until
you try it deep-fried and then glazed! This simple list of ingredients will
yield such amazing results you will hardly believe it was so easy.

INGREDIENTS:

1 package (1 pound, or 454 g) vegan puff pastry

1 can (15 ounces, or 420 g) pitted cherries in heavy syrup

Vegetable oil, for frying

2 cups (240 g) powdered sugar, sifted

¼ cup (60 ml) soymilk

DIRECTIONS:

Thaw the puff pastry according to package directions.
Cut each sheet of pastry into 8 rectangles measuring approximately 5 × 3 inches (12.5 × 7.5 cm). Create a pocket
by folding 1 rectangle in half and sealing the 2 outer
edges with the tines of a fork, leaving an opening at the
top. Add 3 cherries to the pocket and seal the top. Repeat
to make 16 pockets in all.

If you have a deep fryer, this is a great time to use it. If
not, a pot filled with 4 inches (10 cm) of oil will work just
fine. Preheat the oil to 350°F (180°C).

Add 2 pie bites at a time to the oil and fry for 1 to 1½ minutes, then carefully flip over and fry for 1 to 1½ minutes
longer, or until puffy, golden, and crispy. Transfer to a
paper towel-lined plate to absorb the excess oil. Repeat
with the remaining 14 pie bites.

In a small bowl, whisk together the powdered sugar and
soymilk until smooth. Dip each bite into the glaze and
place on a wire rack to cool and dry completely. Place
a kitchen towel or paper towels underneath the rack to
catch the dripping glaze.

YIELD: 16 bite-size pies

RECIPE NOTE

No need to limit yourself to cherries here. Try these
little gals with a number of different fillings—blueberry,
peach, mango, strawberry, banana, you name it. If you
can fit it inside, chances are, it will taste delicious!

PEANUT BUTTER FUDGE COOKIES

You might be of the mind that the fudge and sugar make these more of
a treat, but let us pretend that the oats and whole wheat flour counterbalance
that fact and make this a healthy cookie. What? It is too true. Denial is a great thing.

INGREDIENTS:

1 recipe Peanut Butter Fudge (page 234), chopped, divided

6 tablespoons (90 ml) peanut oil

3 tablespoons (45 g) nondairy vanilla-flavored yogurt

3 tablespoons (45 ml) soymilk

6 tablespoons (75 g) evaporated cane juice or granulated sugar

6 tablespoons (83 g) packed light brown sugar

¾ teaspoon fine sea salt

1 tablespoon (15 ml) pure vanilla extract

1½ cups (120 g) old-fashioned oats

1½ cups (180 g) whole wheat pastry flour

¾ teaspoon baking powder

DIRECTIONS:

Preheat the oven to 350°F (180°C, or gas mark 4). Line 2 baking sheets with parchment paper or silicone baking mats.

Using a mixer, combine 1½ cups (390 g) of the fudge, oil, yogurt, soymilk, both sugars, salt, and vanilla until emulsified. Stir in the oats, flour, and baking powder until combined.

Divide the dough into packed ¼-cup (80-g) portions: you should get 12 large cookies. Press down onto the prepared baking sheets because these do not spread much while baking. Press down 1 tablespoon (13 g) of the remaining fudge into each cookie. (This is optional: if you'd rather not add fudge on top, it's fine too!)

Bake for 14 minutes, or until the cookies are golden brown around the edges. Let cool on the baking sheets for 10 minutes before transferring to a wire rack to cool completely.

YIELD: 12 large cookies

SALTY SWEET OAT COOKIES

These are a cross between scones and cookies, great to grab when you're on the go!

INGREDIENTS:

⅓ cup (73 g) packed light brown sugar

¼ cup (50 g) evaporated cane juice or granulated sugar

½ cup (112 g) nondairy butter

¼ cup (60 g) plain or vanilla-flavored nondairy yogurt

1 teaspoon pure vanilla extract

3 cups (300 g) Salty Sweet Oats (page 24)

1 cup (120 g) whole wheat pastry flour

½ teaspoon baking powder

6 tablespoons (66 g) vegan mini semisweet chocolate chips or any add-in

Heaping ¼ teaspoon fine sea salt

DIRECTIONS:

Preheat the oven to 350°F (180°C, or gas mark 4). Line 2 baking sheets with parchment paper.

Using an electric mixer, combine both the sugars, butter, yogurt, and vanilla.

In a separate medium-size bowl, combine the oats, flour, baking powder, chocolate chips, and salt. Add the dry ingredients to the wet and stir to combine.

Using a scant ½ cup (105 g) of dough, shape 8 cookies. Pat down gently on the baking sheet and flatten a little because these won't spread much while baking.

Bake for 16 minutes, or until golden brown around the edges. Let the cookies firm up on the baking sheet for at least 10 minutes before transferring to a wire rack to cool.

YIELD: 8 large cookies

SUGAR RUSH CEREAL BARS

Who says that rice crispy treats need to be made from rice crispies? We use Cap'n Crunch here, but the fun thing is, they can be made with any cereal!

INGREDIENTS:

½ cup (112 g) nondairy butter

1 package (10 ounces, or 280 g) vegan marshmallows, such as Dandies

12 ounces (336 g) crispy corn cereal, such as Cap'n Crunch or Gorilla Munch

1 cup (176 g) vegan semisweet chocolate chips

DIRECTIONS:

Line a 9 × 12-inch (23 × 30-cm) baking dish with waxed paper.

Melt the butter in a saucepot over medium-low heat. Add the marshmallows, and stir to melt. It may take a few minutes to melt vegan marshmallows. Stir constantly to prevent burning. The melted mixture will be shiny, fluffy, and uniform, almost resembling a meringue.

Add the cereal and chocolate chips to a large mixing bowl and toss together. Add the marshmallow mixture and toss to coat. The chocolate chips will begin to melt and swirl throughout the mixture.

Press the mixture into the prepared dish and press flat with a spatula. Let cool completely before cutting.

YIELD: 12 bars

WHITE CHOCOLATE ALMOND BARS

The crunch of almonds paired with an aromatic orange flavor
makes for one irresistibly chewy dessert or snack.

INGREDIENTS:

⅓ cup (75 g) nondairy butter

10 ounces (283 g) vegan white chocolate chips

½ cup (120 g) nondairy plain or vanilla-flavored yogurt

⅔ cup (80 g) powdered sugar, sifted

Zest of ½ medium-size orange

1 teaspoon pure orange extract

1¼ cups plus 2 tablespoons (165 g) light spelt flour or
1¼ cups (150 g) all-purpose flour

1 teaspoon baking powder

½ cup (80 g) dry-roasted whole almonds,
coarsely chopped

DIRECTIONS:

Combine the butter and chocolate in a microwave-safe bowl and microwave in 1-minute increments, so as not to burn the chocolate, until melted. Stir to combine.

Add the yogurt, powdered sugar, zest, and orange extract to the chocolate mixture and use an immersion blender to combine. Let cool to room temperature before proceeding.

Preheat the oven to 350°F (180°C, or gas mark 4). Lightly coat an 8-inch (20-cm) baking pan with cooking spray.

Stir the flour and baking powder into the wet ingredients. Gently fold in the almonds; the batter will be thick. Spread the batter evenly into the prepared pan.

Bake for 40 minutes, or until set. The edges should pull away from the pan and the surface will look shiny. Place the pan on a wire rack and let cool completely before slicing. These taste especially great straight out of the refrigerator, which will also make them easier to slice.

YIELD: 12 bars

RED-EYE TREATS

Rest assured that the quantity of coffee in these crispy treats won't be enough to keep you wired all night long; it merely adds a touch of caramel flavor here.

INGREDIENTS:

¾ cup (192 g) natural crunchy or creamy peanut butter or any nut butter

½ cup (172 g) brown rice syrup

½ cup (120 ml) pure maple syrup or (168 g) agave nectar

1 tablespoon (4 g) instant coffee or coffee alternative powder

⅓ cup (27 g) unsweetened cocoa powder

1 teaspoon pure vanilla extract

6 cups (96 g) puffed grain, such as brown rice or kamut, plus more as needed

DIRECTIONS:

Combine the peanut butter, rice syrup, maple syrup, instant coffee, and cocoa powder in a medium-size saucepan and cook over medium-low heat for a couple of minutes to dissolve the coffee powder and to make combining easier. Stir occasionally. Remove from the heat, add the vanilla, and stir to combine.

Add the puffed grain to a large bowl, pour the wet ingredients on top, and mix well until it is coated with the sticky mixture. Add more puffed grain if you are looking for denser treats, or if the mixture looks too wet.

Line an 8-inch (20-cm) square pan with parchment paper. Add the mixture and press down firmly, using more parchment paper to flatten.

Chill in the refrigerator or freezer for about 1 hour, then cut into 8 pieces. Store in the refrigerator or freezer.

YIELD: 8 treats

RECIPE NOTE

If your wrists aren't getting any younger and you're afraid of stirring a dense, sticky situation, use your stand mixer—it won't crush the puffed grain.

PEANUT BUTTER CUPCAKES
WITH PB FROSTING AND PB CUP CHUNKS

Pushing peanut buttery goodness to the limit and loving it, these cupcakes will show no mercy to even the most king-size of cravings! The frosting makes enough to cover all 12 cupcakes, but you may want to consider doubling it if you're going for that bakery-style thick slather. (You've got our vote.)

FOR THE FROSTING:

½ cup (100 g) vegan white chocolate chips

2 tablespoons (42 g) agave nectar

4 ounces (113 g) nondairy cream cheese

¼ cup (64 g) natural creamy peanut butter

FOR THE CUPCAKES:

1¼ cups (295 ml) soymilk

1 tablespoon (15 ml) apple cider vinegar

1 cup (256 g) natural creamy peanut butter

⅔ cup (133 g) evaporated cane juice or granulated sugar

½ teaspoon fine sea salt

2 teaspoons (10 ml) pure vanilla extract

1½ cups (188 g) all-purpose flour

2 teaspoons (9 g) baking powder

2 teaspoons baking soda

⅔ cup (116 g) chopped Peanut Butter Cups (page 232)

DIRECTIONS:

To make the frosting: In a microwave-safe bowl, combine the white chocolate and agave. Microwave in 20- to 30-second intervals, being careful not to let the chocolate scorch, until melted. Stir to combine. Add the cream cheese and peanut butter and, using an immersion blender, blend until perfectly smooth. Chill until ready to use.

To make the cupcakes: Preheat the oven to 350°F (180°C, or gas mark 4). Line a standard muffin pan with paper liners.

Combine the soymilk and vinegar in a medium-size bowl: It will curdle and become like buttermilk.

In a large bowl, whisk together the peanut butter, sugar, buttermilk mixture, salt, and vanilla until perfectly smooth. Sift the flour, baking powder, and baking soda on top of the wet ingredients. Fold the dry ingredients into the wet, being careful not to overmix. Fold in the chopped peanut butter cups.

Divide the batter evenly among the paper liners, filling each almost to the top.

Bake for 22 minutes, or until a toothpick inserted into the center comes out clean. Let cool for a few minutes in the pan before transferring to a wire rack. Cool completely before frosting. (And if you have any leftover peanut butter cups, use them as a topping!)

YIELD: 12 cupcakes

VANILLA PUDDING CUPCAKES

Believe it or not, Jell-O brand instant vanilla pudding is vegan! We know, wha-wha-what? But it's true! (In fact, the following instant pudding flavors are all vegan according to PETA: Pistachio, Banana Crème, Lemon, and Vanilla—so that means lots of options for rich, moist cupcakes!)

This recipe creates a dense moist yellow cupcake that reminds us of a really rich pound cake. It tastes perfect topped with a mile-high pile of your favorite butter cream or cream cheese frosting.

INGREDIENTS:

1 box (3.4 ounces, or 96 g) French vanilla or vanilla instant pudding mix

2 cups (240 g) white whole wheat or (250 g) all-purpose flour

½ teaspoon baking soda

½ teaspoon baking powder

¼ teaspoon salt

1 cup (200 g) evaporated cane juice or granulated sugar

⅓ cup (80 ml) vegetable oil

¾ cup (180 ml) nondairy creamer or nondairy milk (plain or vanilla)

½ cup (120 g) nondairy sour cream, store-bought or homemade (page 211)

DIRECTIONS:

Preheat the oven to 350°F (180°C, or gas mark 4). Line a standard muffin pan with paper liners.

In a large mixing bowl, combine the pudding mix, flour, baking soda, baking powder, and salt.

In a medium-size mixing bowl, combine the sugar, oil, creamer, and sour cream until smooth. Add the wet ingredients to the dry and stir to combine, being careful not to overmix. Divide the batter evenly among the paper liners, and smooth out the tops.

Bake 20 to 25 minutes, or until golden brown and a toothpick inserted into the center comes out clean. Let cool for a few minutes before transferring to a wire rack to cool completely. Top with your favorite frosting.

YIELD: 12 cupcakes

GRAHAM CRACKER CAKE

Roasted marshmallows on top of a moist cake so tender and tasti-fying, you will have to put it under lock and key if you want to save a piece for yourself.

INGREDIENTS:

7 ounces (198 g) vegan graham crackers or 1¾ cups (198 g) crumbs

1½ cups (180 g) all-purpose flour

1 cup (120 g) powdered sugar, sifted

2 teaspoons (9 g) baking powder

½ teaspoon fine sea salt

1 teaspoon ground cinnamon

¾ cup (180 ml) unsweetened nondairy milk

½ cup (120 g) nondairy plain or vanilla-flavored yogurt

2 tablespoons (30 ml) vegetable oil

2 teaspoons (10 ml) pure vanilla extract

½ cup plus 2 tablespoons (110 g) vegan mini semisweet chocolate chips

½ cup (25 g) vegan marshmallows, such as Dandies (optional)

DIRECTIONS:

Preheat the oven to 350°F (180°C, or gas mark 4). Lightly coat an 8-inch (20-cm) baking pan with cooking spray.

Using a food processor, grind the crackers into crumbs. Add the flour, powdered sugar, baking powder, salt, and cinnamon. Pulse a few times to combine.

In a large bowl, combine the milk, yogurt, oil, vanilla, and chocolate chips. Stir the dry ingredients into the wet, being careful not to overmix. Scrape the batter into the pan and smooth the top. Cover evenly with the marshmallows.

Bake for 30 minutes, or until a toothpick inserted into the center comes out clean. Let cool in the pan for 30 minutes before transferring to a wire rack to cool completely.

YIELD: 8 to 10 servings

BANANA CREAM PIE CAKE
WITH CHESTNUT GLAZE

Super-tender banana cake meets sweet chestnut glaze. It's love at first bite, and this union will have you living happily ever after. Or, you know, until more cake is made. If you like your desserts slightly less sweet, drop the glaze and simply spread some Chestnut Cream Spread on top of the cake, or sandwich it between 2 pieces of cake.

FOR THE CAKE:

2 bananas

½ cup (112 g) nondairy butter

¾ cup (150 g) evaporated cane juice or granulated sugar

½ cup (56 g) coconut flour

6 tablespoons (30 g) coconut flakes

2 teaspoons (10 ml) pure vanilla extract

½ teaspoon fine sea salt

1 cup (120 g) whole wheat pastry or all-purpose flour

2 teaspoons (9 g) baking powder

FOR THE GLAZE:

¼ cup (63 g) Chestnut Cream Spread (page 218)

1½ cups (180 g) powdered sugar, sifted

DIRECTIONS:

To make the cake: Preheat the oven to 350°F (180°C, or gas mark 4). Lightly coat an 8-inch (20-cm) square or round baking pan with cooking spray.

Using a mixer, combine the bananas, butter, sugar, coconut flour, coconut flakes, vanilla, and salt until smooth. Add the flour and baking powder and stir with a rubber spatula until combined. Scrape into the prepared pan and smooth the top.

Bake for 25 minutes, or until a toothpick inserted into the center comes out clean. Let cool in the pan on a wire rack for 15 minutes, then transfer directly to the wire rack to cool completely before applying glaze.

To make the glaze: Using a mixer, beat the cream and powdered sugar together until combined. Chill for 1 hour before spreading on cake or cupcakes.

YIELD: 1 (8-inch, or 20-cm) cake or 12 cupcakes

RECIPE NOTE

Make 12 cupcakes out of this recipe by lining a standard muffin pan with paper liners, filling each liner three-fourths full, and baking for 22 minutes.

OLD-FASHIONED COCONUT CAKE

Two luscious layers of coconut-ty goodness lathered in more coconut-ty frosting goodness.

FOR THE CAKE:

3 cups (375 g) all-purpose flour

2 cups (240 g) sweetened coconut flakes

¼ cup (32 g) cornstarch

1 teaspoon baking soda

1 teaspoon baking powder

½ teaspoon salt

2 cups (400 g) evaporated cane juice or granulated sugar

½ cup (112 g) nondairy butter, softened

6 ounces (170 g) plain or vanilla-flavored soy or coconut yogurt

½ cup (120 g) nondairy sour cream, store-bought or homemade (page 211)

1 cup (235 ml) full-fat coconut milk

2 teaspoons (10 ml) pure vanilla extract

FOR THE FROSTING:

6 ounces (170 g) nondairy sour cream, store-bought or homemade (page 211)

½ cup (112 g) nondairy butter

1 tablespoon (15 ml) pure vanilla extract

1 pound (454 g) powdered sugar, sifted

2 cups (240 g) sweetened coconut flakes

DIRECTIONS:

To make the cake: Preheat the oven to 350°F (180°C, or gas mark 4). Spray two 9-inch (23-cm) round cake pans with cooking spray, or line with parchment paper.

In a large mixing bowl, combine the flour, coconut, cornstarch, baking soda, baking powder, and salt.

In a separate large bowl, with an electric mixer, beat together the sugar and butter until fluffy. Add the yogurt, sour cream, coconut milk, and vanilla and beat until creamy. Slowly beat the dry ingredients into the wet and mix until smooth, being careful not to overmix. Spread the batter evenly into the 2 cake pans.

Bake for 35 to 40 minutes, until golden and a toothpick inserted into the center comes out clean. Remove from the oven, allow to cool for 10 minutes, then transfer to a wire rack to cool completely before frosting.

To make the frosting: Using an electric mixer, beat together the sour cream, butter, and vanilla until creamy. Beat in the powdered sugar, a little at a time, until smooth and silky. Keep refrigerated until ready to use.

Preheat the oven to 450°F (230°C, or gas mark 8). Line a baking sheet with parchment paper or a silicone baking mat. Spread the coconut evenly on the baking sheet.

Bake for about 5 minutes, until just beginning to brown. Be sure to keep a close eye on it, because it can burn quickly.

Level the bottom layer of cake, spread a layer of frosting on top, and place the other cake layer on top. Frost the entire cake with the frosting, and then press the toasted coconut evenly all over the cake.

YIELD: 8 servings

PEANUT BUTTER ROCKY ROAD POUND CAKES

These cakes bake up wonderfully in mini loaf pans, which makes them perfect for gift giving!

INGREDIENTS:

3 cups (375 g) all-purpose flour

1 cup (80 g) unsweetened cocoa powder

1 tablespoon (12 g) baking powder

1 tablespoon (12 g) baking soda

½ teaspoon salt

2 cups (470 ml) nondairy milk

1½ cups (300 g) evaporated cane juice or granulated sugar

1 container (6 ounces, or 170 g) plain or vanilla-flavored nondairy yogurt

½ cup (120 g) nondairy sour cream, store-bought or homemade (page 211)

½ cup (128 g) natural creamy no-stir peanut butter

¼ cup (60 ml) canola oil

2 tablespoons (30 ml) pure vanilla extract

1 bag (10 ounces, or 280 g) vegan marshmallows, such as Dandies

1 cup (120 g) pecan or walnut pieces

DIRECTIONS:

Preheat the oven to 350°F (180°C, or gas mark 4). Coat 8 mini loaf pans with cooking spray.

In a large mixing bowl, combine the flour, cocoa powder, baking powder, baking soda, and salt.

In a separate medium-size bowl, combine the milk, sugar, yogurt, sour cream, peanut butter, oil, and vanilla, and beat until creamy.

Add the wet ingredients to the dry and stir to combine. Fold in the marshmallows and walnuts. Fill the loaf pans three-fourths full. Place the loaf pans on a baking sheet to catch any drips.

Bake for 40 to 50 minutes, or until a toothpick inserted into the center comes out clean. Let cool on a wire rack.

YIELD: 8 mini loaves

RECIPE NOTE

Reserve 3 or 4 marshmallows and a small handful of nuts to place on top of each loaf before baking, for extra gooey roasted marshmallow tops.

JUNE'S SWEDISH DESSERT BLENDER PANCAKES

Joni's sister June, also a vegan, makes these for Joni when she visits. They are her signature dish, and she makes several varieties. This one is Joni's favorite!

FOR THE SWEDISH PANCAKES:

1 cup (125 g) all-purpose flour

¼ cup (50 g) evaporated cane juice or granulated sugar

1 tablespoon plus 1½ teaspoons (12 g) Ener-G egg replacer whisked together with 6 tablespoons (90 ml) warm water, the equivalent of 3 eggs (see note)

2 tablespoons (28 g) nondairy butter

2 cups (470 ml) soymilk

1 teaspoon pure vanilla extract

¼ teaspoon ground cinnamon

¼ teaspoon salt

¼ cup (56 g) nondairy butter, for frying

FOR THE BANANA CRÈME FILLING:

8 ounces (227 g) nondairy cream cheese

8 ounces (227 g) nondairy sour cream, store-bought or homemade (page 211)

½ banana

½ cup (60 g) powdered sugar, sifted

1 tablespoon (15 ml) pure vanilla extract

FOR THE SLICED BANANA TOPPING:

1 tablespoon (14 g) nondairy butter

2 tablespoons (28 g) packed brown sugar

1 banana, sliced into rounds

Powdered sugar, for sprinkling (optional)

Chocolate Syrup (page 227), for drizzling (optional)

DIRECTIONS:

To make the pancakes: Blend all the ingredients in a tabletop blender, or in a mixing bowl with an immersion blender, until very, very smooth.

Melt 1 tablespoon (14 g) of the butter in a frying pan over medium-high heat. (Or use cooking spray between each batch, spraying away from the stove when the pan is warm, and carefully holding the pan.) Once the butter is melted and the pan is hot, pour in enough of the batter to coat the bottom of the pan, and swirl to make a thin crêpelike pancake. Cook for 2 to 3 minutes, and then flip and cook the other side for 2 to 3 minutes. Repeat to make 4 to 6 pancakes in all.

To make the filling: Place all the ingredients in a blender and process until smooth and creamy.

To make the topping: Melt the butter and brown sugar in a pan over medium heat. Once the sugar is completely dissolved, add the banana slices and toss gently to coat, continuing to cook until sticky and warm.

Assemble the dessert by placing 1 pancake on each of 4 to 6 plates. Add equal amounts of filling to the center of each pancake and roll up the pancake around the filling. Top with the sliced bananas. Sprinkle with the powdered sugar and drizzle with the chocolate syrup. Serve immediately.

YIELD: 4 to 6 servings, depending on the size of your pan

RECIPE NOTE

If you don't have access to egg replacer, use 1½ tablespoons (12 g) cornstarch and omit the water.

MATÉ MADNESS MARGARITA

LOW FAT   **SOY FREE**   **QUICK AND EASY**

Yerba maté (pronounced mah-tay) is a South American tea that packs a powerful caffeine punch. Be careful: you can't really taste the alcohol in these, which, in our case . . . is very dangerous!

INGREDIENTS:

6 cups (140 ml) brewed yerba maté tea, cooled

½ cup (120 ml) freshly squeezed lime juice (about 4 limes)

½ cup (120 ml) freshly squeezed orange juice (about 2 oranges)

⅓ cup (112 g) agave nectar

1 cup (235 ml) Triple Sec

1½ cups (355 ml) tequila

Raw or sparkling sugar, for the glasses

6 lime wedges, for garnish

DIRECTIONS:

In a large pitcher, stir together the tea, juices, agave, Triple Sec, and tequila. Keep chilled until ready to serve. Serve over ice in a sugar-rimmed glass (or mason jar) with a wedge of lime.

YIELD: 6 servings

PINEAPPLE GINGER LASSI

GLUTEN FREE   **QUICK AND EASY**   **LOW FAT**

Here's a tasty beverage to enjoy alongside Indian-style curries or dishes, or to put some pep in your step first thing in the morning. Add the optional ice cubes for a thicker beverage. As far as sweetness goes, adjust the amount of agave depending on how sweet the yogurt is.

INGREDIENTS:

6 ounces (170 g) nondairy plain yogurt

½ cup (80 g) frozen pineapple chunks

¼ cup (60 ml) fresh pineapple juice

2 to 3 teaspoons (14 to 21 g) agave nectar, or to taste

½ to ¾ teaspoon ground ginger, or to taste, or grate fresh gingerroot, to taste

2 ice cubes (optional)

DIRECTIONS:

In a blender, process all the ingredients until smooth. Serve immediately.

YIELD: 1 serving

PINK PUCKER

LOW FAT **SOY FREE** **QUICK AND EASY**

Not a drinker? That's okay: the whiskey is totally optional. However, if you decide to make these virgins, you may want to cut back on the sugar a bit.

INGREDIENTS:

4 cups (940 ml) water

1 cup (200 g) evaporated cane juice or granulated sugar

10 ounces (280 g) fresh or frozen whole strawberries

2 cups (470 ml) freshly squeezed lemon juice (about 8 lemons)

1½ cups (355 ml) whiskey (optional)

DIRECTIONS:

In a medium-size pot, combine the water and sugar. Cook over medium-high heat until all the sugar is dissolved and the mixture is just about to boil.

Add the strawberries and continue to cook for about 5 minutes, stirring constantly. Remove from the heat and stir in the lemon juice. Carefully transfer to a pitcher and chill in the refrigerator before serving. You can strain out the strawberries if desired, but we think they taste yummy, so we leave them in.

Serve over ice, stirring in ¼ cup (60 ml) of whiskey for each drink.

YIELD: 6 servings

RECIPE NOTE

Try this as a refreshing summertime slushy by not doing any cooking. Use frozen strawberries and blend all the ingredients until satisfyingly smooth. Add extra ice for a thicker beverage.

Acknowledgments

Jill Alexander, for making this project sound irresistible and for convincing us to dive into it head-first; our editor and friend Amanda Waddell, for being such an inspiration and a joy to work with; and Will Kiester, Rosalind Wanke, and Karen Levy: We couldn't have done it without your expertise and kindness!

We are, as always, most grateful and forever indebted to the Official Testing Team: Courtney Blair, Monika Soria Caruso, Kelly Cavalier, Michelle Cavigliano, Anne-Laure Chevallier, Amy Gedgaudas, Jenny Howard, Annika Lundin, Shelly Mocquet-McDonald, Monique and Michel Narbel-Gimzia, Constanze Reichardt, Josiane Richer, Keri Risse, Nina Stoma, and Liz Wyman (a.k.a. Missus Super Tester who tested approximately 70 of our recipes!).

Joni would like to thank her Gramma Jo: My grandmother, Joann, has fed me many meals. She is solely responsible for my oversized portions and my tendency to make WAY too much food. She has cooked for many people, for many years, and through her I have been inspired to take on the world with a knife and fork! Thank you, Gramma, for inspiring me, having faith in me, and teaching me so much without even trying. I love you!

Celine would like to thank her parents and Chaz for wearing their cheerleader outfits at all times, shaking their pom-poms at her even when she acts like a professional stress ball. Thank you, Jeanette (www.jeanettezeis.com), for providing the props made by your very own two insanely talented hands.

About the Authors

Joni Marie Newman is a Southern California native, and currently resides in Orange County with her husband, their three rescue mutts, and Michael, the cat. She is the founder of Justthefood.com, the author of *Cozy Inside* and *The Best Veggie Burgers on the Planet*, and the coauthor of *500 Vegan Recipes* and *The Complete Guide to Vegan Food Substitutions*. You can get in touch with her at Joni@justthefood.com.

Celine Steen lives in California with her favorite dude and their two crazy cats. She is the founder of Havecakewilltravel.com, as well as the coauthor of *500 Vegan Recipes* and *The Complete Guide to Vegan Food Substitutions*. You can get in touch with her at Celine@havecakewilltravel.com.

Index